THE FOREWORD

In the years I have known Ferrell, I have always admired her and her tenacity to accomplish the mandate that God has given her. She is an example of what it means to act when Jesus speaks. When God told Ferrell to start buying homes, she did not have the money that was needed. Ferrell and her husband had just used their savings to buy their 1st home and soon after God was asking her to redevelop an entire community. Immediately Ferrell started looking into how she could accomplish this mandate. She took all that knowledge and put it in this book. Ferrell has written everything she wishes she had known as a first-time investor. She shares her personal experiences and provides step-by-step guidance for how you and I can invest in real estate regardless of our age, income and most importantly background.

As a 26-year-old first-generation investor that moved to America at 10 years old, this book has provided me with so much knowledge in the field of real estate that I plan to use in my home country of Zimbabwe. I've always dreamed of owning property and building hospitals in my native country, an area in need of development, particularly in the healthcare industry. I always thought I had to wait until after I became a doctor to start investing, but already, I have started investing in real estate with the guidance from this book. I now have a plan to set up my future children with the best life possible through real estate. Being a mother of two, Ferrell is on a mission to leave a legacy for her children. Multiple times in this book she mentions the importance of generational wealth. Real Estate is one of the easiest vehicles in which to leave wealth for your children and their children. Your real estate investing journey doesn't end with reading this book. Join the Comma Club Community, a community of like-minded people adding commas to their net worth through real estate investing.

- Rudo Duri, a first-generation investor.

WE MUST OWN

Ferrell Fellows

COMMA CLUB

Copyright © 2022 by Ferrell Fellows

Comma Club Publishing

Dallas, Texas

www.commaclubcommunity.com

Contact the author: Invest@CommaClubCommunity.com

ISBN (Print): 979-8-9868095-0-2

ISBN (Ebook): 979-8-9868095-1-9

All rights reserved.

No part of this publication may be reproduced, stored in a retrieval system, stored in a database and / or published in any form or by any means, electronic, mechanical, photocopying, recording or otherwise, without the prior written permission of the publisher.

Disclaimer: Please be advised that the author is offering this book and its contents for educational purposes only and the information contained herein is NOT to be construed as legal, financial, tax or other pertinent advice for making a particular investment decision. The information and data contained herein this book is provided to the reader as a general guideline only to assist them in gaining knowledge in their personal pursuit of evaluating and participating in potential real estate investment. All of the content provided herein, including but not limited to general and specific formulas, charts, data, diagrams, graphs, graphics, principles, theories, recommendations, materials, samples, examples, and other information is for illustrative purposes only and NOT to be relied upon by the reader in making a prospective investment. Each prospective opportunity will have its own unique set of factors and circumstances to evaluate and take into consideration, and the author specifically offers no warranty or assurance on the reliability of the information contained herein for any one instance. The author highly recommends that each prospective investor seek their own independent legal, financial or tax matters advisor prior to making any major investment. There is NO GUARANTEE and NO WARRANTY that employing the same techniques, ideas, strategies, products, or services that are detailed on www.wemustown.com and CommaClubCommunity.com or any books or materials will produce the same results for you. Examples that may be provided in books, workbooks, articles, videos, and other sources on the site are just that – examples. They may or may not work for your specific situation and are not to be interpreted as a guarantee or promise of earnings. The level of success you reach employing these techniques and ideas is entirely dependent upon your skills, financial resources, and the time you devote to achieving career & investment success. Because of this, we cannot guarantee your level of success, nor do we in any way, whether directly or indirectly, do so. Forward-Looking Statements: Materials in this book may contain information that includes or is based upon Forward-Looking Statements give our expectations or forecasts of future events. You can identify these statements by the fact that they do not relate strictly to historical or current facts. They use words such as "anticipate," "estimate," "expect," "project," "intend," "plan," "believe," and other words and terms of similar meaning in connection with a description of potential earnings or financial performance. Any and all Forward-Looking Statements here or on any of our promotional materials are intended to express our opinion of earnings potential. Any such statements are considered accurate at the time they were written but may no longer be at the current time or in the future, and We Must Own, wemustown.com and commaclubcommunity.com disclaim any duty to update said statements. All links are for information purposes only and are not warranted for content, accuracy, or any other implied or explicit purpose. We do not warrant or guarantee the work or advice of any affiliated businesses, referrals, or companies referenced in any book or site published by comma club community, coaches, or partner

ACKNOWLEDGEMENTS

Nicholas, Kingson & Glory, I thank you for allowing me to spend two years of late nights and Saturdays writing this book so that my passion for ownership could impact more than just our household. All the times I looked away and you needed my gaze, I was looking to the future seeing the hopeless, impoverished, and broken communities of our world restored.

Rudo, my Editor-in-Chief, this book would not be possible without you. Thank you for your willingness to invest in my dreams while you awaited the manifestation of yours. I'm often baffled by your selflessness and your humility.

To the KLC team, you have given me my time back and allowed me the freedom to flourish in more areas than one. Thank you for your dedication to create a Kingdom Legacy and build the Comma Club Community from just an idea into what it has become.

Ty and Brent, thank you for saying yes when everyone else said no.

Mom, turning into my mother has been my greatest accomplishment. Your journey in business built my faith to become an entrepreneur because of the countless miracles I've witnessed in your life.

Dr. Joseph Mwenya, thank you for imparting your many graces on many occasions too numerous to count. I will never discount the impact of your presence in my life and your teachings on my businesses and my family. You revealed Jesus and that changed everything!

Becky Hennesy, thank you for being my biggest cheerleader. Through your leadership of the Reformers Collective, you are raising world leaders who will thrust against the status quo until transformation emerges on every mountain of society. I'm grateful you came along on this ride to restore South Dallas with me!

Cindy Jacobs, thank you for imparting your grace for writing books that Peter Wagner imparted to you. Your prayer gave me the fire to complete the second half of my book.

Special thanks to Anthony German, JTaylor Studios, and Gloria Ashby for your contributions to this book.

I can't forget Dustin Heiman, Tamera Nalls, Phylicia Goings, Frances Franklin, Trevor Turnbo, Victoria Strange, Cory McFarlane, Ed Paramo, Luther & Kenneth Huggins, Jasz Anderson, Natalie Strong, Liz Guillen, and Jeanette Fellows for your role in where I am today.

DEDICATION

I dedicate this book to those of you who have taken responsibility for your communities. May all of you be empowered to govern the territories that God gives you with knowledge, wisdom, compassion, and understanding. I pray God gives you great wealth that will endure many generations.

TABLE OF CONTENTS

INTRODUCTION
    About the Author
    About Comma Club Community
    Creating Access to Wealth
    The Comma Club Vision

SECTION 1: A MENTORSHIP IN OWNERSHIP
    Why We Must Own
    Facts About Real Estate
    The Action Plan
    Establish Your Vision

SECTION 2: THE BASICS OF INVESTING
    Investment Strategy Review
    Property Types and Classifications
    Understanding Your Target Market

SECTION 3: PREPARING TO INVEST
    Financing Options
    Preparing Your Personal Finances
    Forming a Business Entity
    Building Your Team
    How to Know When You are Ready to Invest

SECTION 4: CLOSING & MANAGING YOUR INVESTMENT
    Property Selection
    Step-by-Step Process from Offer to Closing
    Generating Income on Investments
    Tax Considerations for Real Estate Investing
    Commencement

Glossary
References

INTRODUCTION

ABOUT THE AUTHOR

I am Founder and CEO of the Comma Club Community, author of "We Must Own," and instructor for the Comma Club Beginner Real Estate Investor Course. I am a Licensed Texas Real Estate Broker, Investor, Developer, Sponsor, Coach and Owner of Kingdom Legacy Real Estate based in Dallas, Texas. I am professionally designated as a REALTOR, Certified Loan Signing Agent, Certified Tax Professional, Accountant, and Notary Public. I hold an MBA degree from Florida A&M University and am a proud graduate of the most prominent historically Black College and University in the country. None of these titles or degrees individually prepared me to invest in real estate, and none of them are required to be successful.

My range of career and life experiences and my faith in God, together with my passion for teaching, enabled me to launch countless everyday people into success as new real estate investors. My professional career began as a Global Sourcing Manager for Procter & Gamble controlling an annual spending budget of $50 million for capital expenditures in product manufacturing and supply chain developments throughout the United States, Europe, Asia, and Latin America.
On my first day of work as a recent graduate, I was given the assignment to negotiate a $5 million contract with a French supplier via a translator. So much of the negotiation was lost in

translation, and I am not referring to our language differences. As a newbie, I did not understand the contract that I was responsible to negotiate, and I was intimidated by the process, the size of the financial figures on the paper, and the amount of responsibility given to me so quickly.

From working at a multi-billion-dollar company I learned that millions are just a drop in the bucket and my ability to scale a vision was unlocked! I also learned that as a twenty-three-year-old black woman that I was far more capable of managing wealth than I had ever been taught growing up in the rough streets of South Oak Cliff, Texas.

I know what it feels like to be totally intimidated to enter an unknown business world where you feel like an outsider. I sat in a corporate office, one of only two black women in a room full of hundreds of middle-aged white men. I will never forget the day I did the big chop and took the brave route to wear naturally textured hair to work. My male colleague balked at me, "Why did you cut your long straight hair? You look better that way." I was mortified, only further revealing that not only was I in a world I did not understand, but that world also did not understand people like me.

I reflect on this experience because I want to prepare you for the world of commercial real estate investment and development that is less than 2% minority and less than 1% non-white women. The disparities in property ownership and the absence of diverse leadership in the commercial real estate industries is unremarkably reflective of trends you see across the board in so many other prominent industries. The wealthy are getting wealthier, and they are looking less and less like me.

When you enter a bank office or a boardroom to lead an investment pitch, the people sitting around the table who lead the financing decisions are often from lineages of wealth and out of touch with the communities where they invest their dollars. It can be extremely intimidating to pursue information that has been long-hidden and made exclusive to those who attend Ivy League colleges or their private family retreat where wealth secrets have been passed down from one generation to the next. I want to acknowledge that I would not be here today if it were not for courage to enter realms that intimidated me. I expect the readers of this book to push beyond your fears and pursue ownership because no matter how impossible or difficult it may seem; it is very possible to build wealth and change the trajectory of your entire life through real estate.

In 2010, I walked away from my corporate career as a Global Sourcing Manager for Procter & Gamble, from a promotion, a pay raise, and an offer to become a higher-level manager for the Beauty Care segment of my division, from traveling the world doing a high-powered job that I would surely love. Instead, I chose to become an entrepreneur. I left that company at the young age of 25 to set out on my own.

Following the voice of God, I began a creative career of writing that I still enjoy till this day. Though born into a lower middle-income family, abandoned by my absentee father, raised by a single mother, and having barely tasted a life of six-figure earnings, something in me was driving me to dream bigger than my corporate salary could offer me. I wanted the freedom to live my life on my own terms. The thought of waiting for retirement to pursue my passions and dreams was suffocating, so I walked away from the certainty of a hefty paycheck to take a chance on myself, believing there was something in me bigger than a corporate office and a prominent work title. I went from caviar and corporate expense accounts to cans of tuna fish. I maxed out credit cards quickly, but I never regretted my decision. Twelve years later, I am still here - thriving, building, and becoming all that God destined for my life.

In the tough times of entrepreneurship, I looked for creative and honorable ways to earn money and began tutoring college students in subjects that I studied during my five-year MBA program, that is how I survived so many years while my companies were forming. As a passionate tutor, I tutored college level accounting, economics, and business courses for over fifteen years at various universities including Florida State University, Southern Methodist University, and my own alma mater, FAMU. I never realized at the time that those years of hustling to pay the bills cultivated my ability to teach complex financial topics in a way that others could easily understand. I helped hundreds of students graduate from challenging business programs because of this gift to teach. For the last six years, I transposed that gift into teaching first time home buyers and investors to purchase property. Watching others rise out of financial hardship into stability, and even prosperity, laid the groundwork for the Comma Club Community investor network and the writing of this book.

The disparity of wealth, ownership, and real estate investment education bothers me. There is such widespread ignorance that leaves so many out of the game. I remember as part of my signing bonus for my first job, my company offered to pay my down payment and closing costs to purchase my first home. I turned it down because the idea of property ownership frightened me. I felt I was too young to own property because I had seen only one other person my age own property and he was an anomaly.

I fret at the misinformation that is so widely distributed through minority communities about when it is appropriate to purchase property. Property can be owned at any age. I placed a key in my son's hand at the age of five and told him, "Son, this house is yours." When I assisted two black businessmen in my community to acquire their first business office, I watched as they grabbed their firstborns and did the same. Let's be clear. This book is not about a get-rich-quick money scheme; it is about the slow methodical process of building multi-generational wealth using real estate as a mechanism to change the trajectory of your great-grandchildren's future.

I tell the stories of my journey into the world of real estate throughout this book, which is mostly technical real estate information and some anecdotal color about my personal experiences. I have been told no so many times. I have been ignored, had my properties robbed, and had crews walk off the job. I have experienced failure and had to rework the plan and keep going. I emptied my bank account countless times. My husband and I have known what it is like to count change for dinner just to feed our family. I have maxed out credit cards and lived with nothing. White-collar conspirators tried to swindle my company out of millions of dollars, but I was saved by discernment.

I have faced discrimination. Most bankers see me and do not realize that I am the person they are coming to meet. I built teams and managed crews. I ran a company with staff, built from the ground up. I raised financing, managed investments, and sponsored deals. I developed impactful community projects, stood before city councils and fought for the people of my neighborhood.

In essence, I have survived the uncharted territory of being a black woman real estate developer in the city of Dallas and lived to tell about it. How? Because I am compelled by a force within me to do something about the ails that I see around me that I despise. I live in a community surrounded by distress, poverty and homelessness. I see the same individuals panhandling on the corner by my home, and I am unsettled from my peace to watch them continue as housing prices rise and the city grows more comfortable in their riches just a few miles north. "Somebody must do something about all of this poverty and hunger," I yelled. The silence yelled back, "That somebody is you." I learned through prayer and petitioning God to change things in my community that the things we most despise are within our power to defeat.

I initially entered real estate as a traditional salesperson seeking to sell luxury homes, earn high commissions, have a flexible life of travel, and retire to a life of homemaking and motherhood. Boy was that fantasy off target. Through a series of divine events, I saw how people in extreme poverty live in one of the wealthiest cities in the nation, and I abhorred that reality. I realized that the ills of my community were a direct result of property's ownership. I believed that if I owned the properties that were defunct and appalling, then I would do better by them and the people that they housed.

It started with an idea that if I could own my community, my community would be different. I started a company called Kingdom Legacy Company and purchased my first investment. That investment changed my entire life and that of my family. My vision kept growing into a massive idea that I would eventually own my entire community. This career path has had its challenges, but I now own a portfolio of commercial and residential properties that are setting the standard of quality in my community. I am even leading projects that the Mayor and City Manager of Dallas recognized. As CEO of the Kingdom Legacy Company, my vision is to purchase and rehabilitate every available distressed property in our target area in the next decade.

As a Real Estate Broker, I was honored as Real Estate Salesperson of the Year (2020) and ranked in the top sales categories for multiple years for on-market and off-market sales. I have had the pleasure to consult as a specialist for multiple land trusts and community development corporations advocating for economic development in the Dallas communities. Currently, I volunteer on the Dallas Housing Policy Task Force, the St. Philips Development Advisory Committee, and consulted for the 10th Street Land Trust. I regularly volunteer feeding and clothing the homeless residents of South Dallas and actively work to dismantle systems of poverty and systemic racism through development, advocacy, and policy reformation in my community.

I live, work, and serve in the community where I invest. Therefore, I am personally and financially invested in the progress of one of the oldest minority communities of Dallas. As a real estate consultant, I sit on several development company boards or consult as partner, co-investor, or broker. I hear the development decisions that are inspired by wealthy, out-of-touch investors and company leaders. I am able to speak to the needs of the community because I know the people and the needs personally. I have both rebutted many projects that would be harmful or detrimental to the people as well as advocated for the citizens to participate and co-invest in the projects coming to our community.

Specifically, I advocated for equity in each venture to be set aside for community members to own a piece of every project. Project leaders and developers are stunned at the idea of allowing the community members to invest. It is as if they never imagined that the people who live in a community would want to invest and benefit from the income that commercial development yields. On a recent board call with a community bank, I was appointed to identify and spearhead a group of minority business owners within this community to give them first right of refusal to invest in five grocery stores and two hospitals under development. These kinds of opportunities rarely come to minorities.

What makes me most successful as an investor and developer is that I care about the people impacted by my business decisions. I have this great contrast from working with some of the wealthiest and most powerful individuals in Dallas to serving the poorest, most vulnerable ones. I have served the homeless on a dangerous corner in Dallas and personally speak to those battling addictions, women oppressed by sex trafficking, and mentally ill war veterans. I helped open a transitional home for chronically homeless women called Rahab Refuge Center of Texas and serve as the Board President.

Community development and advocacy have become passions of mine. I see that the most essential element to transformative social change is active involvement with the people in a community. That is why, when I formed the Comma Club Community, I emphasized developing a platform that teaches community-centric investing where wealth builders would be personally connected to a mission in their local community and inspired to use property ownership as a means to bring justice and solutions to the most difficult areas of the United States.

As Founder and CEO of the Comma Club Community, our mission is to *Create Commas and Communities*. For me this is more of a mandate than a mantra. I must possess the land. I must do well with it and cause it to prosper for the benefit of those I have been given to protect and the generations that will come after me. I see the tenants and families under my care as extensions of my household. I accept the problems of poverty and homelessness in my neighborhood as *my* responsibility. Therefore, building wealth is mandatory. I believe I am called to restore my community and, as I teach Christ-centered investment principles, I can lead other like-minded investors to do the same.

Thank you for joining me in this journey to create reformation throughout communities around the world.

- Ferrell Fellows

ABOUT COMMA CLUB COMMUNITY

Comma Club is a real estate investor network offering wealth building strategies, training courses and a community of support for novice and first-generation investors to launch their journey into the world of real estate investment and development. This community provides a forum where members share their experiences, seek guidance and access expert training, coaching and a network of industry professionals. The purpose is to help participants excel in their investment journey and build long-term multi-generational wealth.

Our programs are digital, meaning you can learn on a computer, a phone or tablet. Comma Club members have access anywhere in the world to learn at their own pace. The course content is relevant anywhere in the United States. Though we share global events that impact the real estate markets, our primary investors reside and/or invest in the U.S. markets.

Currently a Beginner Real Estate Investors course and the *We Must Own* workbook is available for additional guidance and practice. As we expand our platform, we will offer a breadth of course topics where expert investors, developers and industry professionals share their expertise to grow the knowledge base of the Comma Club community members. Members who enroll in our Beginner Real Estate Investor Course will review the fundamentals of the real estate industry, the various types of investment options, and the process from start to closing of the deal.

As members prepare to take the leap into their first deal, they can build their confidence with advanced courses and niche topics such as commercial real estate, flipping houses, multifamily rehabilitation, hotels, community development, homeless solutions and more. Our industry professionals have gathered a plethora of resources for business formation, property inspection, taxation, deal financing and property management for end-to-end support throughout the process, making services available to our members at a preferred rate. This digital community of like-minded investors was created so that ordinary, everyday people can access the long-hidden knowledge about real estate investing and start their investment journey immediately.

CREATING ACCESS TO WEALTH

Look around. Everywhere your footsteps, from the towering cities to the grassy fields, from the farmland to the forests and all the concrete in between, someone owns all of that property. Why not you? If everything you see is owned by someone, then isn't it about time that you get your slice of the earth?

My primary motivation for creating Comma Club is to create a mentorship for ownership, where new investors find the confidence and motivation to start investing in real estate. Comma Club is an evolving network of like-minded investors who motivate one another to own land and property, build commas and communities as we grow so that we can be in a position to create the world that we want to live in and pass to our children.

Build Wealth at Any Experience Level

As a young professional, I began to ask myself, "Why didn't anyone teach me to invest?"

Real estate investment training is rarely taught in primary and secondary schools. If you are fortunate, you inherited properties from a family member, but chances are they did not pass along their wisdom. Unfortunately, most of the population have little to no practical knowledge and experience in real estate investing.

They even understand little about buying and owning a personal home. I know because I have coached countless people to purchase their first home, then their first investment property, and ultimately to build residual income outside of their everyday career. Many of these individuals successfully built a portfolio of real estate properties after following the steps and strategies that I provided in the training courses.

Build Wealth at Any Age

As a college junior, I worked as an assistant for a real estate developer in my college town. Guess what? He was 25 years old, a student at my college, and was awarded a contract by the city to redevelop an entire neighborhood. After successfully revitalizing a neighborhood, he developed an entirely new community with homes valued at $500k and up. I watched how a young student with no career experience or background in real estate built a multi-million-dollar company eventually developing properties all over the country.

As a 30-something woman, I began working for a broker who was 24 years old and owned nine properties. He never had to work for anyone again because he had a million-dollar net worth before the age of twenty-five. That broker inspired me because he was earning residual income and had the freedom to enjoy it.

When I began my journey as an investor, I met a man under the age of 40 who owned 91 rental properties. He did nothing but drive around and collect rent checks from his tenants and reinvest his earnings to grow his portfolio. He taught me the methods of his business which I quickly applied and began to purchase his properties, thus building my portfolio.

I quickly learned that investing in real estate is not about age. With fundamental knowledge anyone can do it. I would like to teach you, regardless of your experience, or age. You do not need to be a real estate agent or broker to start investing in the real estate market. In fact, most real estate agents know little about real estate investing even though they work in the industry. The investment courses we offer teach simple to understand processes and end-to-end strategies for success.

Build Wealth at Any Income Level

Do you think you need to be rich to invest in real estate? Fortunately, you do not have to be rich or even have a high paying job to invest in real estate. You can start to build wealth regardless of your annual income. Through my real estate coaching, I helped a 20 something temp-employee purchase two rental properties using the information from this book. I have helped novice investors learn to pool capital and buy a portfolio of properties using the syndication method. I have helped successful entrepreneurs take profits from their business and reinvest them in real estate to grow their wealth at a faster rate. But most importantly, I united like-minded community members to raise capital to transform their community with small dollar investments that made a big impact. Regardless of your income or employment, you can become a successful investor. The Comma Club is here to help you build wealth through real estate.

THE COMMA CLUB VISION

By creating the Comma Club Community, I hope to enable, educate, and inspire everyday people to own within the communities where they live and to take back the reins of control over the lands where they reside. Though real estate markets have historically been reserved for the wealthy, I intend to create a platform of education and access so that everyday citizens like you and me may share in the wealth of this nation as owners of this great land. This is collaborative investing and communal growth. As we build high, let's be intentional to build together.

Section I:

A MENTORSHIP IN OWNERSHIP

WHY WE *MUST* OWN

I believe wealth can be created by anyone - at any age, income, or experience level. Even more, I believe the real estate industry should be accessible to anyone of any race, any economic and social status who wants the opportunity to participate in the markets. Unfortunately, statistics do not agree. There is a 30% gap in homeownership between Whites and Blacks, a 26% gap between Whites and Latinos, and Asian communities fall behind as well. A wealth study from the Social Security Administration reveals the shocking truth:

"Although wealth varies substantially by race and ethnicity, little of that disparity can be explained by differences in income or demographic characteristics. In fact, the wealth gap far exceeds the income gap. The large body of empirical studies on wealth (for example, Wolff 1998, 2000; Hurst, Luoh, and Stafford 1998; and Blau and Graham 1990) shows that white households have at least five times the wealth of minority households yet earn, on average, just twice as much as minority households. Several studies have tried to explain the wealth divide that is greater than $10 trillion at the time of this writing. Smith (1995) reported that it is due in part to lower minority incomes, poorer health, and smaller inheritances. Even after controlling for income and demographic factors, Blau and Graham (1990) found that almost three-quarters of the Black-white wealth gap could not be explained; they speculated that differences in intergenerational transfers and, to a smaller extent, barriers to the accumulation of home and business equity might be responsible.'" Only 10% of black families report receiving an inheritance and 7% of Hispanic families, compared to 30% of white families according to the Federal Reserve. Real estate is an asset that can be transferred intergenerationally; unless there is more ownership today, the future generations will face bleaker statistics than those currently measured. Succession and estate planning is also necessary to preserve wealth to the next generation. When a community member does not own their residence nor own a business or investment in their community, they miss the opportunity to participate in the growth and representation in that community and are left further behind in the economic gap as property values rise over time. It is not only imperative to own residential property, but also critical for business owners to own the properties where they operate for many reasons including business continuity, controlling costs, economic incentives, greater insurance protection, and the opportunity to leverage assets on the balance sheet to fund business operations & expansion. The gap in business ownership between whites and minorities represents 25% of the overall wealth gap in America. Statistics also show only 3% of black families own commercial real estate, a disheartening statistic seeing that black spending power reached its highest peak in 2022 at $1.6 trillion while average net worth of blacks declined by 14%.

Diverse ownership and leadership of commercial real estate companies is a big problem in this country that has somehow stayed under the radar. Commercial real estate companies are at the center of commercial development, brokering major deals and driving economic progress in urban areas and developing markets. There have also been major barriers to entry for minorities and those of lower social classes seeking careers in the commercial real estate industry. According to a study by the Bella Research Group and the Knight Foundation, less than 1% of minorities work in commercial real estate management roles, and just about 2% of all measured development companies were owned by minorities. For women, only 14% of white women served in management roles in

CRE, and less than 1% were women of color. The people who spearhead real estate development are typically limited to a reserved group of elite white males and those deciding the fate of communities often do not even live within the communities they develop nor personally impacted by the decisions made. The outcome of these decision makers has left diverse communities stripped of culture, gentrified, and ravished of its value. Private family offices and investment groups that own and finance major deals pass along intergenerational wealth and knowledge through a private insider only network amassing wealth and property and controlling rents and policy as they grow. While most of the population knows very little about real estate investing, they participate unconsciously as renters, patrons, and low-level employees – left completely in the dark about the prospects of ownership. For those who did not inherit property and whose parents were not property owners, the probability of ownership becomes even dimmer. Those who care to learn have had few resources, because practical training on real estate ownership has not been customary in school curriculums without attending a specialty degree program. Others who are passionate about owning property struggle to finance deals and find resources to get the deals closed and profitable.

There are so many historical wrongs that have led to the current division of property, including the illegal taking of land, government's wrongful use of eminent domain laws to take valuable property owned by minorities, bank redlining and the refusal to make loans in certain areas, restrictive covenants and community by-laws that prevent minorities from owning property, suppressed appraisals that lower property value in minority communities, lower municipal investments into schools and infrastructure in communities of color, government corruption and greedy leaders selling the soul of cities to large corporate interests, poor social welfare policies and an endless list of other terrible travesties. After hundreds of years of restrictive laws and lending policies, and other systemic barriers, it is clear that minorities, women, and those of lower incomes have been left out and left behind. Things have improved as light has been shed on these issues, but still currently 27% of black mortgage loan applications are denied according to the Home Mortgage Disclosure Act.

Though I did not create Comma Club to report the challenges in the industry, it is a reality that has impacted me as a minority woman and an obvious impediment to success that I've had to overcome. When I started a career in real estate, I knew nothing about real estate and had no one to teach me. Fortunately, two minority women took me under their wing and shared their knowledge so that I could quickly get a running start in my career. When I started as a minority woman owned developer, I found myself in the same position struggling to finance deals, evaluate opportunities and get a foot in the door. Had it not been for those in my network, I would have given up with the countless doors closed in my face and phones hung up on the other side. This has compelled me to make the information I've learned as accessible as possible so others can learn the path to success and anyone who wants to can thrive in this industry. The idea for the Comma Club Community came to me during the 2020 global pandemic when I was in quarantine. I was dreaming about expanding the possibilities of how people own property in America, transitioning my mind out of direct real estate sales into citywide development and wanting to position disenfranchised people to have life stability through ownership. I saw how people who didn't own their homes during the pandemic were at risk of eviction while the nations were rocked, but owners felt safer in their home sanctuary protected by emergency mortgage relief. I saw how fragile the economy was, but the real estate markets strengthened to their highest point during times of crisis. The owners came out on top, the renters got pushed further into poverty and the gap between the have and the have nots was widened. People felt the disparities of ownership and there was nationwide upheaval about evictions of the vulnerable population including single mothers, seniors, and people with fixed incomes. There was a huge reality check about ownership where finally people realized that indifference is consequential.

In all this disruption, I took the time to write a nationwide plan to empower people in black and brown communities to own property and be the leaders of community development in their neighborhoods. *We Must Own* is a plea to act and make ownership a priority. This manual targets new and 1st generation owners as a tool to ensure the future generations are not left holding the short stick because of our lack of preparation, education, and effort to learn about real estate and overcome the barriers of ownership. Yes, the barriers are real, but ignorance does not have to be one of them. When I became aware of the massive abuses happening to residents in my neighborhood, my passive approach to real estate ownership became a fiery, unapologetic, relentless pursuit. We MUST own property! We MUST own land! We MUST own businesses! We MUST own houses and commercial real estate! We MUST own investment and development companies! We MUST lead the decisions of our communities if things are ever going to change. My hope is that this manual will equip the reader with all the necessary steps to become an owner. As we collectively pursue ownership, the statistics about wealth, property ownership, and commercial real estate leadership will become more equitable and the wealth gap will be closed.

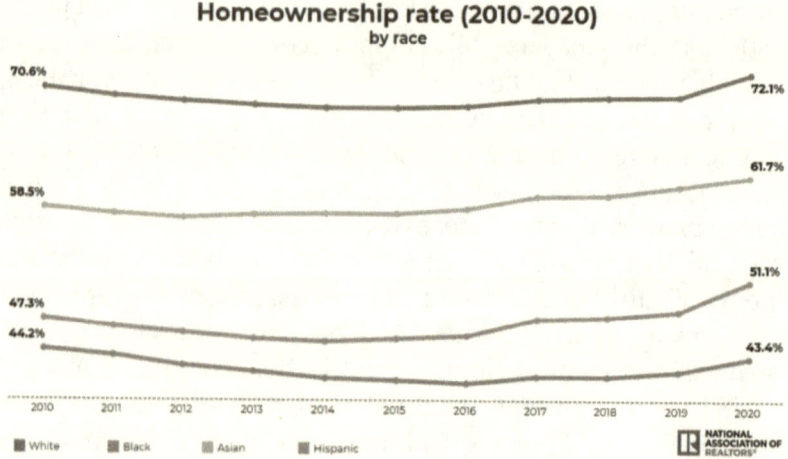

Graph produced by National Association of REALTORs – Feb 2022

FACTS ABOUT REAL ESTATE

- The Federal Reserve reports the net worth of a homeowner is over 40 times greater than that of a renter.

- A 20-year housing study showed that between 2000 and 2008, the average US housing price of $106,000 doubled to $256,000, more than 106% increase.

- As of the second quarter 2022, the median asking sales price for vacant for sale units was $291,600. The median asking rent for vacant units was $1,314.

- The median Black American family has thirteen cents for every one dollar in wealth held by White families, according to Whitehouse.gov.[1]

- Since 2019, home prices rose nearly 30 percent. As a result, a typical home is about $80,000 more expensive than pre-pandemic.

- Black spending power reached its highest peak in 2022 at $1.6 trillion while average net worth of blacks declined by 14%.

- Approximately 40 percent of U.S. housing stock is at least 50 years old, and more than 15 million properties are vacant even as families struggle to find affordable housing.

- Less than 1% of minorities work in commercial real estate management roles.

---

[1] https://www.whitehouse.gov/briefing-room/statements-releases/2021/06/01/fact-sheet-biden-harris-administration-announces-new-actions-to-build-black-wealth-and-narrow-the-racial-wealth-gap/

- 67% of real estate investors are white, 17.4% are Hispanic, 8.4% are Hispanic, 4.8% are Asian.

- In Canada and the U.S., approximately 73% of real estate related degrees (undergraduate and graduate) are obtained by men.

- 68% of real estate investors are male and 70% are over the age of 40.

- 36.7 percent of all commercial real estate industry professionals are women according to the National Association of REALTORs, a number that has not changed significantly in 15 years.

- Women in commercial real estate earn 10.2% less than men overall, Black, Hispanic, and Asian women earn 80-86 cents for every dollar that men earn.

- The 400 richest American billionaires have more total wealth than all 10 million Black American households combined according to a Brookings study.

- There is a 30% gap in homeownership between whites and blacks, which is higher than it was in 1960.

- In 2019, the gap in business ownership between Black and Latino households, relative to White households, accounted for 25 percent of the overall racial wealth gap between these groups.

- Nearly 30 percent of White families report having received an inheritance or gift, compared to about 10 percent of Black families, 7 percent of Hispanic families, and 18 percent of other families according to the Survey of Consumer Finances by the Federal Reserve

- 28% of the Black renter households spend more than 50% of their income on rent.

- As of the second quarter of 2022, just 48 percent of Hispanic Americans and 45 percent of Black Americans own their own homes, compared to 74 percent of White Americans. All other races average 57.3 percent homeownership.

- Among younger families under 35 years of age, about 46 percent of White families own their home, compared to just 17 percent of Black families, according to the Study on Consumer Finances.

- White households are 40% more likely to be able to afford to buy property compared to Black households.

- While the typical Black or Hispanic family has $2,000 or less in liquid savings, the typical White family has more than four times that amount. Other families fall somewhere in the middle, with the typical family holding $5,000 in liquid savings.

- The Federal Reserve reports that the average homeowner in 2016 had a household wealth of $231,400, compared to the average renter having a household wealth of just $5,200.

- In a 2019 survey of Consumer Finances completed by the Federal Reserve, White families have the highest level of average family wealth: $983,400. Black and Hispanic families have considerably less wealth than White families. Black families' average wealth is less than 15 percent that of White families, at $142,500. Hispanic families' mean wealth is $165,500.

- The gap between the appraised value of homes in predominantly White neighborhoods compared to comparable homes in predominantly Black and Latino neighborhoods nearly doubled between 1980 and 2015.

- For homeowners, the typical White families' home value is $230,000 and the typical other families' home value is $310,000. The typical Black and Hispanic families' home values are lower, at $150,000 and $200,000, respectively.

- Loan Denial rates for Black Americans are higher for home purchase loans. According to the Home Mortgage Disclosure Act (HMDA), nearly 27% of Black Americans' loan applications for a home purchase were denied.

- 19% of Hispanic/Latinos and 18% of Asian/Pacific Islanders and 18% of Black/African Americans purchased multi-generational homes.

- Only 3% of Black households own commercial real estate, compared to 8% of White households, and their holdings are much smaller — valued at just $3,600 on average, compared with nearly $34,000 for White households.[2]

- The median Black family under 35 years old has almost no assets ($600). In contrast, the median young White family has a wealth of $25,400. Young Hispanic and other families fall in between, with $11,200 and $13,500 in median wealth, respectively.

---

[2] Brookings Report. "The Devaluation of Assets in Black Neighborhoods," accessed at https://www.brookings.edu/wp-content/uploads/2022/07/Devaluation-of-Assets-in-Black-Neighborhoods.pdf

- According to a 2019 Survey of Consumer Finances by the Federal Reserve, *"Wealth-holding can differ across groups due to the intergenerational transmission of wealth. 30 percent of White families report having received an inheritance or gift, compared to about 10 percent of Black families, 7 percent of Hispanic families, and 18 percent of other families.*

- The total racial wealth gap is $10.14 trillion according to brookings.edu.

- According to the 2015 Commercial Real Estate Women's (CREW) Network benchmark study, women in the industry occupy approximately nine percent of C-suite positions.

- According to a recent Women in Alternatives Investments report by KPMG (Klynveld Peat Marwick Goerdeler), 72 percent of real estate industry professionals agree that achieving gender equity and greater overall diversity is a business imperative.

- Black/African American home buyers reported the highest share of student loan debt at 41%, with a median amount of $45,000.

THE ACTION PLAN

Join
Join our online community at CommaClubCommunity.com to become a member. Stay connected by reading our blogs, tuning in to webinars and posting comments. We want to hear from you!

Learn
Complete the real estate investor courses that will review industry knowledge, investment strategies and take you through a process of identifying, evaluating, and closing on properties.

Pick Your Path
Complete the advanced and specialized investor courses that will offer a deeper dive into the investment strategies, financing options, and risk assessments to build your understanding and knowledge of the process and confidence to get started! Comma Club Courses are in development!

Earn
And when you are in position and ready to take the leap of faith and purchase your first real estate investment, the CC Coaching program will guide you step by step from identifying your property, writing your offer, and closing the deal. We will have supplements and spreadsheets to help you along the way.

Share the Wealth
We want you to share your progress and testimonials within the community. As you earn commas, share your journey so that others can be inspired. Tell a friend, tell a family member, and share on your social networks so we can build wealth generating opportunities collectively.

ESTABLISH YOUR VISION

Take the time to envision your future and write it down. It is written in the Bible, "Where there is no vision, the people perish" (Proverbs 29:18, KJV). I have seen many perishing communities and neighborhoods because no one had a vision to change it. Contrarily, writing down a vision is one of the first steps to manifesting your ideas into reality. It will also guide you in the great big world of real estate to stay focused on the plan that you set out to execute. Let's get started by answering these questions.

1. Why does investing in real estate interest you?

2. How many properties do you desire to own in the next year? 5 years? 10 years?

3. If money were no object, how would that realistically change your vision?

4. What are the top 3 reasons that compel you to invest?

5. What are the top 3 barriers that you believe might hinder your success?

6. Is Generational Wealth Transfer important to you? If so, who will you leave your assets to after you are gone?

7. How much income do you need to earn from investments to replace your income Annually? Monthly?

8. What impact do you hope to have within the community where you invest?

Section II:

THE BASICS OF INVESTING

INVESTMENT STRATEGY REVIEW

Before you begin your journey as a real estate investor, the first step is to select your investment strategy. Investors can implement a variety of investment strategies throughout the life of their investment journey without limitation. However, some investors prefer to specialize in one area and build a portfolio of properties using one tried-and-true method.

Investment strategies can be evaluated based on many distinct factors such as liquidity, time horizon, level of risk, acquisition cost, yield, or degree of investor participation required. Many investors also decide which strategy to assume based on personal interest, comfort level and/or their access to capital. Being that these factors will vary for each student, I am choosing to categorize the various investment strategies by the one factor that is common to all people, and that is TIME. I've learned that time is money, and so I ranked the various investment strategies based on the level of active participation required which directly correlates to the amount of time you will need to invest.

For those who have full-time careers outside of real estate, making a full-time commitment to real estate investing may be unrealistic. Opportunity costs always exist for any time that an individual commits to learning and earning as a real estate investor because everyone's time can always be expended elsewhere. Therefore, it will be important to consider the time required and the cost of that time versus the potential return for each investment strategy. Each person's hour of time is valued differently (some earn $10/hour in their day job and others earn $500/hour), and each person has varying availability; nonetheless, measuring time commitment will be a critical factor in selecting an investment strategy no matter how free your schedule.

Success with any investment is a product of good management. For those who want to implement a certain investment strategy but do not have the time to commit, it will be essential to have an active partner and/or to hire a good team to execute your plan. Many investors do not directly manage their investments and that's perfectly okay. It is still important to note, *you will profit to the extent that your investment is effectively managed.* No one, regardless of their experience level, will manage your money like YOU.

Now, let's explore the investment strategies based on the level of investor participation required. Consider your availability and how much time you can realistically commit and then select an active, moderate, or passive investment strategy that best fits your vision. *Active* means being involved in the regular day-to-day management and decision-making, and *Passive* means as little as writing a check and waiting for the return.

DIFFERENT TYPES OF INVESTMENT STRATEGIES

ACTIVE INVESTMENT STRATEGIES:

- BRR(R) Strategy
- Short-Term Rental Strategy
- Fix and Flip Strategy
- New Construction Strategy
- Land Development Strategy

MODERATE INVESTMENT STRATEGIES:

- Turnkey Rental Strategy
- Wholesaling Strategy
- RRR Strategy
- Buy and Hold Strategy

PASSIVE INVESTMENT STRATEGIES

- Private Lending Strategy
- REIT Investments Strategy
- Joint Venture or Partnerships Strategy
- Crowd Funded Investment Strategy

ACTIVE INVESTMENT STRATEGIES:

BRR(R) Strategy (Buy - Rehab - Rent - Refinance)

A BRR(R) strategy means that you will buy, rehabilitate, and then rent a property to a tenant and hold it for an extended length of time before reselling the property. Investors will typically refinance their investment about six months after completing the renovation and placing a tenant once the property has stabilized in its increased value and is generating income. The purpose of the refinance is to recoup the cash that has been invested during the purchase and renovation process and, in some cases, to cash out the equity that has been earned from the increase in value as a result of time passed and the improvements made to the property. Once the cash is extracted, the investor can recycle the cash by investing into their next deal while still carrying the asset on their books and still collecting rent.

Pros
This strategy is one of the most common and most effective ways to build net worth via a portfolio of rental properties with immediate equity, return of investment, and cash flow with low cost to start. We will discuss financing methods in a later section.

Cons
The Investor will need to be actively involved in the selection, inspection, acquisition, renovation, and rental process which will typically require three to six months of active participation. Once the property is leased the investor will move into more of a passive role. Investors will also need to obtain a working knowledge of the construction and renovation process prior to starting. New investors will typically need to identify, evaluate, and hire a reliable support team of professionals including a real estate agent, general contractor, and property manager among others and be involved in the direction and management of their team.
Step 1 - Buy

The BRR(R) strategies work best when you acquire a property that has been deeply discounted due to its distressed condition. A distressed property will typically show excessive signs of wear, damage, or outdated design features and will typically need a replacement in any or all of the following areas:

- Worn or damaged roof
- Foundation problems and/or settlement cracks
- Plumbing leaks and/or faulty plumbing fixtures
- Electrical issues and/or outdated electrical panel
- Out of date interior finishes
- Obsolete systems and defunct appliances
- Wood rot on fascia, trim
- Worn, damaged or outdated flooring, counters, lighting, cabinetry, and interior design
- Funky layout, enclosed or unusable space (bar areas, theater rooms, formal)
- Severe disrepair or neglect
- Fire and/or water damage
- Poor landscaping, curb appeal and/or drainage

It is important to thoroughly inspect the property prior to closing the deal. Walk through the property with a skilled home inspector and/or contractor to understand the hidden defects that can equate to costly repairs. Check for mold, asbestos, lead-based paint, and other hazardous substances during your inspection process. Schedule specialized inspections if needed to confirm the initial conclusion or to settle your concerns. Local building and property codes require that certain hazardous substances like mold or asbestos be remediated prior to occupancy. Ideally, try to find a property that needs significant cosmetic repair with limited structural repair.

There are times when you find a great deal on a property not because the property is distressed but because the seller is distressed. In these cases, you are capable of purchasing properties in good condition that are well below market value. The same BRR(R) strategy would be applicable with the likelihood of lower rehabilitation cost. There are many situations that cause a seller to be distressed and motivated to sell a property below market value. Here are a few:

- Declining economic markets
- Job loss
- Death/Illness of the owner and/or primary payer in the household
- Divorce
- Foreclosure
- Severe property damage with an under-insured or uninsured owner
- Property tax delinquencies
- Debt
- Liens or court judgements

I do not encourage any investor to prey upon individuals in distressed situations, as a home or property may be the only valuable asset a distressed seller has to be able to overcome their financial or life setback. However, in the event that you identify a property that is available for sale, a fair offer can put a distressed seller back on the right track and be just the opportunity that the property owner needs to cure a whole list of issues in their life.

I have seen many distressed sellers benefit from the right offer at the right time, so do not be afraid to take advantage of a good opportunity. There is a middle ground where investors can snag a good deal and still be able to sleep at night knowing they paid a fair price. As you may soon see, integrity is not a quality inherent to all investors. For those who possess it, God blesses them with longevity and peace to enjoy the fruit of their labor. When you are honest and fair, deals come to you.

Regardless of the source of your acquisition, this is the **formula for your BRR(R) purchase** to determine your maximum price to pay for your property:

Formula to Determine Your BRR(R) Purchase Price

    After Repair Value x 80%
- Estimated Cost of Improvements
- Estimated Closing Costs
- Buyer Paid Real Estate Commissions

    Maximum Price Paid for Property

Step 2 - Rehab

After acquiring the property in a distressed condition, the next step is to rehabilitate it to a condition equivalent to neighboring properties that are sold at or above market value. Thus, you increase the appraised value and create immediate equity growth that exceeds the cost of your improvements.

Have a proper inspection and evaluation of the property condition prior to starting repairs so that you can avoid double work and expensive surprises. Focus on having quality work performed, and do not cut corners. If there are signs of foundation issues that indicate the need for foundation repair, it's more costly to find out after you've already laid brand new floors.

Always add a contingency for unknown issues that may arise during your rehab. Be careful to avoid improvements that are too high end or uncommon for the location and will not add value on an appraisal. Experienced investors learn to make high quality, low-cost improvements to increase the spread between After Repair Value and Acquisition Cost to increase their profit after it is all said and done.

Renovations that create the most dramatic impact on value would be:
- Those that increase the square footage or bedroom/bathroom count of the home. Finishing a basement, guest house, or attic into livable air-

conditioned/heated space can dramatically increase value. Be sure to model top-selling homes in your area.
- Opening the floorplan in the living areas, kitchen, and dining room are top requests for buyers and renters and increase value versus enclosed spaces. Be careful not to eliminate too much structure because buyers need to see defined spaces where they can live and place furniture.
- Bathroom and Kitchen Remodels are necessary. Repainting or reconditioning floors, cabinets, and counters to a more modern color, and adding new draw knobs and handles can totally transform a space. You do not always have to gut and replace; try to restore what exists if at all possible. This will keep costs down.
- Install hardwood or wood-like flooring in your living areas and in bedrooms if this is common in your area.
- Replace the roof and HVAC (if necessary).
- Add walk in showers and walk-in closets where plausible.
- Improve curb appeal by making reasonable modifications to the exterior of the home. Repair rotted trim, soffits and fascia, power wash and repaint exterior siding and trim, repaint discolored patios, fix broken fences, pave gravel driveways, add landscaping shrubs and flowers, exterior shutters that match the trim, and exterior lighting are all nice upgrades that bump up value. Since your property will be rented, do not overspend on landscaping unless you plan to maintain the yard as part of the lease.

You are not expected to perform any of the property improvements on your own. You will, however, need to understand the construction process for the property type that you are renovating and be aware of the main systems and structures of the property. For example, you will need to know…

- that a home is made up of a foundation which can be constructed out of a concrete slab, pier and beam, basement, wood or crawlspace stem wall.
- the various types of roofing that would be common in your market location and the most durable shingle type for your property.
- the basic plumbing, electrical and structural components that go into the property and the standards necessary to meet code in your city or state.
- permitting requirements for additions or modifications to existing structures or walls.

You also need to develop a working knowledge of terminology so that you are not completely taken for a ride by a dishonest contractor. Joining the Comma Club Community, reading our investor content, taking hands-on renovation classes at your local hardware store, watching programs on HGTV, following experienced investors on social media, subscribing to YouTube channels, and reading books on the subject matter are all excellent ways to develop your knowledge of the industry. Overtime, your knowledge will grow, as will your confidence.

Hiring a reliable general contractor (GC) can eliminate a lot of stress because GCs enter into a contract with the property owner/investor and take the responsibility for the construction, improvement, and renovation of the property. The GC assumes the role to hire and oversee the subcontractors and ensures performance and satisfactory completion of the assignment.

You should identify your GC prior to starting work and ask for references, insurance, license information and photos of their finished work. Request a construction estimate upfront and use this as the baseline for your repairs. It is smart to keep construction estimates on file to negotiate future bids, and ask for repairs to be split out between material cost and labor and price/ft. You can bargain shop for materials to save on project cost.

Inspect contractor quotes with a fine-tooth comb if you know details on how they are estimating their price. Keep all invoices and material receipts to submit to your appraiser and in case of insurance claims. Do not be afraid to ask questions or take time before making repair or design decisions. It is better to get a second opinion or have a style savvy friend evaluate your material choices before committing. Stay away from hookups from unlicensed/unpermitted/inexperienced family, friends, or contractors unless you are willing to bear the consequences of their mistakes.

Step 3 – Rent

After completing the renovations, rent the property at the prevailing market rate and hold the property for more than one year, collecting rent at a higher rate of return than the cost of financing. Sometimes the quality of improvements commands an above average rent amount. Even if not, rent prices should be increased annually to follow the market, thus, increasing your yield the longer you hold your property.

A real estate professional should be able to market your property to potential tenants and help evaluate your applicants to ensure you have a well-qualified and dependable long-term tenant. Your real estate professional will also prepare the lease and ensure you have completed the necessary disclosures and registrations to be in compliance with your city or state laws. If you need a referral for a real estate leasing specialist, please reach out to us at Referrals@CommaClubCommunity.com

Step 4 – Refinance

When you believe the value has increased, refinance the loan and cash out your equity.

How You Earn

The BRR strategy allows the investor to benefit through long term property appreciation as values rise over time. Investors who hold the property long term will have an appreciating asset with an amortizing debt that is being paid off by the tenant as the years pass. You benefit by owning the asset, but your tenant pays the debt. The difference between the market value of the asset and the debt owned on that asset is the equity, which you can add directly to your net worth.

In addition to the equity earned, the investor will receive income by whatever spread remains between the rent amount less the mortgage and any property taxes and operating costs. Investors who pay cash or who finance and then hold the property for the life of the loan (10-30 years) will have a property free and clear and will eventually collect 100% of the rent as profit less normal operating costs.

Formula to Determine Your BRR(R) Rental Income:

       Monthly Rent Amount
- Mortgage on Rental Property
- Property Management Fees (If applicable)
- Property Taxes
- Less Insurance
- Reserves for Maintenance/ Repairs
- Utilities or Other Landlord Paid Expenses

Monthly Profit

Formula to Determine Your Equity Growth:

       Market Value of Property
- Outstanding Mortgage Payoff Amount
- Outstanding Debts or Taxes Due on Property

Equity Remaining in Property

Formula to determine Your BRR(R) Return on Investment when selling your property:

Sale Price of Property
- Outstanding Mortgage Payoff Amount
- Selling Costs (Loan Fees, Attorney Fees)
- Closing Costs
- Real Estate Broker Commissions
- Title Fees
- Negotiated Buyer Credits or Concessions in the Contract
- Property Taxes Prorated

Net Proceeds at the time of Sale

- Initial Investment (cash down payment or capital invested)
- Capital Improvements (don't double count if repairs were financed)
- Capital Gains Tax

Net Profit at Sale of BRR(R) Investment

Formula to determine liquidated equity when refinancing your property:

Market Value of the Property x 75% - 80%
- Outstanding Mortgage Payoff Amount
- Closing Costs
- Title Fees
- Unpaid Escrow Balances

Proceeds from cash out refinance at the time of Sale

Fix and Flip Strategy

Fix and Flip properties follow a similar pattern as a BRR(R) strategy; however, there are some notable differences. Like the BRR(R) strategy, the purpose of the Fix and Flip is to identify a distressed property in need of improvement, and then *Fix* the home into a condition equivalent or better than other nearby properties that have sold at the market rate. Once the property has been improved, the investor immediately sells the property with the goal to yield a profit. The profit is formulated as the difference between cash netted at the time of sale and the cost to acquire, repair, and hold the property prior to its sale. This also factors in closing costs to acquire and sell the property.

While the BRR(R) strategy can be implemented with all sorts of property types such as single family, multifamily, commercial retail strips, etc., the Fix and Flip strategy is regularly used for residential properties. Another difference between Fix and Flip and BRR(R) strategy is the remodel choices will typically be higher-end or more luxurious when you plan to sell a property than on a property held for long-term rent. BRR(R) investors will go for lower-level finishes, carpets, and flooring. Flippers will upgrade homes to get the highest resale value. Though both require knowledge of the reconstruction process, Flippers also need to have a knack for design, scheme, and flow, and may often even stage the properties as livable homes to attract ready buyers.

Though other strategies can be implemented by out-of-town investors, let me issue a word of caution. Do not attempt to flip homes in markets where you do not reside. Market knowledge and investor participation is most critical with short term real estate investments.

<u>Pros</u>
Fix and Flips allow investors to turn a profit quickly and recycle their profits into new deals more frequently than other investment strategies. Fix and Flips have been known to yield investors large returns in less than 1 year.

Cons

Success with the Fix and Flip strategy requires skill and velocity. You will need to execute your strategy quickly, as you will typically reduce your profits the longer you hold this investment. New investors without a strong working knowledge of the market and poor management skills have made blunders and lost money with this strategy. Flipping is not for the faint at heart or risk averse and will require active participation until the property is sold.

Step 1 – Buy

Refer to BRR(R) Step 1 with one exception. In order to profit on a flip, you must make significant improvements to the property in order to yield a return in the short term. Modest cosmetic improvements will not yield the same returns as overhauls and complete renovation jobs. Additionally, it is important to note that there are different methods of financing BRR(R) versus Fix and Flip deals that we will review in the financing section of this course.

Financial institutions view properties held for immediate sale as a different risk profile than properties held for rent. They will also typically use different underwriting rules to evaluate the investor's creditworthiness and the approvability of the deal based on the strategy selected. Lenders knowing the property will be sold in the short-term will make short-term interest-only loans during the construction period with the principal due within six to twelve months. Thus, Flippers must be more time conscious because of high-rate interest that inflates after the initial term. Ideally, the investor should look to renovate, market, and close the sale of their flip within six months from the time of purchase.

Formula to Determine Your Fix and Flip Purchase Price
Choose the *lesser of these two formulas* as your maximum purchase price:

Quick Method:

> After Repair Value x 80%
> - Estimated Cost of Improvements
> - Estimated Closing Costs
> - Buyer Paid Real Estate Commissions
>
> ─────────────────────────
> Maximum Price Paid for Property

Or More Detailed Method

> After Repair Value
> - Estimated Cost of Improvements
> - Estimated Closing Costs and Commissions at time of Purchase
> - Estimated Closing Costs and Commissions at time of Sale
> - 6 months Bank Interest
> - 6 months Holding Costs
> - Profit Investor Expects to Earn
>
> ─────────────────────────
> Maximum Price Paid for Property

In the expert counsel of long-time investor Luther Huggins, "Always buy a deal right!" Do not be afraid to pass up an opportunity that appears good when the numbers do not work. In real life the numbers will never exactly fit your financial model, so you will need to make a gut call. However, avoid stressing your model too much because, just like a home, too much stress on the foundation can cause the walls to break.

Understanding your local market will better position you to win deals when competing against other buyers. Cash deals usually win over deals that are financed. When possible, use cash or lines of credit to snag a deal and then refinance if necessary. Higher offers and quick transaction closings also help investors seal the deal. Some investors focus on buying low while other investors pay a premium to secure more deals and save on construction cost through preferential pricing that comes from volume and velocity. Build face to face relationships with agents and wholesalers so that they will come to you first. If you stay in front of your pipeline and remain honest and reliable, wholesalers and agents will continue to come to you when they find a good off-market deal.

Step 2 – Renovate

Refer to BRR(R) Step 2 and the same information will apply. Flipping a house is different from a make-ready where you slap some paint on the walls, clean the carpet, and stick a rent sign out. Be prepared to come with your vision for design, layout, material selection, and system and appliance choices. Be prepared to make all of the executive decisions that your General Contractor will present to you. If you want to save money and do it yourself, be prepared to get your hands dirty too.

As an example, a GC asked if we wanted to excavate the foundation in a home to create a crawl space under the foundation or if we wanted the foundation company to dig holes from the exterior and lift the piers from the side. We asked, "how much does each cost?" and went with the method that was most affordable. Unknowingly, the partial excavation created a slope under the home and when spring rains came there was pooling water under the foundation that threatened to flood the house and cause water damage to our new floors. Ouch!

I found myself out in the rain digging trenches around the home to create escape holes for the water – not a fun day! After having to redo the work that we did wrong the first time, adding gutters to the home, and digging proper drainage, it ended up costing double what it would have cost if we made a better choice in the first place. This is just one of the blunders I have witnessed watching new investors rehab properties. Do not be so married to the bottom line that you cut corners. If you learn nothing else, please take this advice to heart.

On the contrary, do not think the higher the price equals better. Be a cheapskate. Don't count every dime, count every penny. When you show others that you are accountable and focused on your bottom line, others will respect you for it. When you are loose with your wallet and round up on everything, expect to get taken for a ride.

Take time to compare materials and choose options that are similar but cost less. Get multiple quotes on high price jobs like roofing and foundation and negotiate with your contractors. Keep record of your past cost so that you can compare line by line when you are misquoted, or prices change. Push back when something does not add up and ask for warranties to work. This way, if it is not done right, the vendor must return to fix it on their dime.

Flipping is not the time to be pompous. Show up to your work site in jeans and boots and get your hands dirty like everyone else. If you look like you can pay a premium, you will.

Step 3 - Sell

The goal of every flipper is to finish their renovation and watch the home sell with the snap of their fingers. In hot markets, this may happen. However, flippers should make a few considerations before listing.

The first question is, "When is the best time to list?" My experience would say wait until the home is completely finished, staged, and photographed before giving in to the temptation to list. Why? Because you do not want to cheat yourself out of every dime you could profit by selling too early. There will always be a buyer who drives by and who would love to make you an offer. By accepting a quick offer on an unfinished property, you could leave money on the table from other buyers willing to pay higher. Take their contact information and give them an opportunity to submit an offer when the home is complete unless their offer is just too good to refuse.

Having a complete home that lists and sells on the market establishes that area as a hot selling location and creates data for local appraisers to use on future appraisals on pricing, square footage, condition, and days on market data. Off market sales work against you. So, list your properties and populate sales data within your local listing service if you plan to work in that same area in the future.

Flippers who are unable to sell the property or unable to sell at the price they need to yield a profit can opt to move to a BRR(R) strategy and refinance the property as a rental after the renovation. This will allow the flipper to exit the high-rate loan and wait until the market value increases to a level that is favorable to their profit goals. In this case, the investor will wait out the market until the investor is able to sell the property in the future at the price originally anticipated, recouping their profits and rental income along the way. If the investor opts to rent their property, they might be satisfied with renting the home at a price that breaks even with the holding cost. The investor's main objective would be to hold the property at no additional cost so that it does not become a financial burden.

How You Earn

The Fix and Flip strategy allows the investor to benefit through short term appreciation and increase in value as a result of improvements to the condition of the property and local demand for a property of this quality, design features, and price.

Formula to Determine Your Fix and Flip Profit

Sale Price of Remodeled Home
- Outstanding Mortgage Payoff Amount
- Selling Costs
- Closing Costs
- Real Estate Broker Commissions
- Title Fees
- Negotiated Buyer Credits or Concessions in the Contract
- Property Taxes Prorated

= Net Cash Received at Time of Property Sale

- Purchase Price of Property (if not fully paid off at time of close as part of Payoff)
- Cost of Improvements (if not fully paid off at time of close as part of Payoff)
- Closing Costs Paid at Time of Purchase
- Investor Paid Commissions at the Time of Property Acquisition
- Borrowed Funds on Credit Cards or Lines of Credit or Net Accounts Due with Suppliers
- Holding Costs (Electricity, Gas, Water, Utilities Connection Fees)
- Owners Risk Policy Insurance + General Liability Insurance
- Marketing Fees

= Profit Earned on Fix and Flip

New Construction Strategy

Perhaps you are a visionary who loves to start from a blank canvas. Building new construction is an investment method that allows investors to build properties from the ground up and create any property type that they envision. From single family housing, which is most common and accessible, to tiny houses, townhomes, container communities, retail, office complexes and more – you have the option to build anything you want that is allowable within the zoning of your location. Each lot will be subject to present zoning regulations and must conform to the designated use(s) for that address, unless a non-conforming use permit or exception is granted.

Oftentimes new investors discover this method of investing when they inherit a lot of land or an existing lot that they own has gone unsold for some time. Undeveloped land in a city area is unproductive to the owner and the community around it. Vacant or undeveloped lots in the inner city often end up used for parked vehicles, junk storage, or overgrown grass and litter. Of course, this is not always the case, but if the land goes undeveloped or unleased, it will not benefit the owner financially until it is sold. Meanwhile, property taxes and association fees continue to be charged. While unimproved land in rural areas might best be used as agricultural land, windmill, solar or cell farms, the highest and best use of platted lots in the inner city is most often construction of a property for residential or commercial use.

New construction may seem daunting to approach as a new investor, but it can be a very profitable path if done correctly. First time investors should seek individual lots in densely populated areas near major roads or highways with existing utilities. The closer you get to a city center, the less supply of vacant lots available for purchase. In the case where affordable vacant lots cannot be purchased, investors may choose to purchase homes that are in such disrepair that they can be torn down to rebuild from scratch and then resold for a price high enough to justify the cost of doing so.

Investors who purchase raw land and then build its infrastructure such as roads, lighting, water, sewer and electricity, would be called *Developers*. Developers parcel the land into multiple lots with different intended uses such as single-family housing, senior apartment living, community centers, walking trails, and retail. After dividing the land, the developers resell groups of lots to new construction builders, who then construct properties according to the developer's community masterplan. The Comma Club vision is to inspire investment in community sized developments; therefore, we will discuss this process in more detail in the Land Investment section of this lesson and will offer a mini course on New Construction and Development for those interested in this strategy.

Pros
New construction is a very profitable industry with large margins. New properties are generally valued higher on bank appraisals than existing construction and considered more desirable for home buyers and renters. While the masses of investors compete for existing distressed properties to flip or rent, new construction builders can avoid the bidding wars between Flippers by purchasing lots and building to suit the lot.

Cons
New construction requires a greater depth of knowledge and higher costs invested in architectural planning, building design, permitting, construction, and safety. It is more regulated by local zoning and building codes than existing construction. New construction requires more active management of the construction schedule and crew. Locations are often less ideal than existing construction. Investors are susceptible to fluctuations in profit driven by volatility in the global commodity markets tied to the construction industry. Bank financing is also more restrictive, as most banks require a larger down payment and a higher credit score for a new construction loan.

Step 1 – Acquire Land

In order to build a home or commercial property, you must start with identifying a lot of land. You may start by searching for a lot zoned for the intended use that you desire to build. Or you may begin with a lot that you own, and build based on the land's permitted use. If the existing use is not the highest and best use for the area, you can request an exception from your current zoning board, which will often require community support. Local real estate agents can assist you with identifying lots within your desired market area and budget.

When it comes down to where you should build, remember the number one rule of real estate: Location, Location, Location. The location of your lot determines value, more so than what you decide to build. Be sure to review the market value of nearby new construction within a quarter mile of the land that you have identified. Look at recent sales and historical sales of completed construction to ensure that there is a demand for the property that you intend to build with at least six recent sales or leases at the price you desire. If there is no market, strongly consider the difficulty or ease of making a market in that area. Be prepared to adjust your pricing or holding costs accordingly as you wait for your customer. See the financing section for methods to finance land.

Step 2 – Plan Your Vision

Building new construction will require a team of industry professionals in order to pass through the various building code requirements and to successfully complete your building or home. Local permitting and building code offices create building standards and inspection requirements to ensure that what you build is safe for occupancy without major defects or hazards as a result of faulty construction. Begin your process by learning the local and state building codes and consult specialists as needed. Rules vary per municipality. Most building permit offices will require that you submit your plans for approval prior to beginning the job. As you complete various stages of your property construction, inspection fees will be due before the city inspector will provide your permit to proceed.

Architectural firms prepare renderings of your design vision. They provide blueprints, which are formal construction plans that can be presented for approval at your local permitting office. Create a budget for your construction project based on the design and adjust design features as needed to contain your project within the decided budget. The market sets the sales price ceiling and that is something you cannot control. What you can control (to an extent) is project cost by limiting design choices and changes.

Once the construction plans are completed, the General Contractor will use them to guide the crew according to the dimensions and measurements listed on the plans. Find a trustworthy, reliable and experienced General Contractor to manage your construction process. In some states, it is required that General Contractors be licensed. Beware, in some states it is not required.

If you are an experienced laborer wanting to get into the business on the investment side, you can serve as the GC for the job yourself, subcontracting jobs as needed. The benefit of using a General Contractor is that they receive wholesale discounts on materials due to relationships and scale of business with vendors. With the construction labor force shrinking and demand so high, having a GC with a network of dependable subcontractors helps speed your build job along versus waiting for one-off subcontractors to arrive at their availability.

Step 3 – Build Your Vision

Here is a quick summary of the 10 major phases of the process to build your home.

1. Prepare Construction Site and Pour Foundation
2. Complete Rough Framing and Roof
3. Complete Rough Plumbing, Electrical HVAC

4. Exterior materials and Insulation
5. Complete Drywall and Interior Fixtures Start Exterior Finishes
6. Finish Interior Trim, Install Exterior Walkways and Driveway
7. Install Hard Surface Flooring, Countertops, Complete Exterior Grading
8. Finish Mechanical Trims; Install Bathroom Fixtures
9. Install Mirrors, Shower Doors, Finish Flooring, Exterior Landscaping
10. Final Walk-Through

This summary of the construction process is indeed just that – a summary. We will explore New Construction and Development in a later section.

How You Earn

Formula to Determine Your New Construction Profit

Completed Construction Sales Price
- Lot Acquisition Cost
- Total Hard Costs (Site Work, Foundation, Framing, Systems, Finishes, Final)
- Total Soft Costs (Survey, Design Fees & Blueprints, Permits, Legal Fees, Warranty)
- Holding Costs (Insurance, Utilities, Interest Expense)
- Real Estate Broker Commissions
- Title Fees
- Negotiated Buyer Credits or Concessions in the Contract
- Property Taxes Prorated

Profit

Land Development Strategy

As mentioned earlier, investors who purchase raw land and then build its infrastructure such as roads, lighting, water, sewer, and electricity, are called *Developers*. Developers often parcel land into multiple lots with different intended uses such as single-family and multi-family housing, senior living, recreation centers and parks, or retail and industrial uses. After dividing the land, the developer's resale groups of lots to new construction builders who then construct properties according to the developer's community masterplan. In some cases, developers will sell lots individually after creating an owner's association for keeping the community within the developer's original vision.

Finally, a land developer may choose to continue as the property developer and actually construct the project themselves. The Comma Club mission is to create community-sized impact. Therefore, we will discuss Community and Land Development in much greater detail in a separate minicourse. For the sake of this section, we will focus on the land development investment strategy where acreage is parceled and sold as developed lots.

Land developers are true visionaries because they explore new frontiers and often convert overlooked and unwanted territory into productive, vibrant spaces for housing and commerce. Being a developer is like being an artist with a blank canvas. You must be able to see what has not yet been established. You certainly must exercise faith in your vision with confidence to invest in an idea that may take years before the vision is brought to fruition or a profit is generated. This strategy of investment requires active engagement for longer periods than other investment forms.

<u>Pros</u>
One benefit of land development is that the cost of undeveloped land is less expensive than developed land and appreciates in value after the infrastructure has been placed. With a vision, developers have the opportunity to impact hundreds to thousands of people.

Responsible, good-hearted developers can make a positive ripple effect beyond their intended development site. Development increases local property value, creates jobs, stimulates economic growth for the surrounding community, expands the market for existing and future businesses, and draws new residents, who, in turn, increase the local tax base that invests in schools, roads, and amenities.

Cons

Investors' first disadvantage is that land is in limited supply and there will never be any more created. Undeveloped land is typically sold by the acre and can require larger investments to purchase acreage in a premier location with a longer term before turning a profit. Investors will face added layers of municipal regulation required to approve development projects and require political and community support. Opponents may argue that development infringes upon natural habitats and ecosystems, creates added traffic, pollution and waste, and changes the existing landscape. Therefore, developers need to prove how their project will enhance the community beyond the environmental impacts.

Step 1 – Secure Your Land

Remember, the first rule of real estate is always, Location, Location, Location. Identifying the best land to develop is a factor of proximity to major roads and highways, school systems, office and retail, where population is growing and demand for housing and new development is forthcoming. Even when the most ideal locations are discovered, the developer must take into account project cost and potential income based on the allowed zoning and needs within that area. Another consideration is the ease or difficulty of project approval that may be influenced by the political landscape or influential members of the community.

Once the area has been identified, the next step is determining suitability of a particular parcel of land. The developer must take into account the topography and natural features while determining if the parcel is feasible for the intended use. Once the ideal parcel of land is available, the developer must go about securing an agreement with the landowner and placing the land in escrow with a sufficient due diligence period to research and obtain the necessary entitlements to move forward with the deal.

Step 2 – Obtain Land Entitlements

Before a developer can move forward with their development plan at the location they secured, they must obtain land entitlement. Entitlements are the legal rights conveyed by approvals from governmental entities to develop a property for a certain use, density, building type or placement (reference land century.com). Entitlement details the use, function, density, and setback of a given property according to the municipal regulations. Depending on the existing zoning of the parcel, this process can take a few months to over a year.

This process is lengthy and arduous, but land entitlement is an essential element before moving to the next steps. Citing an article on Loopnet.com, the typical entitlement process usually requires a developer to submit a formal proposal, conceptual design package, and various environmental and technical studies to the local planning department. The project will then be reviewed against existing zoning regulations, planning codes, and local laws. It will also be evaluated to ensure there are no major environmental impacts, reviewed by various local state and federal organizations, and subject to a vote by the city council to ensure community support. Each municipality will have its own entitlement process, so be sure to check with your local city planning and development office.

According to LandCentury.com, the forms of entitlement can be described below:
- Rezoning: A property's zoning dictates what you can and cannot do with the land. If the area is not zoned for your intended use, you may need to go through the rezoning

process. This can be complicated and lengthy. Sometimes, rezoning is not possible.

- Zoning variances: This can include the number of parking spaces, building heights and setbacks.

- Use Permits: You may be required to obtain a conditional use permit for your project.

- Utility Approvals: If utilities are not already at the site, you may need to seek approval for them. You may also need to donate land to the city for utility entitlements.
- Road Approvals: If there are no existing roads that connect the property, you may need to seek approval for the creation of these as well. You'll also need to consider easements and access.

- Landscaping: Your local planning and development agency may also need to grant you approval for your landscaping.

Step 3 – Building Infrastructure

Once entitlements are granted, the developer can move forward with laying in infrastructure. Based on the existing topography of the land, the developer will decide where roads will run through the community, entryways, and curbs. You will also facilitate the process with public and private entities to add sewer storm water connections, gas lines, and electric, water, and telecommunications pipelines. The developer will also decide shared areas like sidewalks, traffic signs, landscaping, walking trails, parks and community amenities.

If the vision is for housing development, the developer will parcel and design the lots into the most feasible arrangement that meet the size and setback requirements prescribed by their city. You will create building pads and run utility connections throughout the community. Sometimes the developer will establish an owner's association which is a regulatory board made up of the owners of the community. An owner association establishes the covenants and restrictions of the community that each new owner is bound to uphold.

Step 4 – Sell the Parceled Land

As developer you establish the community master plan, which is the overall vision to be built, how the lots will be parceled, the size and use of each lot, and the desired anchor tenants or businesses you want to occupy your commercial spaces. The developer can make early on agreements to lease space or land to end users and can obtain a ***Professional Service Agreement*** (PSA) from the city to review the proposed site plan and master plan in comparison to the existing plans of the city.

The developer then either designs and builds the various home or commercial sites as a single vertically integrated firm or hands that plan off to be completed by third party building companies. If the latter is the method of choice, then one large property consisting of multiple acres of land will be platted into individual properties and then sold with a separate legal description and address per lot.

Land developers may choose to phase their sale into groups of lots over time, knowing that the land they continue to hold will rise in value as outside builders complete housing and business sites and residents move into the community. Some of the initial investment into the infrastructure such as water and wastewater management systems, can be recouped over time through the creation of a Municipal Utility District or Planned Improvement District. In this model, residents pay a special tax or assessment annually to pay off the bonds that funded the development. These financing options are only available in certain states.

How You Earn

Formula to Determine Your Land Development Profit

Cash flow from Sale of Developed Lots
- Cost to Acquire Undeveloped Land, Escrows & Fees
- Cost of Environmental Studies
- Cost of Land Survey
- Cost for Architectural Planning
- Third Party Appraisals Fee
- Attorney Fees
- Engineering and Design Costs
- Professional Service Agreement with Municipality
- Permits & Fees
- Insurance and Bonding Costs
- Cost of Infrastructure Materials and Labor
- Landscaping and Maintenance of Property
- Selling Costs and Commissions
- Other Holding Costs

Profit on Land Development Deal

Short-Term Rental Strategy

Short term rentals have become an increasingly popular method of generating income using real estate. With this method, an investor will purchase or lease a house, condominium, or apartment, and then rent it to guests who are seeking daily, weekly, or monthly occupancy. Investors choose this method versus a long-term tenant because they can earn more income renting furnished rooms by the night than by the year like a standard lease. Investors often choose locations that attract travelers to the local market such as a condominium with a beach view or a spacious house within walking distance to the nearby sports arena.

In order to market competitively in a location with a plethora of options from competing hotels/motels and B & B's, savvy property owners decorate their places in themes that are memorable and attractive. For investors with a knack for decorating and interior design, this investment strategy will allow them to employ their most creative talents and furnish properties with living room, bedroom, office and dining furniture, appliances, décor and the essentials for life away from home. It's important to remember that guests often seek entertainment and relaxation, so ensuring your property is peaceful and offers amenities is a necessity!

Short-term rentals are classified like hotels. Properties that earn income by the night may be subject to a hotel or occupancy tax in many states. Like hotels, new guests rotate as often as daily and require support to check in, check out, learn their way around the home, connect to internet and smart devices, and find local food options and travel information as part of the recurring management of the rental. When issues arise such as plumbing issues, noisy neighbors or damage, the owner will be responsible to ensure the guest is accommodated and the problem resolved quickly. Additionally, units must be thoroughly cleaned between guest stays, all towels and bedding laundered, and wet areas properly sanitized. Property owners must always take health and safety protocols because of the increased liability caused by frequent visitors.

In one investor horror story, the cleaning staff failed to check the drawers of the unit prior to reletting the unit to the next guest and their family. When the new arrival opened the nightstand, they found a loaded gun. Fortunately, it was found by an adult and reported, but it was an extreme oversight that could have ended in a number of disastrous ways. It also cost the investor negative reviews, and they had to forfeit revenue from that guest's stay.

One instance like this could cost an investor dearly. A child could be endangered; financial and criminal liability could be incurred; the property could be kicked off its hosting platform and all future bookings canceled. Remember, regardless of who stays in your property, it is still *your* property. The safety of your guests falls upon you as the owner. The liability is always yours. Hiring a qualified property manager is highly recommended; nonetheless, be sure you set strict protocols and be certain that whomever you hire follows them.

Investors often market their properties on sites like Airbnb, VRBO, and Trip Key. These are a few of the many available platforms to attract visitors and manage bookings. These sites tend to be more guest-oriented than landlord-oriented. Therefore, property owners often feel pressured to make concessions, waive fees, or reimburse lodging costs in order to garner positive guest reviews and 5-star ratings, even if the guest is not entitled to the accommodation or their request is unwarranted. Since investor income is tied to guest experience, it is important to provide consistently great guest experiences and take a "customer is always right" approach. Though you may experience short term losses, fully booked calendars will outweigh the concessions you make.

Any homeowner can employ this method to earn rental income by leasing spare bedrooms, even if they do not consider themselves a real estate investor or plan to move out of their home. Homeowners can use this method to ensure their home is occupied while they are traveling or vacationing somewhere in the world and earn money while they are away. If you are a homeowner interested in using this method, be sure to check your Homeowners Association rules and restrictions. HOA's commonly restrict short-term rentals to thirty days or less. This method is best employed in neighborhoods that are not bound by a mandatory owners' association.

There is a new business model called Rental Arbitrage where investors rent a property on a long-term basis for the purpose of re-renting the same unit by the night. This is a low cost, high cash flow investment strategy with few barriers to entry since you do not have to purchase a property. Rental Arbitrage is permitted by apartment complexes and condominiums managers who have vacancies they need to fill and are open to assuming additional risk by allowing unscreened tenants to stay on their properties. For the investor, the requirements to start would be the same as any other rental process: submit an application, pay a security deposit, sign a lease, furnish the apartment and list the property on a booking website.

Though simple and affordable, this method comes with its quirks. For one, make sure you have permission from the property manager before listing your unit for rent. Doing so without permission could result in eviction which will negatively affect your rental history for years ahead. The lease could also have an acceleration clause if the lease is terminated, where the full amount of the rent for the lease term becomes immediately due and payable and you have to vacate the unit.

Secondly, make sure you have permission in writing within the lease agreement to rent the unit as a short-term rental. If property ownership or management changes, or guests cause issues in the building, then this lease will protect you from being forced to stop running your business during the lease term.

Finally, the unit may not be covered by the property's insurance. Be sure to have renters and liability insurance to protect your unit against damage to the interior. Though this method has the advantage of lower overall costs to begin with, it forfeits the benefits of property ownership such as equity and tax write offs, which are the most advantageous parts of investing.

The time commitment for the short-term rental strategy requires 24/7 daily on call management in order to be effective, to consistently receive great reviews, and to maintain full booking calendars. The best approach is to secure a dependable property manager. Build their fee into your financial model so that you can have a life outside of managing guests and their endless needs. Trust me, I learned the hard way.

Pros

Ease of entry. This method can be implemented by anyone who owns a property or has access to rent a property that allows rental arbitrage. There are several booking websites to enable property owners to attract guests and manage their bookings easily.

Cons:

Requires active engagement in guest management, increased liability due to revolving guests and limited screenings. HOA's and some cities are becoming increasingly more restrictive to short-term renters.

Step 1 – Find Your Property

For short-term rentals or vacation properties, find a property located near an attraction or hub where visitors frequent. Some property location ideas include near a: busy airport, sports and events center, downtown area where business goers frequent, beach or lake area, tourist location, or hospital. All guests are not staying for entertainment, some guests such as travel nurses and flight attendants seek quiet spaces to rest in between long work sessions. For these sorts of guests, having dark rooms and quiet surroundings will be critical for guest satisfaction. If your location is in a busy nightlife area, these guests will look for walkable lodging close to restaurants and bars in a safe but easily accessible area. Find a property that is not subject to restrictive HOA regulations or city ordinances.

To have the best overall guest experience, find a property that is newly renovated with cosmetic upgrades. Unless you are providing a historical experience like hosting guests in an old castle or a place that commemorates a historical event or architectural style, it is ideal to choose a property that is in good condition. Most guests will prefer a modern touch with new bedding, appliances, and up-to-date plumbing, lighting, flooring, and décor. Most guests will not appreciate drafty windows, noisy pipes, creaky floors, and outdated, faulty light fixtures and appliances. For the sake of managing costs, I recommend purchasing a turn-key property that has been gutted and the major systems and appliances have been recently replaced with a warranty so that you do not inherit the maintenance the prior owner failed to perform.

Step 2 – Decorate Your Property

Short-term rentals must be furnished because the guests are renting a room for a brief period and will expect the same accommodations that they have at home. Airbnb was originally created as a bed and breakfast where guests stayed in homes as a personal guest, eating breakfast at the table with the family and having a cultural experience by partaking in the foods and customs of the community where they are visiting. Unfortunately, the model has changed and now the service is used mostly for private stays. The guests not only want their own bedroom, but they also want a living area, entertainment space, and a kitchen to cook their own food. They do, however, appreciate a space decorated to provide a cultural or artistic experience that may be far different than what they are used to at home. For this reason, many property owners design their spaces in very eclectic themes that would not be typical of a normal family home. They may use color, textures, paintings, lighting, and patterns to express a certain mood or emphasis in the space.

If you do not know how to decorate and create interesting spaces, hire someone. Avoid assuming any old couch or curtains will do. You may feel strongly about your personal tastes, but smart investors will ask for outside opinions before listing online or committing to their design choices. Keep in mind that this is an investment for public consumption and that hundreds of visitors with individual preferences may or may not agree with you.

In this business model, guests book off of pictures and reviews. So, invest in high quality photography and capture photos when the property is in prime condition and clean. Design your lighting to make colors pop in photos by being mindful of natural light and the time-of-day photos are taken. Choose angles that positively reflect the spacing of your rooms so that furniture and walls do not appear oblong or narrow. Also, be careful not to photoshop or doctor your photos in a way that would be misleading to your guests. If you turn a twin bed into a king or a murky brown pond into an aqua blue oasis, your guests will rip you apart with negative reviews once they arrive and realize your photos were deceptive. Just be honest and let guests book according to what is the most accurate depiction of your property.

Step 3 – List Online

Identify various websites to host your property and synchronize your booking calendars so that when a guest books on one site, it auto-updates all of the other sites. Create your online profile and list the details of your property description accurately sharing as much visual and written content as possible. Include photos of every room, bathroom, and closet so that guests can get a great idea of what their experience will be like in real life. Show televisions, kitchen equipment, laundry facilities, and whether the property has a bathtub or shower.

Create a property manual that explains how to use the technology, internet, systems and appliances so the guests have instructions to make things work. Share your house rules and expectations such as no parties, no visitors, or no smoking. Notify guests if you have audio or video recording equipment and be sure not to record in private areas like bathrooms and bedrooms. Leave tips for local restaurants and attractions that guests may enjoy. Set your nightly rate and take into consideration weekends, holidays and peak seasons when you may be able to garner a higher rate because of demand.

Finally, tell the guest about yourself. Let them know why you are hosting this home for them. Tell them about your life, pets, hobbies and interests, and put a professional photo of yourself that shows them they are booking with a real person. People love to stay in a home where they feel safe and welcome and there is a host who will provide on the spot assistance to answer questions and help manage problems.

How You Earn

When you own a property and use it as a short-term rental (versus renting), you not only profit from monthly rental cash flows, but you also benefit from the increase in equity over time. Remember, equity is the difference between your asset value and the debts you owe to operate your business. Over time, your equity in the property grows because you are using the monthly rental income to pay off your debt obligations each month while simultaneously the home is rising in value due to market appreciation. Even if the market experiences decline, over extended periods of time the market rises consistently, and properties become more valuable.

Formula to Determine Your Equity Growth

```
      Market Value of Property
  +   Value of Furnishings, Appliances, and Equipment
  -   Outstanding Mortgage Payoff Amount
  -   Outstanding Debts or Taxes Due on Property
  _____
      Equity Remaining in Property
```

Formula to Determine Your Short-Term Rental Profit

Cash flow from Nightly Rentals
- Web Hosting and Booking Fees
- Monthly Rent or Mortgage Expenses
- Utilities (Lights, Water, Gas, Cable, Internet)
- Furniture and Equipment Rentals (If applicable)
- Property Management Fees (paid per booking or % of revenue)
- Cleaning Fees (Fee Per Booking X Number of Bookings)
- Landlord or Renters Insurance
- General Liability Insurance
- Subscription Services (Netflix, Hulu)
- Landscaping, Pool Cleaning and Maintenance of Property

- Refunds and Guest Concessions
- Repairs
- Parking Fees (If applicable)

_____

= Monthly Profit
x 12 months

_____

= Annual Profit

Formula to Determine Liquidated Equity When Refinancing Your Property:

Market Value of the Property x 75% - 80%
- Outstanding Mortgage Payoff Amount
- Closing Costs
- Title Fees
- Unpaid Escrow Balances

_____

Proceeds from Cash Out Refinance at the Time of Sale

MODERATE INVESTMENT STRATEGIES

Turnkey Rental Strategy

Buy and Hold of turnkey rental properties is a strategy where the investor purchases a rent-ready property for the joint benefits of cash flow and long-term asset appreciation. Investors who engage in this method typically yield a greater return in the long-term than short-term investment methods like Fix and Flips. The goal is to purchase a property that can produce continuous cash flow for many years while growing in value over the long-term as the market rises in value. To be considered long-term the investor must hold the property for more than 12 months. The property type can be single family and multifamily rented to individuals and families or commercial properties leased to business tenants.

We will explore strategies for investors to buy and hold land and distressed properties in a later topic which varies slightly. Regardless of asset type purchased, the Buy and Hold strategy of Turnkey properties is a tried-and-true method used for long term wealth creation. I highly encourage first time investors to consider this option over all the rest.

Buy and Hold is similar to the BRR(R) strategy that we learned earlier but differs in that you purchase a *Turnkey Property* that is already income producing or is vacant but rentable in its present condition with no major repairs required. Recently renovated turnkey properties save the investor a great deal of time and eliminate the risk of renovation. Turnkey properties sell for market value, with an adjustment for condition; distressed properties can be purchased well below market value. Nonetheless, the benefit is that your financing terms are more favorable, and the process of acquisition is simpler if repairs have already been completed.

The motivation for Buy and Hold rentals would be the potential for long-term gain. During the term, the tenant's rent payment is covering the cost of the mortgage and any expenses to upkeep the property. Over an extended period of time, the tenant has paid down the mortgage while the market value of the property has appreciated due to inflation. As the investor, you benefit by receiving the equity that you can cash out when you sell or refinance the property. Generally speaking, the longer you own the property, the more wealth that is created. It is important to properly maintain the property to protect the asset valuation.

I once met a businessman who purchased a rental property shortly after the birth of each of his children. When one of his children graduated from high school, he sold their rental property and used the profits to pay their college tuition. If the child received a scholarship to school, the businessman used the profits to pay for their housing and contributed the balance to pay for their first home or business upon graduation from college. Talk about a solid plan for success! This man thought about his children's education and careers twenty years ahead and properly prepared his finances to ensure his kids would start out their adulthood debt-free. His children were then in a position to be a homeowner and/or business owner in their twenties, so they could continue the cycle and create generational wealth for their families to come.

Pros
This long-term investment method has a greater propensity for substantial wealth creation than other methods. Great for new investors seeking residual income. Limited experience, knowledge, and time commitment required to begin. Moderate time commitment that can be reduced by hiring the appropriate staff.

Cons
Longer time horizon to yield large returns, initial cash investment will be returned over time. Requires solid property management and dependable tenants.

Step 1 – Acquire Your Property

Identify a property that is in a promising market that has potential for growth and development in the surrounding community over the next five to ten years. Rather than looking at the property alone, look at the surrounding community and determine if this location is a place where you see value and in which you want to invest your time and money. Look at neighboring properties and the upkeep of the exterior, yards, and streets. You may like a property, but you cannot change the neighbors.

Consider the proximity of your ideal market to grocery, retail, and business districts. If the property is commercially zoned, look at the diversity of businesses operating nearby and the demand for your business type. Would you acquire a retail strip zoned for personal services when there are six barber shops within a one-mile radius? Research local schools and the distance from your subject property to the nearest elementary, middle, and high schools. Understand upcoming road and zoning changes in the area and drive the nearby streets to see if future development is underway. Once you have approved the location, then approve the property.

The ideal property to Buy and Hold has been recently renovated, and all the major structures and systems are in good condition. Cosmetic updates are nice but beware of the age and functionality of the major systems of the house including electrical systems, plumbing systems, roof, foundation, and HVAC units. These are big-ticket items that are often neglected in rental properties. Ask for maintenance records, warranties, and receipts. Do not let the previous owner's deferred maintenance become your problem, unless the price is reflective of that. Do not assume that because the listing data says the HVAC unit or water heater has been recently replaced that it is new. Cheap property owners often replace old equipment with refurbished equipment that does not have a manufacturer's warranty. When in doubt, check the serial numbers.

For occupied properties, identify who owns the kitchen appliances and furnishings. Unless you are purchasing a multi-family unit or you are in a location with desert temperatures, seriously think before buying investment properties with pools. The maintenance is expensive, and potential liability and obvious risks exist. Inspect for prior water damage, mold, asbestos, and harmful materials and toxins. Ask the tenants about their experience and concerns living there, and if at all possible, talk to the neighbors. Nosy neighbors are the best informants.

Evaluate the rental market and identify at least six comparable properties to support the assumed rent on your property of interest. This will typically require the support of a licensed real estate agent. As a note of caution: public real estate websites often report inaccurate and out of date market data, so hire a real estate agent who knows the market. Remember this saying, "A cheap man pays twice." REALTORs have been trained in market analysis and have access to a depth of market data that average investors cannot readily access; do not pridefully assume your research is valid without the eyes of an expert in your market.

If the property is currently rented, the existing lease must be honored until the completion of the lease term. Review the lease and be sure the tenant is paying market rate rent and adjust the rent amount accordingly upon renewal. If the property is commercial, be sure to thoroughly evaluate the business plan of the tenants and review bank statements and performance data to justify the viability of the business before you execute a long-term lease. If the property is residential, research the HUD (Housing and Urban Development) rental rates for the zip code to know what the government is willing to pay on a voucher program for that area. Typically, government housing programs provide a maximum rent chart by the zip codes in your county.

In most cities there is a shortage of affordable housing and a waitlist of ready tenants who have housing vouchers to assist with payments. These voucher programs are excellent options for property owners to receive guaranteed rents and tenants usually stay in the property long-term. Ignore the negative and often unjustified banter about the type of people that use housing subsidies. There are far too many families in need of dignified housing that will properly care for your property if given the opportunity. Regardless of where you source your tenant, appropriate screening and management is necessary. Set rules and penalties and communicate in writing to new and existing tenants so they understand the cost of breaking your rules.

As soon as the property is acquired, the investor can immediately begin earning income on the investment and does not have to front the interest and carrying costs during a construction period. If the property is in an active lease agreement at the time the investor closes the purchase, a proration of the current rent and the security deposits will be credited to the investor at closing, thus reducing their closing costs at the time of purchase. This has proven to be a great benefit for new investors who have limited cash to invest and are seeking ways to stretch their dollars. I've been there and I understand.

Try to close toward the beginning of the month after rent has been collected by the seller per the lease agreements so a majority of the monthly income will be credited to your account. For example, if you purchase a four-plex that is earning $8000 in rental income monthly plus a $2000 security deposit per unit and you close on the 5th of the month, you should receive a credit of $14,933 at the closing table. This could cover a chunk of your closing costs and get you a whole lot closer to ownership with less money out of your pocket.

We will discuss financing the deal in greater detail in the topics to come. A savvy real estate agent can guide you through the acquisition process. If you need a referral for a real estate agent in your area, please reach out to us at Referrals@CommaClubCommunity.com

Purchasing multiple rentals in a concentrated area is a smart way to control the market and ensure the quality of your investment. I knew a wise investor who owned eight houses on the same street. The proximity of his rentals allowed him to collect rent, manage his rentals and maintain his landscaping with ease. He controlled the market on his street because he set the going rent rate. When it came time to refinance his rentals, he had sufficient off market data to establish the market value for his bank-ordered appraisals.

Step 2 – Manage Your Property

Upon closing your deal, hire a dependable property manager to collect rent and manage maintenance schedules and repair requests. If you are managing a handful of units, you may be well capable of being your own property manager. Tenants keep their properties in better condition when they know their landlord is making visits and checking in regularly versus an impersonal management company that only sends letters. There is one caveat to managing your property yourself: tenants may play your heart strings when difficult times arise. If you have a personal relationship with your tenants, it can make it hard to evict for non-payment, impose fines or late fees, and/or increase the rent annually. A property manager has a business relationship with the tenant and easily enforces these rules.

The full scope of the property manager's duties should be outlined in a property management agreement to inform the PM the requirements and limitations of their role. Some duties include setting, billing and collecting rents; attracting and screening tenants and preparing lease agreements; maintaining the property; record keeping and conducting routine inspections; managing the operating budget and expenses; and administration and communicating with tenants. The Property Manager should be well versed in federal, state, and local tenancy law and will represent the landlord's legal interests while providing care to the tenants. Property managers are often paid as a percent of gross rent and may also be paid a fee for new leases that they secure.

Set aside reserves in your operating budget for maintenance and unexpected repairs. In the long term, deferred maintenance leads to asset impairment, increased repairs, and higher costs. Inspect your property on a quarterly basis to check for damage, infestations, or hazards, and take photos for records. If the pet agreement says no pets and you find a new dog, be sure to enforce the lease violation penalty or you may not be able to enforce it at a later date. If the lease says non-smoking and you identify evidence of smoking in the unit, address the violation in writing and inform the tenants if deposits will be lost due to their violation.

In regard to safety, ensure that the property meets the safety codes and that your tenants can readily exit the unit during the event of a fire or emergency. Add fire alarms, sprinklers, and extinguishers as required by law; remove bars from windows unless they can be unlocked from the inside; and ensure the driveways have the necessary clearance for emergency vehicles and that no one is allowed to block fire hydrants. Check pet breed restrictions with your insurance carrier as some companies will not protect you from liability caused by an aggressive breed. Disclose all known present or past hazards in the property and whether anyone has been harmed or died in the property due to a defect in the home.

Step 3 – Expand or Divest at the Appropriate Time

If your desire is to accumulate a portfolio of properties so that you can retire, set your financial goals and strategic plan upfront. Here's a place to start: take your annual salary and divide it by your expected profit/ cash flow per property. This is the number of properties, on average, that you must acquire to replace your annual income. For example, if your annual salary at work is $100k and you intend to cashflow $5,000 in rental profit, you will need 20 properties in your portfolio to replace your income.

Let's assume the number is twenty properties. This may seem like an impossible or extremely far off goal; however, there is power in writing a vision down and speaking about it in prayer to God and to *faith-filled* friends. Begin speaking and decreeing what you intend to do and watch as you accomplish your goal quicker than you imagined. If you need twenty properties, write a strategic plan and set an annual number of properties to purchase each year to reach your goal. Keep in mind that time is on your side as well as inflation, market development, rent increases, and a windfall of blessings that will come your way to help you achieve your goals.

From a strategic planning perspective, purchasing multiple rentals in a concentrated area is a smart way to control the market and protect the values of your investment. I knew a wise investor who owned eight houses on the same street. The proximity of his rentals allowed him to collect rent, manage his rentals and maintain his landscaping with ease. He controlled the market on his street because he set the going rent rate. When it came time to refinance his rentals, he had sufficient off market data to establish the market value for his bank ordered appraisals.

If your desire is to impact your community growth and stimulate your local real estate and economic market, the more properties you own within the same zip code or even within the same block will increase your influence. Large institutional investors may lean away from "placing their eggs in one basket." However, Comma Club's vision is to build Commas AND Communities through an emphasis on community-centric investment strategies. As part of your decision matrix, do not overlook the positive and negative impacts of your decisions on the community.

As a fundamental aspect of my business model, I decided that I will only invest in properties that fall within a particular map area that represents about five square miles. Pray for your property value to rise and for transformative development in your neighborhood. You will understand the power of prayer when you start to see grounds breaking in your community.

When I purchased my personal residence, it was next to a busy highway with noisy traffic as cars entered the onramp to the highway. At this intersection, which I could see directly from my newborn daughter's bedroom window, there were dozens of homeless panhandlers and a rundown commercial strip. There was a hair salon and tire shop located directly behind the home and so many reasons to say, "this won't work!"

However, as I stood in the home for the first time staring out of the master bedroom window and looking at the downtown view, I remember thinking, "My God, why do I feel like this is where I'm supposed to be?" Little did I know God sent me to this neighborhood because I would become an intercessor and prayer advocate to drive change in the area.

I began standing in my daughter's bedroom at night praying that God would bring change to that corner. Months later I became part of a prayer team that went out to the streets to feed and pray for the homeless. We saw countless people delivered from addictions and prostitution. Even the head drug dealer quit the business. We never saw him again after the day we prayed for him, and he gave his life to Christ.

On another random day, when I stepped foot in my front yard, the Lord said, "That highway will no longer be there. Soon the exit ramp is going to be moved, and you won't be able to access the highway from this street" I heard His voice clear as day. About a week later my next-door neighbor called me over to his yard to tell me the city had approved a plan to reroute the highway and that noisy area was going to become a greenspace with trees and beautiful landscaping. The day I received the city plans in the mail; I almost fell out of my chair! They showed a hundred-million-dollar city and highway infrastructure improvement and a park right next door to my house. The increase in value would be unimaginable.

Two years after moving in, the hair salon I had prayed to own went up for sale when the owner of 50+ years decided to retire. Wow! It would be crazy to ignore the link of prayer to the community reformation. I became the Broker for that run down retail strip and was hired to buy that liquor store cash with a blank checkbook. I helped a non-profit company buy that entire city block right outside my daughter's window.

Follow the market to know the appropriate time to divest your properties. The decision to sell should be a well thought out one after consulting your generational wealth plan, financial plan, and tax advisor.

How You Earn

Formula to Determine Your Turnkey Rental Income Profit:

    Monthly Rent Amount   x 12 months
- Mortgage Payment (Principal and Interest Only) x 12 months
- Annual Property Management fees
- Annual Property Taxes
- Annual Insurance
- Annual Maintenance and Repair Costs
- Annual Utilities or other Landlord Paid expenses

Annual Profit/ cash flow from Turnkey Rental Property

Equity Growth Formula:

    Market Value of Property
- Outstanding Mortgage Payoff Amount
- Outstanding Debts or Taxes Due on Property

Equity Remaining in Property

Wholesaling Strategy

Wholesaling of goods or retail wholesaling is a trading practice that is very prevalent in our United States economy and something we participate in as consumers on a daily basis. A wholesaler buys goods from a manufacturer in a large quantity and resells the goods to several retailers in smaller quantities for a higher price. The retailers then repackage the goods, mark up the price, market the goods to their customer base, and resell them at an even higher price. Because of volume, the wholesaler is able to accept a lesser price than the goods may be worth on the retail market. Because they are buying a large volume of goods, the marginal profit per unit adds up to a sizable profit. In this method of wholesaling, the wholesaler is the intermediary between the manufacturer and the retailer, buys goods for a lesser price, and resells them at a higher price than what they paid.

Real estate wholesaling is a similar concept to this retail wholesaling, except that a wholesaler does not have to sell a large quantity of houses to see a worthwhile profit. In fact, the investor can make significant income with each wholesale deal closed. The business model of real estate wholesaling is also known as "The Real Estate Assignment" strategy, because the wholesaler finds a good deal and then "assigns" or transfers the rights to purchase that deal to someone else for a higher amount. The wholesaler becomes the middleman or woman between a property owner and end buyer. He makes a profit by contracting the purchase at a lower price, and then assigning the contract to a new buyer at a higher amount. The wholesaler keeps the difference as a fee for locating and securing the deal without ever repairing, renovating or even closing on the purchase of the home.

The assignment fee can be a fixed rate determined by law or a negotiable amount. According to FortuneBuilders.com, the average assignment fee is $5,000. However, if the wholesaler buys a deal low enough, there can certainly be more profit. I know wholesalers who earn $20-30k per deal.

Depending on the state where you operate, a legal duty to disclose the assignment fee to the homeowner at the time of closing may exist. This could clearly create a shock when the property owner realizes they sold their home for less than it was worth. In this strategy, there will be a gray area between what is fair and what is profitable, so be sure not to engage in predatory and misleading business practices. When in doubt, disclose your intention to wholesale the home, especially if you are a licensed real estate agent or hold a professional license of some sort.

Oftentimes homeowners are unknowledgeable and lack representation to assist with their decision making. Homeowners typically own distressed properties they cannot afford to repair or are in distressed situations needing cash fast. They are agreeable to sell their home for the prospect of a quick close without having to fix up or list their home on the real estate market. Homeowners may be in a foreclosure process, may have health, relationship, family or life changes or may have received a home via court order or death of a family member. These are just a few of the scenarios where homes become available to wholesalers.

End buyers are home flippers or investors who are seeking an off-market deal for a fair price. Wholesalers should build relationships with flippers so that when a deal is contracted, they have a ready pool of end buyers to whom they may assign their contract. This investment strategy requires little upfront costs, if any, and is something that novice investors can implement without a depth of knowledge in real estate or investing. Even if wholesaling is not your main method, it should be understood so that if you happen upon a wholesale deal as an investor, you know how to snag it.

How is this possible? Is this legal? It is both possible and legal. According to Fortune Builders, "a subject property owner signs a contract with an investor that gives the investor the rights to buy the home. That's an important distinction to make, as the contract only gives the investor the rights to buy the home; they do not actually follow through on a purchase. Once under contract, however, the wholesaler retains the sole rights to buy the home.

That means they may then sell their rights to buy the house to another party, also known as an assignment of rights. Therefore, when a wholesaler executes a contract assignment, they aren't selling a house, but their rights to buy a house. The end buyer will pay the wholesaler an assignment fee and buy the house from the property owner."

This may seem confusing but think back to our scenario about the wholesaler of goods. The wholesaler buys a pack of skittles from Wrigley Company for $0.50 cents and resells the pack of skittles to Target Stores for $0.75 cents, who then resells that same pack of skittles to customers for $1.50. It is the same pack of skittles but because of the ease of access to what they want, the Target customers are willing to pay three times more than what the skittles may actually be worth.

We do not consider this practice of marking up the price as deceptive or illegal when we purchase goods from retailers on a daily basis, even when they do not disclose the original price paid. However, since wholesaling of properties deals with a much more significant amount of money, it must be guided by the appropriate contract language to protect both the buyers and sellers from deceptive practices.

In a standard real estate contract, there may be language where the buyer on contract can assign the contract to a new buyer before closing on the purchase. If not, the wholesaler must write in the Buyer Name section of the contract special language that, once executed by the property owner, would allow for an assignment to another buyer. See below:

Buyer: Comma Club LLC, **and/or assigns**

If there is language that prohibits the assignment of the contract, then the two parties must agree to an assignment before the contract can be transferred to a new buyer.

Pros
Highly profitable investment strategy with little upfront costs, if any, and an ease of exit from the investment. Novice investors can easily implement this strategy without a depth of knowledge in real estate or investing.

Cons
Difficult process to find off-market deals. Requires a network of end buyers to exit the deal quickly and effectively. In practice, profiting from the ignorance of an unwitting seller may make this legal method seem a bit unscrupulous to a principled investor.

Step 1 – Find the Right Property

The most difficult part of the wholesaling strategy is finding off market deals. Though there are houses scattered on streets across America, finding a good deal can feel like trying to find a needle in a haystack. When you find one, contract it fast!

So, what is a good deal? Typically, wholesalers will be seeking a distressed property in need of significant repairs or a distressed seller willing to sell well below market value in exchange for a quick and easy closing. The home should be in an area where there are sufficient comps to support the After Repair Value (ARV) and, where once repaired, can be easily resold for a profit. Though the wholesaler is not actually completing the purchase of the home, they are finding a deal that another investor will be purchasing. Therefore, the deal should meet the same criteria as a profitable Fix and Flip or BRR deal. The criteria for purchase should encompass a review location, property condition, cost of repairs, hazards and defects, recent nearby sales, resale values, rental rates, days on market, holding costs, selling costs and fees. Review the information on finding a property in those previously discussed topics for more information on how to evaluate a property.

Now that you know what to find, the question for most new investors to the wholesaling business is where can I find these properties? The answer is not the location but the method you use to find them. Wholesalers use multiple methods to attract and identify properties. I know one successful agent who found all of her properties by walking the streets and knocking on doors wherever she saw distressed homes in groups. These areas included clusters of homes with falling roofs and signs of disrepair. She asked the person at the door if they were interested in selling their home, and if they would pass her contact to any neighbors who might be interested in a cash offer.

Others used post card mailers to address lists or zip codes, posters, street signs, billboards, radio ads, and car stickers. Some people cold call foreclosure lists and others hound real estate agents with automated text messages, phone calls, and emails offering cash for any of their off-market listings. Yet, the best way I have seen was the one a man named Mr. Huggins used.

Mr. Huggins built his multi-million-dollar business through face-to-face relationships with real estate agents and investors. He sat down for coffee or lunch with people on a regular basis and called to check in on them on personal dates like birthdays and holidays. He asked them to make him their point of contact when they had a distressed listing. Because of his track record and reliability, real estate agents called him first and he made a cash offer. Mr. Huggins did not have to hunt down deals; his phone was always ringing with people bringing the deals to him.

As a special note, do not attempt to wholesale publicly listed properties on the MLS that are already being brokered by a real estate agent unless your research shows this home has been severely overpriced and you can contract it for a deep discount AND you disclose that you are wholesaling the home. Do not deceptively lie and tell the listing agent that you are a cash buyer so that you can attempt to assign the contract to an actual cash buyer. If you have a cash buyer in your network that is paying you a referral fee to negotiate MLS listings and get them under contract for them, this is a different story. Unfortunately, many novice wholesalers tie up MLS public listings for weeks at a time with no real capability to purchase the home. This is deceptive. Furthermore, this is not a viable business strategy.

Do not be discouraged if you have a challenging time finding properties. Just keep at it. More than a handful of deals fell in my lap when I was not looking for them. Wholesaling should not be your bread and butter. It should just be your butter. In the beginning of your wholesaling journey, have other sources of income, and allow wholesaling to be the bonus that grows your wealth more expediently.

After networking and proving yourself as a reliable deal closer, your business model will grow where you consistently receive a pipeline of leads, and you are constantly closing deals. I say this for all the young entrepreneurial investors who have been sold a pie in the sky, get-rich-quick wholesaler scheme. This business takes a lot of sweat equity, grit, negotiating skill, and integrity. Laziness gets you nowhere. So, get your feet to the pavement and go out and earn it. Desperation impedes results. Relax. Let the Holy Spirit lead you in all things, even where you find deals and how you earn money. Everything we win, we win in the Spirit first before it manifests naturally. I'll write a full book on this later.

It is also important to discuss liens and encumbrances to the property and understand if there are clouds on the title which may prohibit the sale or significantly slow down the process. A lien is a right to keep possession of a person's property until a debt is paid. Consider, these questions:

- Who is the true owner of the property? Is it the person listed as seller on the contract or are there other siblings, family members, or heirs who may have a legal right to the property?

- Are there back taxes, city fines, or liens that may need to be paid before the property can sell? Is the seller aware of these fees and which party on the contract is responsible for paying these fees?

- Does the seller have personal judgements, or liens that must be paid at closing? A few examples might be an IRS tax lien for unpaid back taxes, a Department of Revenue lien for unpaid state taxes, HOA liens, Materialman liens, divorce judgements, and child support liens. If a seller finds out their $20,000 in back due child support has to be paid at closing, they may refuse to sign at closing.

If the property has a lien on it, there may be additional costs to consider as part of your offer or due diligence needed to determine if this is a worthwhile investment. Take this into account when writing your offer and the amount of time you option the home.

It is always a good starting place to ask the seller as many questions as possible about the home, such as how they acquired it, why they are selling, and any mortgages or debts associated with the property. It is also wise to have a title attorney or title company run a title search on the property to see what liens come up for the property before marketing it to another investor. If negative findings arise during the initial days of the option period, go back and renegotiate the price.

Step 2 – Execute an Option Contract to Purchase the Property

Familiarize yourself with the standard real estate purchase agreement in your state. Find a blank form that you can fill in, or have an attorney prepare a customized assignment agreement with specific provisions that you decide. Keep these documents on hand so that when a deal presents itself you can be ready to get paperwork signed immediately.

An option contract is an agreement between two parties to facilitate a potential transaction involving an asset for a set price and date. The option agreement is a provision within a standard real estate purchase contract and gives the buyer *the right to purchase a property*. Note that the option contract is a right and not an obligation to purchase a property. The option gives the buyer a period of time to evaluate the property and move forward with the purchase at the previously agreed price or terminate the contract without penalty.

The option period may be referred to as a feasibility period or contingency period. It provides for a length of time to evaluate the property and terminate the purchase agreement without penalty. During the option period, the seller cannot execute a contract with any other potential buyers, thus giving the first buyer a holding period to reserve the home without competition. During the option period the seller cannot terminate the contract because they receive a better offer.

This option must be purchased by the buyer for a fee, sometimes called the option fee, in order for the holding period to be legally in effect. The option fee in the state of Texas is a negotiable and non-refundable amount that ranges from $100-200. However, this fee may vary state to state.

Here is an example of an option period clause as provided by Securities Exchange Commission SEC.gov:

*1. FEASIBILITY PERIOD. Purchaser shall have a sixty (60) day feasibility period, commencing upon the Effective Date (as hereinafter defined) (the "**Feasibility Period**"), to undertake at Purchaser's sole expense such engineering, development, marketing and other studies as Purchaser may desire. If Purchaser is not satisfied with the Property or the transaction evidenced by this Agreement for any reason or no reason at all, Purchaser may as a matter of right, terminate this Agreement by written notice to Seller at any time prior to the end of the Feasibility Period, in which case the Deposit (as hereinafter defined) shall be returned to Purchaser within five (5) days of such termination (less $100.00 paid to Seller as consideration for entering into this Agreement), and thereafter the parties shall be relieved of further liability from performing hereunder, with the exception of Purchaser's obligations to Seller that survive any termination of this*

Agreement. If such notice is not given prior to the end of the Feasibility Period, Purchaser's right to terminate pursuant to this Paragraph 1 shall expire at the end of the Feasibility Period. Time is of the essence with respect to the giving of any such notice by the Purchaser. All engineering, development, marketing and other inspections, tests and examinations shall be conducted by parties qualified and, where applicable, licensed to conduct such inspections, tests and/or examinations. Purchaser shall pay the costs of all tests, inspections, examinations, investigations, and reviews conducted pursuant to this Agreement. After the performance of any tests, inspections, examinations, investigations and reviews, Purchaser shall promptly repair any damage to the Property to substantially the same condition as existed prior to the conduct of said tests, inspections, examinations, investigations and reviews, and this obligation of Purchaser shall survive any termination of this Agreement. Prior to undertaking any activity or exercising any rights granted in this Agreement, Purchaser shall obtain, and subsequently maintain in full force and effect throughout the duration of this Agreement.

If you find a property that has potential, go ahead and execute a contract with the property owner quickly. Set a longer option period to give you plenty of time to evaluate the property and find an investor to assume the contract. You will need sufficient days to prepare a deal presentation, pitch the deal via email, and schedule showings, and give investors advance notice to tour the property. Leave yourself some wiggle room just in case an investor does not bite the first go round. Fourteen days would be tremendous. Depending on the urgency of the seller, you may only get a couple of days, so be prepared for the deal before it comes.

Contract the property at a price lower than what a flipper would pay to leave room enough for your wholesaler fee. For simplicity, use the same formula used to compute the purchase price of a flip and then deduct your fee from that number. Therefore, the price offered will need to reflect the cost of needed repairs, holding costs, and other selling costs that the end buyer will pay while still leaving the flipper a sizable profit that is worth their time. As Mr.

Huggins likes to say, "You have to leave some meat on the bone." If you contract the deal too high, no investor will buy the deal, and you will have to terminate the contract or reduce your wholesale fee to make it work.

Step 3 – Identify an End Buyer and Assign the Contract

Once you have a deal under contract, you need to get moving to identify an end buyer so you can assign the contract. Be prepared with a contact list of cash buyers who are seeking distressed properties to renovate. This can include Flippers , Buy and Hold Investors or Do-It-Yourself home buyers. The bigger your network, the more likely you can assign a deal when you find one and the higher price offer you will get. Remember, competition drives value. If you have ten investors bidding on the same deal, you may get one willing to pay $5-10k more than another, which immediately becomes your profit.

Even as a new and inexperienced wholesaler, start building your network now. Attend local investor events and introduce yourself as a wholesaler. Reach out to real estate agents and take them for coffee to introduce yourself. Let them know you can be a resource to them if they have a property for sale or they have a buyer looking for an off-market deal. Attend other wholesaler showings and network with investors there, handing out cards and making connections. Remember, wholesalers sell to wholesalers sometimes. If you can't sell a deal, sometimes someone else with a different network can and you can agree to split the profit.

If there is one thing I have learned as a real estate agent and broker, it is that relationships mean *everything*. Novices get hung up on the fact that they have not done a deal yet, so they fear making bold introductions and networking like an industry professional. However, a scripture says, "From the days of John the Baptist until now the kingdom of heaven has suffered violence, and the violent take it by force" (Matthew 11:12, ESV). The end of that verse means that if you want to take hold of something, you must seize it forcefully. The best time to prepare for an opportunity is before the opportunity presents itself. You have to already see yourself as a successful investor and align your network before the property presents itself to you. I avidly believe that many times God does not allow an opportunity to come until you are in a position to manage it. Regardless of which strategy you select, this holds true.

When you are ready to present the deal, be prepared to provide a list of comparable sales so that the cash buyers know the market potential in that area. You will also need to provide a title report to show the title is clear or has a path to closing. It is also smart to provide an estimate of repairs so that investors can quickly decide if the deal will work for them. As stated before, your option period should be long enough for you to complete the necessary research and then leave time for the investors to evaluate the property and view it.

In hot markets, deals sell themselves. If you cannot wholesale a deal, use your network of real estate agents to have them list the home on the market with permission from the owner; however, you may need to negotiate your fee with the seller directly because listing brokers cannot pay a referral fee to unlicensed individuals. If you are a wholesaler and a licensed real estate agent, you can contract off market houses and wholesale them yourself. I do this all the time. If I find a distressed property or a potentially marketable listing that will be a repair headache for the seller, I reach within my network of investors and pitch the deal to them first. If they want to make a cash offer, I add a commission in the deal and get paid without doing any work listing and marketing the home. In this case, I write up a listing agreement and then add a commission rather than write a purchase and option agreement and assign the contract. However, it is essentially the same process.

After you identify a property, identify a cash buyer and execute an assignment of contract agreement. Email it to the title company so that they can prepare for closing with the correct buyer information.

Step 4 – Collect the Assignment Fee when the Home Sells

Now it's time to get paid. Some wholesalers collect an upfront deposit when they assign the contract to another buyer and then receive the remaining portion of their fee at closing. Make sure the end buyer is present for closing (or has a notary scheduled) to close the deal. The buyer should be prepared with the funds needed to close on the original purchase plus the pre-agreed upon assignment fee. After the property seller and end buyer close the deal, the title company provides your check or wires your funds directly to your account.

How You Earn

Formula to Determine Wholesale Deal Profit
Choose the *lesser of these two formulas* as your maximum purchase price:

After Repair Value x 80%
- Estimated Cost of Improvements
- Estimated Closing Costs
- Your Wholesale Fee

– Maximum Offer for Wholesale Deal

Or

After Repair Value
- Estimated Cost of Improvements
- Estimated Closing Costs and Commissions at time of Purchase
- Estimated Closing Costs and Commissions at time of Sale
- 6 months Bank Interest (purchase price * current int rate (6/12)
- 6 months Holding Costs (insurance, all utilities)
- Profit Investor Expects to Earn (you can use an estimate like $40,000)
- Your Wholesale Fee
_____
Maximum Offer for Wholesale Deal

Your wholesale or assignment fee is your profit if you can get the deal to close!

RRR Strategy (Reside, Rent, Refinance)

The RRR is my self-titled go-to investment strategy that is so easy everyone can do it. This homeowner turned investor model is a simple method to convert a primary residence into rental property with the snap of your fingers. And you can do it over and over again. This method of buying homes, residing in them for a period of time, and then converting them into rentals is an awesome method for young people who are flexible and willing to move every year or so. You can easily acquire a handful of properties with little money out of pocket, while building a portfolio of rentals. No need to be a rich businessperson to execute this plan, I helped a temporary employee in her early twenties start this method and earn $75,000 in equity in 3 years. By year 4 she sold one property with a $180,000 profit.

Again, this is so simple that investors of any age or income bracket can execute this strategy with the right mindset. Unwittingly, most first-time homeowners buy homes with the wrong point of view. Often people delay home ownership until their 30's or 40's when they are more settled with marriage, families, and long-term careers. Many people wait until they are more financially secure to offset the worry about responsibility for upkeep or maintenance. They often question the point of having a 4-bedroom house when they are a single individual without a family of their own. Due to this reasoning, many young people waste time and money renting when they could start building their portfolios as soon as they are eighteen years old and employed.

Another wrong mindset is this "forever home" concept. When more mature buyers are ready to own, they often think of their first home as their forever home, the place they want to reside for many years. While owning a home is the American dream, most people limit their goal to owning one house without realizing they can repeat the process.

All these things I mentioned happen because of one essential flaw in people's understanding. They do not realize that every house is an investment -- not just a place to live. The same market factors of inflation, appreciation, and value creation benefit homeowners the same as investors. Many have found themselves at a closing table with a large cash out upon selling or refinancing their asset. So why do this haphazardly? Why not intentionally use this method strategically?

Buying homes as a primary residence is a smart way to acquire a large asset with little upfront capital required. The concept of leverage means buyers can put a small amount of cash down in proportion to the overall cost of the asset, while using the bank's money to finance the balance. When you occupy the property as your primary residence, even if only for a brief period of time, you qualify for the much lower interest rates, the requirement for cash reserves is eliminated, and the underwriting standards become less stringent than typical investment loans. You eliminate many of the barriers that investors face with bank financing by simply choosing to occupy your property for the initial years.

After you meet the occupancy requirements, you can rent out the property and start earning income over and above the mortgage amount. Then purchase another home, occupy it for a period of time and repeat. There is no limit to how many times you can execute this plan. Many first-time homebuyer programs allow buyers to purchase homes with zero down payment. In some cases, these programs are eligible to reuse as second homes, when you relocate to a new area. After a certain number of years have passed, buyers become eligible again. Check your local area real estate expert for information on grant programs to lower your upfront costs.

As you grow your portfolio of houses, you will need to show the lender that your homes are leased, and the rents will be counted as income to offset debt owed for those properties. It will be essential to produce a lease agreement and to keep bank statements and deposit records for rents. Many homeowners are surprised to learn that they can qualify for multiple home purchases without showing additional income from their day job. This is a huge game-changer for workers in careers without much salary growth or those who feel underpaid but love their work and do not plan to switch careers. Adding rental properties to your portfolio can increase your annual income without having to change jobs.

As a REALTOR for many years, I can tell you that purchasing a primary residence that you occupy is the easiest way to finance your investments of all types. The real estate market for 1-4 units presents the lowest cost for down payment and fewest requirements for qualification.

Let me be clear ... you must occupy the residence as your primary home. Buying a property with the intention to convert into an income property *immediately*, **while telling the bank that it is a primary residence represents** *mortgage fraud for which* **you could be subject to jail time, fines, and/or penalties.**

Additionally, if your mortgage company discovered that you were not occupying the home according to the lending requirements, your note could be accelerated and become immediately due in full. **This is a warning for those creative financiers who think that this section of the book is about cheating the system. It is not.**

However, every system contains legal loopholes that you can exercise to obtain the outcomes you desire. Most lenders have a minimum occupancy duration to meet the primary residence requirements of the loan. Make sure you ask questions and read your loan documents in advance to be sure you operate within the rules. If you follow these guidelines, you should be free and clear to purchase numerous properties.

In my experience lenders require you to reside in the home for six months – 2 years. Beyond that point you are free to rent your home as an investment. Because life happens, homeowners sometimes must move out of their homes sooner than expected and even before they have met the lenders occupancy guidelines. Various circumstances include job changes requiring relocation, marriage, divorce, relocating to help an elderly parent, medical reasons, financial changes, or a myriad of other reasons. Other moves can be more voluntary such as when buyers do not feel safe in the neighborhood, do not like the drive time to work, have issues with the house itself, want to move children into a better school district, or found a dream home across town and just simply can't wait. In these circumstances lenders allow homeowners to convert their homes to rentals and those homeowners can often purchase a home in a new area – even if it is less than the required time. The rationale for buying your next home in such a short amount of time would need to be explained during your underwriting process, but life circumstances happen, and underwriters understand when the explanation makes sense. Here are a few examples of common reasons why buyers might be justified in buying another primary residence and converting their existing primary residence into a rental investment property soon after buying:

Example: Christie is a 28-year-old young professional in a dating relationship, and she doesn't want to keep paying rent while she sees where her relationship is headed. She realizes that she can save $300/month by owning a home in the same zip code as her apartment and she needs a backyard for her poodle Lola. She applies for a first-time homeowner program and then finds her first home in Oklahoma City! She closes and is happy as can be in her pink paradise with her puppy. Six months later her boyfriend Adam proposes, and they decide to get married in Cancun on Valentine's Day. The two decide that it's best to buy a home together and since John has never owned a home, he uses a first-time homebuyer program being offered by a local mortgage company. Christie decides to convert her primary residence into a rental property and the happy couple go house hunting together to find their next home where they will live together in Oklahoma City! Christie has a new husband and a new rental property and is happy as can be because she is earning $800/month profit renting out her pink paradise to her best friends Jill and Wendy. Two years later, Adam gets a job in Dallas, and they decide to convert their primary residence into a rental instead of selling it, which their REALTOR tells them is a smart move! They can earn equity long-term and earn residual income by keeping their homes as rentals. Since they have owned their home for 2 years, the lender tells them that they qualify for first time homeowner programs again (no way!), so they only put a small down payment down (3.5% of the purchase price) to buy a new home in a suburb of Dallas. They buy their third house and are loving it when Adam finds out his former job wants him back in Oklahoma. They think long and hard about it, but since his former job offered him a bigtime promotion and Christie's best friends are back in OKC, they both agree to return. There's only one catch, they have a 2-year lease in place with the tenants of both of their houses in OKC and legally they can't break it just because they are moving back. This time, they decide to purchase their fourth house in Edmond, Oklahoma since it is about 20 minutes from downtown and they think it will be a wonderful place to start a family. Because they are moving more than fifty miles away from their primary residence in Dallas, they can qualify for a low-down payment program again! Wow! It's been 3 years and they own four houses, and they are technically investors all while simply moving as life changes happened! They realized that being a proprietor is simpler than they ever thought it would be and they are earning $1500/month in rental income all while building equity in their houses as the tenants pay down the mortgage and as the housing market appreciates annually. Since they've got the hang of it, they plan to stay where they are and purchase more investment property in a few years with the goal to own ten houses before they turn forty.

Pros
Easiest method to acquire properties with the lowest upfront cost for first time homeowners. Simple financing process and funding is very accessible for most buyers. Existing homeowners can become investors immediately by converting their existing property into an income property.

Cons
The homeowner must move out of their residence every time they acquire a new property. Subject to various bank underwriting restrictions. This method is typically practical for young adults or

empty nesters. It may not be suitable for families with children or people who cannot easily uproot from their home or neighborhood for a financial interest.

Step 1 – Qualify for Mortgage Loan as a Primary Resident or Occupying Borrower

For current homeowners, the good news is that you can skip to Step 2. If you have owned your property for one year or more and reside in it as your primary residence or own a single-family residence that is rented out, you may qualify to purchase your next residence. Refer to our section on *preparing your finances for investment*. If you feel you are able to qualify for a mortgage loan, or would like to determine your readiness, apply with a mortgage lender.

Most mortgage loan applications are taken online, and the application can be completed within an hour. Lenders take two to three days to review your application and give you a determination about your approval. Feel free to shop around with as many mortgage lenders as you wish to identify the lowest interest rate options available to you and the lowest down payment requirements and mortgage fees.

When you purchase a home as a primary residence you do not have to put 20% down. This is a common misconception. Ask about first time homebuyer programs and No Down Payment programs. These programs are often available to people who earn under a certain income threshold or live within certain income tracts that are primarily low-to-moderate income or primarily minority demographically. Do not disqualify yourself. Ask what programs are available to you.

I once qualified as a borrower in a two-income household earning six figures. Many buyers that I represented as their REALTOR have been shocked to find that they qualified too. Mortgage lenders are in the business of making loans, so go ahead and apply. In the worst-case scenario the lender will point you in a direction to become qualified in the future if you do not qualify at the time.

Ask the lender about their occupancy requirements and how long you must reside in the home to consider it a primary residence. Do not tell the lender that you want to rent your home or become an investor because this may throw up unnecessary red flags. A loan officer once called me to explain that they declined a loan simply because the borrower sent them an email saying they wanted to become an investor and were considering renting the home as opposed to occupying. It's not necessary to disclose your future plans. Just ask the lender to explain their occupancy requirements so that in the event that you want/need to move in the future you can know the guidelines.

Ask the lender to provide copies of closing documents that you may have to sign so you can read them in advance. You can even tell your loan officer that you may consider renting the home in the future and want to know what their rules are for renting the home *in the future.* I have had some lenders say that whatever you do after closing day is none of their business. Other lenders provide copies of occupancy declarations that are signed at closing spelling out their program rules.

It is important to read the lender documents, particularly when you are accepting government subsidies or other down payment assistance funding. Sometimes these programs have a forgivable grant that is amortized based on how long you live in the home or how long you own the home. This means that if you sell the home before a certain number of years, the assistance must be repaid out of the equity in the home. These rules may or may not apply when you retain ownership of the home and rent it out, so please be sure to read before signing. Some rules allow you to convert the home to a rental but regulate the income of the renter to ensure you keep the home affordable.

Once approved, it is time to hire your Real Estate Agent and evaluate homes as a long-term investment. For new investors hoping to get started with this method, begin with the standard first-time home buyer process. I encourage you to consult your local real estate agent as you begin your process. If you need a referral in your city, email referrals@CommaClubCommunity.com.

REALTOR's home buyer services are free to you, and they often have insight about the best mortgage lenders that offer first time home buyer programs in your local area. Do not worry if you already own a home; let the mortgage lender know that you already own a home, but you would like to purchase a new primary residence and have them walk you through their process to do so. Be sure to let your REALTOR know that you are seeking a primary residence to live in, but that you want to purchase a home that could become a "sound investment" in the future.

Ask the real estate agent to pull reports of the rental rates in the same area as the home that you decide to purchase so that you can understand your potential profit before you decide to purchase. Do not assume that because the house is nicer or more expensive that it will make a more profitable investment. In my experience, the opposite is true. What you are looking to determine is the net profit between the mortgage payment and the rental amount.

Since you are pre-approved, ask your lender for the estimated mortgage payment of your home. Be as specific as you can. If you cannot give them an exact address that you intend to purchase, give them a purchase price in the zip code so that they can estimate the tax rate and insurance for homes in the price range where you plan to buy. This ensures that the mortgage estimate you use is as close as possible to what you will actually pay. Find out if your mortgage payment includes principal, interest, property taxes, homeowners' insurance, mortgage insurance, and any other fees monthly. If not, compute what these amounts should be for your home.

Compare the mortgage payment to the rental rates of homes in the area where you decide to purchase and see if they are sufficient to cover the mortgage and expenses with money left over. Any overage represents your profit or your rental income. For example, if the rental rates for your home are $1800/month for a three bedroom two-bathroom home of like condition in your zip code and your mortgage (PITI, or principal, interest, taxes, and insurance) is $1200 a month, then you have a $600 profit margin before factoring in maintenance reserves and lawn care expense. After deducting another $200 to cover these anticipated property owner expenses, you would net $400 profit once you convert this home to a rental. Based on these figures you can decide to buy this home as a primary residence, knowing in the future you will be capable of earning some residual income.

If you compute the rental rates in your target area and find that the homes rent for less or equal to your mortgage payment, then that home will not make a worthwhile investment to earn rental income. Do not skip this step. Do not rely on the word of your REALTOR.

Ask for reports of rental income. Find at least six comparable rental homes within a quarter mile of the area where you are looking to buy your primary residence. Estimate and average the rental rate for these homes and be as conservative as possible. If the net difference between the average rental rate and the estimated mortgage payment is equivalent to a profit amount that you deem sufficient and favorable, and the home checks off everything you need to live in it, then move forward.

Once you purchase the home, then move in, turn on the utilities in your name, forward mail to your new address and simply live life. Set a maximum time period to stay in this home *before* you move in so that you are already preparing yourself to buy your next home. Avoid getting comfortable and forgetting your strategy. Remember, the goal is to eventually convert the home into a rental and buy a new primary residence in the future. If you absolutely adore the neighborhood and do not want to move, then buy the home across the street.

Step 2 – Convert the Primary Residence into a Rental Property

Now that you own the home and you reside in it, it's time to get a game plan to finally become an investor. **Hire a REALTOR!** Recheck leasing prices in your neighborhood and see how much your house can be rented for based on the market data your REALTOR provides. I do not advocate relying on web-based market information or leasing on your own. There is nothing more reliable than a professional who does this for a living, and MLS data is more comprehensive and more accurate.

Have the REALTOR provide you with a report of at least six recently rented, nearby houses of like-kind and take a conservative average. Do not list your house for the highest number you can think of –do not be that obnoxious person who ignores market data and thinks your house is the best thing since sliced bread. Look at the lease price per foot and compare it to your square footage. Look at the features of the home that is rented versus yours. Do they have a pool? An extra bedroom? Are you on a cul-de-sac or facing a golf course? Did they do major updating to their kitchen and master bathroom while your house features original interior design? Talk through a reasonable lease price so that your home doesn't sit on the market for lengthy periods of time because it's overpriced.

Once you decide your price, list your home and wait for the applications to roll in. The REALTOR has access to software to screen the tenant on your behalf and is an objective pass through to help you identify shady tenants. You have every right to meet your tenants in person, interview them, or review all application materials yourself. Ask lots of questions and verify everything on their application. Review their check stubs and compute if they earn 2.5-3x the rent as a rule of thumb. Call their employer to verify their job and income. Call references to see what type of family they are – domestic violence and criminal activity may be disqualifiers. Call their former landlords to verify that they pay rent on time and did not break their lease or damage the previous rental.

Keep in mind, renters often have lower credit scores and sometimes have spots on their credit from mistakes in the past. It is important to consider these things critically and dig into the details. Did they have a bankruptcy twenty years ago while going through a divorce? Do they have outstanding medical debt due to a child getting sick unexpectedly, but all other bills are on time? Did they lose their job in an economic downturn, but seem to be steady on paying debt over the last two years? There are no perfect tenants; otherwise, they would own the home next door and not rent yours. Ask the right questions; evaluate their honesty and integrity; and decide to rent your home to someone who you feel will upkeep your home, pay rent on time, communicate well and keep their commitments.

While you prepare to rent your home, you will also be preparing to purchase your next residence simultaneously. There is no fixed rule on whether you should rent your existing home first or first find your next home to purchase. That decision depends on your local housing market conditions and the living options available to you. When you are ready to buy again, go back to Step 1 and follow the steps to be pre-approved for a home loan. Remember to inform the lender that your home will be rented and be prepared to show them a copy of a signed lease agreement and a security deposit or first month's rent. The lender will use the income for the property to qualify you for your next purchase.

If you start your new home search before renting your existing home, the lender will likely require as a condition of closing that you send them a copy of a signed lease agreement showing you rented your existing home. Lenders usually credit 75% of the rent amount as additional income, so be sure you are renting your home for at least 25% more than your monthly mortgage amount. Be prepared to explain to the lender or underwriting department why you are moving out of your primary residence into a new one (such as you need to be closer to work, family reasons, bigger house, want a pool, growing family, etc.) As long as you occupy your next home as your primary residence, you will qualify for the preferential rates and terms that occupants get.

Remember, mortgage lenders are in the business of making loans and homeowners have every right to move and purchase a new home as often as they choose as long as they can qualify under the underwriting guidelines of their mortgage lender. Every bank has different underwriting criteria upon which they choose to make loans. If one bank does not offer you the terms you desire, or they decline to offer you a mortgage loan, shop around and find another bank.

Step 3 – Refinance Your Properties

This last step to refinance your home is optional and the timing of it could be prior to or after Step 2 based on your investment goals, economic conditions, and/or the housing market at the time of your decision. To refinance means that you take out a new loan on your property, paying off the original note in an effort to cash out the equity that has been built over time or to lower your monthly payments to increase your monthly cash flow.

A *Cash Out Refinance* allows you to borrow up to 75% of the value of the home or, in some cases, up to 80%. If you have been renting your home for several years, your tenant has been paying down your mortgage loan, meaning there may be equity in the home that you can liquidate. In addition to the reduction in principal balance, the housing market may have increased in value in your market area and/or improvements made to the home may have increased its value. These two factors could mean there is equity you can cash out and use to expand your real estate portfolio or for any other expenditure you may select.

In order to cash out the equity, you follow a similar process to the one you followed in Step 1. Instead of getting a loan to buy the property, you apply for a "refinance." The lender orders an appraisal of your home to see the new market value based on an independent appraiser's opinion of value. If your home increased significantly in value over the original loan amount, the lender will allow you to borrow up to 80% of the new appraised value. They will deduct the amount of the original note and cost of closing fees and cut you a check for the difference.

I have seen some borrowers cash out hundreds of thousands of dollars and turn to invest the funds into faster appreciating investment vehicles or buy additional properties. It is a terrific way to finance new real estate acquisitions and one of the cheapest forms of debt you can borrow. Since the funds are unrestricted, imagine consolidating high interest rate debt, opening a franchise business, or buying a small apartment building with the cash that is locked in the savings account of your home. These are just ideas, but possibilities are endless. Since the money you receive at cash out is technically debt, it is tax free, and the origination points and closing costs are tax-deductible.

Sometimes when your home is reappraised, your *LTV, or loan to value,* drops to 80% or below. When that happens, *Private Mortgage Insurance*, also called *PMI or MIP,* is removed from your mortgage payment, thus reducing the monthly amount that you owe. If the house is rented to a tenant, doing a *rate and term refinance* could be a simple step to lower your payment and increase your monthly cash flow. When rates are low, check your interest rate versus what banks are offering and apply for a rate and term refinance to see how much you could save, OR how many years you could shave off your mortgage by lowering your rate.

Step 4 – Repeat Step 1 - 3

How You Earn

Formula to Determine Your Rental Income using RRR

      Monthly Rent Amount
- Mortgage on Rental Property
- Property Management fees (If applicable)
- Property Taxes
- Less Insurance
- Reserves for Maintenance/ Repairs
- Utilities, Lawncare or other Landlord Paid expenses

Monthly Profit that Property Owner Keeps

Formula to Determine Liquidated Equity When Refinancing Property:

Market Value of the Property x 75% - 80%
- Outstanding Mortgage Payoff Amount
- Closing Costs
- Title Fees
- Unpaid Escrow Balances

Proceeds from Cash Out Refinance at the Time of Sale

Buy and Hold Strategy - Land and Distressed Property

Investors seeking to store excess cash while obtaining tax shelters and earning long term capital gains might implement a *Buy and Hold* strategy. Buy and Hold is a long-term passive strategy in which investors typically hold their land and properties for ten or more years with the anticipation that the land and property will appreciate, even though markets may fluctuate in the short term. These buy and hold investors do not make improvements to the land or property, and often generate no cash flows during the holding period. Likewise, they incur few expenses to maintain the property. Expenses like property taxes, and grounds maintenance become losses that reduce the investor's existing tax liabilities due from other business or investment income, thus creating a savings to the investor. Because the property has not been improved and often remains in a distressed and unoccupied status, taxes remain low throughout the years and maintenance cost is limited to keeping the grounds cleared and safe and in compliance with city rules and regulations.

Since many new investors seek residual income, this strategy would be better suited for someone seeking long-term wealth accumulation and who is in a financial position to wait for it with no cash flow earned for many years. Investors implementing this strategy are not seeking a cash flowing investment vehicle; more so they seek to retain their existing income through tax savings. Generally speaking, these investors already have substantial amounts of taxable income, so short-term cash flow is not their primary motivation for purchasing property.

While a developed property could better serve the people in the community, the investor may choose to leave it undeveloped for personal monetary interests or until the neighboring properties have been developed in order to enable sustaining the business model the investor has in mind. Regardless of their intention, the investor gets a good deal. He makes the initial investment and receives a tax benefit from the expenses of maintaining the property. Then, when ready to sell, the property has appreciated to such an extent that it offsets the holding costs and creates a profitable return on investment.

Buy and Hold investors initially seek inexpensive investments in promising areas that they expect will "turn" in ten to twenty years from unwanted property to prime real estate. I knew of an investor in Atlanta, Georgia, who purchased a series of industrial buildings in his mid-twenties for $300,000. At the time of his purchase, the properties were in a crime-ridden, deserted area with little business or residential activity. In his mid-forties, he sold one building alone for $3 million dollars. Over the years he never improved the properties, nor did he generate any cash flow. He simply paid the taxes and maintained the grounds, waiting for the time when the area would improve, and his investment would pay off. As the population grew in Atlanta, developers began to move into his local market and build high-end restaurants and office complexes around his building. By simply buying a property and holding it for twenty years, he benefited from the development of the surrounding community and made a fortune.

The best news about this investment strategy is that it requires no minimum investment. I met a successful investor who purchased a single-family residential lot in a city area for $500 at a tax auction. Less than ten years later, lots in the same area were selling for $60,000 per lot. The genius to this method is not the amount of the investment, but the propensity for growth in the area you select and the amount of time you wait to see the investment turn.

Given the amount of time it may take to see a significant profit, it may behoove you to create a living trust or name your heirs on the property title. This allows the property to automatically remain in the possession of the heirs and avoids unnecessary probate issues. It is unfortunate when heirs cannot afford to probate wills in order to receive their inheritance. A greater misfortune is when heirs do not understand the future value of inherited property and sell for short-term profits, leaving the big profits to a savvier investor. A living trust can transfer ownership of the property to heirs in the event of death but direct the use of property or create a time requirement before divestment.

Pros
Investments grow in value over time with little to no management or operating costs required. Investors' time commitment is limited to identifying a property to acquire and keeping taxes paid on the property. This method requires little working knowledge and can be effective on small dollar acquisitions such as residential land and buildings that have come to ruin.

Cons
This investment usually takes many years before the investor yields a profit. Investors must be able to cover holding costs while receiving no cash flow on the property.

Step 1 – Purchase Your Property

Acquire land or a distressed/vacant property in a promising location. Consider proximity to major cities, highways, schools, and retail centers. Research city planning initiatives and review budgets for future development. Oftentimes city planning meetings and votes are open to the public or available to view online. Highway changes follow population growth and are often discussed five to ten years before the construction commences. It's best to know ahead of time what the city deems as developing locations so that you can invest there earlier.

Consider land that could be rezoned from a lower-level use to a commercial use. Mixed use or industrial property is often re-zoned for apartments, retail and office uses and causes the land value to become more profitable. Another option is to purchase infill lots in an already developing residential location. As homes are built, new construction investors will come seeking lots to build and your lot could be the perfect individual lot to build infill housing.

Step 2 – Hold the Property

Hold the property and/or land for an indefinite period of time until the market value of the neighboring properties increases to an amount that will yield your desired return. With the Buy and Hold strategy, your property need not generate any income during the term that you hold it. However, there are many practical ways to lease the land for profit if you intend to earn money while holding.

For rural land, research agricultural exemptions that may be available in your area. Consider the benefits of leasing the land to solar or windmill farms or cell tower companies which typically pay a long-term lease for use of vacant land. If you intend to hold your land for twenty to fifty years, consider reforestation of the land by planting trees that can be harvested in decades to come as well as create substantial income from timber for yourself and generations to come. Crop land is valued higher than pastureland. Therefore, you may want to consider planting crops or leasing land to farmers. These methods can increase the value of the property over time, while initial costs are underwritten by private or government funding.

Step 3 – Sell the Property

Sell the land and/or property when its market value increases to the desired amount. At that point you can mortgage the property, sell it for a profit, or develop the real estate to sell or lease the land. If an outside developer approaches you about developing the property, consider selling a majority interest but negotiate a stake of equity in the completed project.

How You Earn

Use the following formula to measure the potential earnings that could be received if the property is sold. As you hold the property year to year, continue to estimate the unrealized gain or loss and consider selling in the year most advantageous for your bottom line and tax filing. Consider tax savings and liabilities separately.

Consult a tax accountant or real estate tax specialist to determine the appropriate time to divest.

Buy and Hold of Land/Distressed Property Profit Formula:

      Market Value of Property
+   Value of Improvements
-   Initial Investment
-   Holding Costs
-   Interest + Financing Costs (If applicable)

    Unrealized Gain/Loss in Property

Formula to determine your Buy and Hold Rental Profit
*If property is occupied and rented.
  Monthly Rent Amount
-   Mortgage on Rental Property
-   Property Management fees (If applicable)
-   Property Taxes
-   Less Insurance
-   Reserves for Maintenance/ Repairs
-   Utilities or Other Landlord Paid Expenses

Monthly Profit that Property Owner Keeps

Equity Growth Formula:

Market Value of Property
-   Outstanding Mortgage Payoff Amount
-   Outstanding Debts or Taxes Due on Property

Equity Remaining in Property

PASSIVE INVESTMENT STRATEGIES

Private Lending Strategy

Private lending is a concept where an individual uses their available cash to function as a bank, lender, or passive investor. People who opt for this investment strategy have access to capital that is in a savings account earning low interest or in an investment account yielding returns lower than what they could potentially earn through real estate investments.

This passive investment strategy allows individuals to make use of excess cash without the need to be actively involved in the process of real estate. We are all familiar with the concept of banking because we use banks in our daily lives. We deposit funds at banking institutions, and we withdraw funds as needed through the use of debit cards. We borrow credit and repay it, but in most cases, we rarely ever earn significant interest from the funds that we have on deposit with the bank. Private lending allows the deposit holder to make effective use of their cash by depositing it into a trusted real estate vehicle and awaiting a return on investment based on whatever negotiated terms have been secured.

Active investors and moderate investors can partner with passive investors to utilize this private lending strategy. For example, an investor completing a fixed and flip might obtain their funding from an individual who operates as a private lender. I know a woman in Virginia who has become successful in fixing and flipping properties and her source of funding is an 80+ year old retiree. The retiree had access to a sizable retirement savings account and a vision for transforming and developing their local community. The fix and flipper is a young spunky real estate agent with an eye for interior design and a knack for remodeling houses. Together the duo has completed some hefty remodeling projects in Richmond. The flipper now has the eye of a local bank and has given several talks to other female deposit holders on how to invest in real estate using creative financing methods. This example serves as a motivation to anyone who has a vision and is willing to partner with others who believe in their vision and have the capital to support it.

When one person has money and the other person has passion and skill, these two can become a powerful team in the real estate investment industry. If you are interested in a more active strategy but lack access to capital, look around your network and see who may be in an opposite situation. These individuals can serve as partners where you both can benefit through collaboration.

Though it is like a partnership, with this particular strategy the active investor would be the borrower and the passive investor would be the lender. The borrower signs a promissory note with a fixed interest rate and a term obligating them to repay the debt. In most cases the debt will be secured by the property itself, meaning that the lender has an investment that is backed by the security of the asset that they have funded. In the event of a default by the borrower, the lender may have a deed of trust or some other security instrument to provide them legal support to reclaim their money.

As a private lender you will not be a true business partner in the ownership of the assets and the equity that may be gained, nor will you receive the cash flows if the investment is rented. You simply receive a payment of interest in addition to a repayment of principal within an agreed upon set period of time. This method allows you to earn a greater amount of interest on your money than typically earned in a bank savings account. However, if you are interested in participating and earning a greater return, read more in the partnership section.

A cautionary note to investors interested in becoming a private lender: Beware that who you invest in is just as important as what property your money finances. Everyone with a vision, skill set, and a great idea is not the ideal receptacle for your hard-earned money. Beware of people who may sell you a big idea without the credibility and integrity needed to follow through. Pay attention to the minute details, read over your contracts thoroughly, engage legal and tax accounting advisors, and ask questions until you fully understand the deal. Most private lenders have little knowledge or experience in the real estate market; however, they have a general understanding of the business, the market in which they are investing, and/or a strong trust in the person that leads the investment.

Pros
Private lending allows an investor to gain a return of investment larger than what they might typically receive by holding their cash with a banking institution. Private lending allows an investor to participate in the real estate market without the time commitment and activity needed in other methods discussed. This method is typically secured by the asset, thus giving the investor the confidence that their money will be returned and, if it is not, they have access to assume control of the asset which may be more valuable than the money they invested.

Cons
It may be easier for con artists or people with bad intentions to swindle or take advantage of private lenders. The return on investment is generally lower than what could be earned in a more active investment type. The investor also has less control because they are simply handing over cash without being in control of its use, the quality of the work, the teams selected, the execution timeline, and often not privy to the day-to-day details of the investment process.

Step 1– Set a Budget
Identify a certain amount of funding you can budget and risk losing for this investment purpose. Though no one anticipates losing their money, I always encourage investors to limit their risk to the amount they could lose and still recover from. Once an amount is set you are ready to move on to the next step.

Step 2 – Structure Your Investment Terms
Now it's time to structure your investment. It's important to understand how much interest income you currently earn on your

existing deposits. Talk with a wealth advisor, financial advisor, and your banker, and pull your savings records. These are all resources for researching the activity and amounts of interest that you earned over the last few statements.

If you earned less than 1% interest on your funds that are being held on deposit at your local bank, consider what rate of interest you hope to obtain by investing in a riskier vehicle such as real estate. There is no correct number. This is a subjective decision of risk versus rewards. Depending on the level of risk you evaluate in an investment opportunity you can determine what rate of return you deem is required to put your money into that investment. In most cases anything greater than what you earn from existing investments will be a gain. The next thing to consider is the term. The term represents the length of time that it will take for your investment to yield the return you desire and for your principal to be repaid in full. It is important not only to consider the timeline that you desire but also a reasonable timeline that it should take for real estate investments of each kind to generate the return that you are asking. You want to ensure that the terms that you set are actually possible and that both parties are set up for success.

For example, a fix and flip on average may take three to six months to acquire, renovate, and sell. Therefore, you may set the term between six and twelve months to allow the investor a reasonable amount of time to find a property, renovate it, manage delays, and to sell in order to return your capital without defaulting.

Speaking of defaults, address that possibility in your contract or agreement. In the event your borrower is unable to repay the debt in the amount of time outlined in the agreement, outline what will be the remedy, legal course of action, and the penalty. Oftentimes in private money agreements, the penalty increases the rate of interest over the original amount charged. For example, a hard money loan may charge 12% annual interest if repaid between month one and month twelve. However, if the principal is not repaid by the twelfth month the rate may increase to 18% interest. This incentivizes the investor to make good on their promises, and it leaves you in a solid investment in the event that your funds take longer to be returned than expected.

Step 3: Identify Your Borrower

Find the right borrower. Now that you outlined your deal, you are ready to find the person to bring it to life. Attend local networking events where real estate investors gather. Pass out your business card or reach out to experienced investors whose work you have seen, and you are confident they know what they are doing.

Everyone is always looking for more capital for investment, so finding someone seeking a capital infusion into their real estate deal should not be difficult. Finding someone worth investing in is the focus. This will take research, discernment of character, and trust. Do not be afraid to invest in someone new or with whom you do not have a long personal relationship. Do the appropriate due diligence because someone you know well could have illegitimate intentions. The right candidate could be someone you meet at a business meeting and strike a relationship that is mutually beneficial.

How You Earn

Formula to determine your Private Lending Investment Profit:

```
      Loan amount
   x  12% interest for the term of 6 months.
   ─────────────────────────────────────────
      Interest on amount loaned
```

REIT Investment Strategy

Another common passive investment strategy is *a real estate investment trust* (REIT). REITs were established in the 1960s by the United States Congress with the goal to make real estate markets more accessible to common investors.

A REIT is a company that owns, manages, and finances income-producing commercial real estate assets. It allows numerous individual investors to pool capital and then earn dividends without the individuals having to buy, manage, or finance any of the properties on their own. Properties in a REIT portfolio may include hotels, apartment buildings, retail centers, restaurants, health care companies, warehouses, storage buildings, or other large commercial complexes.

You may already be invested in a REIT through a mutual fund or exchange traded fund (ETF) in your 401K, IRA or pension plan. As of 2021, approximately 145 million Americans live in a household already invested in a REIT but likely do not know it. Fifty percent of REIT shareholders are mutual funds and ETFs; however, 21% are individuals that have direct stock ownership. This section of our investment strategy will focus on direct stock ownership of a REIT.

Investors who are already invested in stocks may want to consider investments in REITs to diversify their existing portfolio. According to a 20-year review of stock performance ending December 2019, REITS outperformed other stock market indexes of large cap-stocks by yielding 11.6% return annually versus the Russell 1000 which yielded 6.29%. Investing in a REIT would be a similar process to investing in publicly traded stock through a trading platform such as eTrade, Fundrise, or TD Ameritrade. Most REITS are traded publicly, and investors can buy them like stocks throughout the trading session.

REITS are considered strong investment categories because the stock is backed by actual real property and that property is income producing. The value of the stock is measured by the anticipated appreciation of the assets, the income produced by the assets, and the yield. There are more than two hundred publicly traded REITs in the United States. To evaluate each company, you can consider their asset management team, their track record, the earnings per share, and the dividend yield.

Not all REITS are publicly traded though. Some are considered public non-traded REITs and/ or private REITS. Public non-traded REITS are registered with the Securities Exchange Commission (SEC) but are not offered publicly on the national securities exchange. They typically are less liquid than publicly traded stocks and are more stable because they're not subject to market changes. Private REITS are not registered with the SEC, do not trade on national exchanges, and are sold only to large institutional investors.

I am not directly promoting any platforms, please seek professional advice regarding the most appropriate platform and REIT or fund for your investment goals.

There are three types of REITs. Most real estate investment trusts fall within the category of equity REITs. Equity REITs own and manage income-producing real estate; their revenues are generated primarily through holding property long-term and not reselling the property for profit. Secondly, mortgage REITs hold mortgages on real property; they lend money to real estate operators and owners through mortgages and loans or indirectly through the acquisition of mortgage-backed securities. The third category is hybrid REITs, which use both equity and mortgage investment strategies.

Alternatively, you could invest in private equity funds (PE Funds), which also pool institutional investors' funds to invest in private commercial real estate investments. Collectively, United States private equity funds raised $287.8 billion dollars in 2021 and aggressively sought to acquire real estate assets based on their capital providers' view of real estate as a safe, tax-efficient investment vehicle. The minimum investment to participate in a private equity fund starts at $250,000 and is exclusive to high-net worth investors. Funds are not regulated like REITs and the investment must remain in the asset for years, versus REITs which can be sold on the public market like stock.

Type of REIT	Holdings
Equity	Owns and operates income-producing real estate
Mortgage	Holds mortgages on real property
Hybrid	Owns properties and holds mortgages

Referencing Investopedia, here are the requirements for a company to qualify as a REIT with the Internal Revenue Service:

- A REIT must primarily own income-generating real estate and distribute the income to the shareholders.

- The company must invest at least 75% of the assets in real estate, cash, or U.S. Treasury Bonds.

- 75% of income must be derived from real estate rents, interest on mortgages, or real estate sales.

- A minimum of 90% of their taxable income must be paid annually to shareholders as dividends.

- Entity must be classified as a corporation for tax purposes.

- The entity must have a Board of Directors or Trustees.

- The entity must have a minimum of 100 shareholders.

- No more than 50% of company shares can be held by five or fewer individuals.

Pros
1. REITs offer annual dividends because 90% of the income generated must be distributed to the shareholders each year.
2. There is potential for long term capital appreciation. As rents rise year over year yields may also increase year over year.
3. REITs have outperformed stock indexes on the average and present a great option for portfolio diversification.
4. REITs can be easily purchased on most public exchanges.
5. REITs are liquid and can be sold much more easily than owning a physical property as an individual investor.

Cons
1. Dividends are taxed as regular income for shareholders.
2. Since REITs are traded on public exchanges, they are subject to market risk and fluctuations.
3. REITs have potential for high management and transaction fees.
4. Only 10% of the REITs taxable income can be reinvested back into the business; this means that REITs are limited in their ability to bring new properties into the portfolio so that growth might be slower than if you were to own property directly.
5. Non-traded and private REITs are illiquid; they may need to be held for prolonged periods of time before seeing a return.

Step 1 – Research

Since there are more than 200 real estate investment trusts on public exchanges and many public non-traded REITs with new investment platforms being introduced regularly, the first step should certainly include research. Research and evaluate the available options before diving in on your first REIT. The last few years introduced a wave of viral investments in which novices invested in anything posted online as the latest, greatest stock. Retail investors rejected the fundamental tenets of investing by buying what is popular and subjecting themselves to market fluctuations based on changing opinions. There has been a lot less emphasis on research and a lot more emphasis on trends. While this worked out for some, the stock market experienced wild swings in valuations as investors bought and sold at the command of a Twitter post or a meme. Do not do this. Do your own research. Look at trends in REIT performance. Contact an investment broker. Find out what your mutual funds and 401k is invested in currently.

Step 2 – Join an Investment Platform and Purchase Shares

Purchase shares in the REIT of your choice through a broker.

Joint Venture/ Partnership Investment Strategy

A real estate partnership involves multiple individuals or businesses that come together to create a new entity called a partnership. The partnership can be structured differently for each individual company and the individual needs of the partners.

Some partnership agreements include both a general partner and a limited partner. Collins dictionary defines a general partnership as a form of partnership in which the partners are all liable for the activities of the partnership. Active owners, called general partners, have unlimited liability for all business debts. The limited partner, however, has no liability for the debt obligations of the business. The limited partner is liable only to the extent of their actual investment in the partnership but is not obligated to repay debts that are secured or borrowed by the business. General partners are fully liable for all debts and losses from the business; they also have full control over the management of the entity.

From the perspective of a passive investment strategy, you would assume the role as the limited partner investing capital exclusively. This approach works well if you have an existing property that you own, but do not have the expertise or the money to turn it into a cash flowing investment. This method is severely underutilized in distressed communities where properties sit abandoned or underperform and simply need an infusion of vision and capital to bring them up to par.

This general partner/limited partner model works well in real estate where you have one primary partner who is actively involved in the day-to-day operations of the real estate venture and a second or additional partners who are silently involved in capitalizing the investment. One partner is a managing partner, and the other partner or partners are the capital partners. Both managing and capital partners receive a share of equity interest and distribute profits according to whatever split was predetermined in the partnership agreement.

Regardless of whether you are the general partner or the limited partner, remember that the terms are always negotiable. The split of equity will be determined based on the amount of capital invested, the amount of risk involved, and the amount of management effort, skill, and time involved in leading the effort to yield a return. All partnerships will be guided by a partnership agreement which is also known as an operating agreement. In this contract both parties will agree to the various terms of management distribution and control. Read your partnership agreement thoroughly and understand the terms outlined. This is a legal contract that guides the distribution of profits and protects you in the event that a deal goes sour or your personal relationship with the partner declines.

In a partnership investment structure, the profits or losses of the partnership are passed along to the individual members of the partnership. The profits are taxed on the individual party's personal tax returns, thus avoiding double taxation of the partnership and personal income. There are many types of partnership entities that can be created and may vary state by state. A limited liability partnership is a different type of partnership where all of the owners have limited personal liability for the financial obligations of the business. Please refer to the section about forming a business entity for more information on entity types. I encourage you to research business classifications and consult the appropriate legal counsel and accountant to make the appropriate decision for your wealth building goals.

A joint venture is a partnership of two existing businesses. Joint ventures are ideal for two parties who are already actively involved in the real estate business but can mutually benefit by teaming together and pooling their resources, experience, and capital for greater profitability. I encourage partnerships and joint ventures because typically there is strength in numbers, and with greater capital there is potential for greater outcomes.

One of my early successes in real estate came from a partnership. As an active real estate agent wanting to explore real estate investment, I possessed the skill, acumen, and market knowledge to be successful as a real estate investor. However, I lacked enough access to capital to move forward with my dreams. Alternatively, my business partner had capital but lacked the time or wherewithal to invest in real estate and manage that process.

Our two business entities came together to form a joint venture. I served as the managing partner, and they served as the limited partner providing investment capital only. This proved to be a successful combination where all parties advanced their individual goals using the resources that the other offered.

I often see partnerships in families, in friend groups, and in professionals who find like-minded individuals with similar goals. To ensure a partnership will be a great long-term relationship, evaluate the person or entity's merits. I consider all business relationships as important as marriages. When you sign your name on a legal agreement that obligates you two to a 30-year repayment of a debt, it is important to think long term. The strength of your relationship will be tested when finances are in play. Disagreements may emerge, tension in difficult discussions will surface, people may see things from a different point of view, and business decisions may have to be made that go against other's vote. However, when the partners are aligned with a mission or vision or financial objective that is extremely clear, you can overcome these challenges.

<u>Pros</u>

A partnership minimizes fiscal responsibility because it is shared among your partners. An additional benefit is that there are more resources and help to get the job done. With this business type you avoid double taxation as profits are passed through to the individual partner's personal tax return. There is more opportunity for shared wisdom and learning among the partners. As the saying goes, two heads are better than one.

Cons

The disadvantage of partnerships is that the profits will be split among multiple parties. Decisions and control may be compromised by the vote of multiple voices. There can be a propensity for disagreement, and in the event of a dispute, the business may suffer or dissolve.

Step 1 – Find the Right Partner

The first thing to do to establish a partnership is identify the right partner for you. Take time to think about whether you would like to be the general partner serving in a management role or a limited partner operating as a silent investor without input into the investment management. Are you interested primarily in making decisions and executing the business operations, or do you prefer to simply invest capital and wait for the investment to yield a return? How much time can you commit to leading an investment? Is your focus within another career area, school, or family obligation? Do you want to collaborate with another partner with both of you working together and agreeing to decisions by vote? If you are seeking a passive investment strategy that doesn't require much time, you will be the one inserting the cash or asset into the deal. The right partner for you will serve in an opposite function. It is also possible for multiple partners to come together and serve either role.

Determine the fit of a suitable partner based on a variety of alignments including common business goals, target market, the amount of capital required and/or available, skill sets, personalities, and the overall short term and long-term vision of each partner. Financially, the right partner will be someone agreeable to the equity split you hope to obtain and the terms you negotiate in your partnership agreement.

And do negotiate. A partnership must be mutually beneficial for both parties to stay involved and happy. You may have to make concessions to the terms you offer, but you are on your way to a good business relationship when agreements can be made upfront. Beware of settling on something that is a deal breaker for you. If you are disgruntled from the start, you will carry that emotion throughout the partnership. Do not take the short end of the stick unless you can live with it. If you and someone cannot align, that is okay. Move on and the right partner may present themselves to someone new.

But a word of caution. Negotiations should not feel like wars. If you take a concession to gain a partner, this can move you one step closer to your vision. Then, in the future, you can launch out on your own or renegotiate. With completed deals, experience, and more money in your pocket, you will be in a better position of leverage to negotiate better terms the next go round.

Many people partner because they lack a skillset that someone else possesses. Consider bringing on a partner to provide legal, architectural, staging and interior design, or transactional support in exchange for some equity in your business. Financially, it may be cheaper to bring on support from a partner than outsourcing those services.

Personality is a significant factor in working with someone. Trust me, I have had my fair share of friction with people who did not align with my personality or vice versa. Do business with someone you can communicate with honestly and openly and who brings cheer when you see their number flash across your phone. You do not want to cringe at the thought of working with someone.

Consider how a potential partner reacts to negative information and how this person treats their employees or colleagues. A good test is to take them to dinner and see how they treat the waiter. When it comes to business, make sure your partner is in good legal standing and someone scrupulous that you want to be attached to legally. I remember a business colleague came to me excited about a new potential partnership for their housing development venture. As they described their partner, they informed me that they were being investigated for a crime but had not been charged. I immediately stopped them in their tracks and said, "do not sign that agreement."

Every bank loan application asks if you are a party to a lawsuit or involved in a legal proceeding. You may not be, but if your partner is, you can get dragged down in the muck. Not to mention, if your partner is being sued, you do not want to put your assets at risk. Even if there is legal separation through a limited liability company or limited liability partnership, attorneys have cunning ways to come after everything a person is attached to, including your partnership. A *lis pendens* can stop you from selling your property while you wait for the legalities to work themselves out.

So, where does one find the appropriate business partner? That answer differs for everyone. Have you looked in your existing business network? Who do you most often find yourself talking to about real estate investing? Who is most interested in discussing your interests and in sharing their ideas and visions regarding real estate investments? Have you considered investing with family members who have like-minded interests and are trustworthy? Oftentimes people are leery of investing with family or friends because they fear destroying a relationship; but honestly, who can you trust more than those who are closest to you already?

I'm not encouraging you to invest with your friends or family, but do not be opposed to considering it. Friends and family can be the least supportive, especially when they think you are going off the rails with an out-of-the-box, pie-in-the-sky vision of real estate investment. Trust me, I purposely avoided telling people close to me about my investment dreams until after I was profitable. I owned five houses and was closing on a million-dollar commercial development before I told my mother the gist of what I was doing. I simply did not have the wherewithal to be challenged with negative opinions. I am saying this to encourage you if you do not have the financial, operational, or emotional support from those in your inner circle. That's okay, the right partner is somewhere on this planet waiting to find you.

Frequently, people say "I do not know anyone with money." I have found that when you create a solid business plan, money suddenly appears. If you do not know anyone in your primary network who is willing to be your business partner or capital partner, you may find that person in a local real estate investment club or in an online networking club. Attend local real estate events, seminars, or business meetings where investors and real estate professionals typically spend time together.

Again, heed this warning. Consider your partner with as much or even more care than you consider the business opportunity at hand. Check into the credibility of the person seeking to be your partner. You can go as far as doing a background check if you feel that it is necessary to fully understand the credentials of your potential partner. Ask for financial records, credit reports, historical deals, transaction records, and closing disclosures for past acquisitions or sales. Ask for a resume or references. Meet in person and meet their family. But whatever you do, be willing to provide the same for yourself.

Step 2 – Create a Partnership Agreement

Once you find your partner, create a partnership agreement that guides your business relationship. A partnership agreement will address business formation, parties, ownership, management, control, taxation, and dissolution. All of these matters should be discussed, agreed to, and written in a formal contract that is signed by both parties.

FORMATION will state where your business is formed and where it will operate. You would hate to give $50,000 to your partner for them to go invest it in an igloo in Antarctica. Typically, your business will need to be registered with the state and local municipality where you will be investing.

Your partnership agreement will list out the **PARTIES** who are members in the partnership. You can invest as an individual or you can come together as business entities. One party can be an individual and the other party can be a business entity.

The partnership itself will become a new business entity so be prepared to give it a **NAME**. How about Million Dollar Investments LLP?

Within your partnership agreement you will have to decide where you will **OFFICE** what will be your **ADDRESS OF RECORD**.

You will decide the **TERM** which simply means the length of time that you would like to be in partnership with this other party.

Address the **PURPOSE** of your partnership in your agreement? We list that our company's purpose in business is *to acquire, improve, lease and sell, construct, and manage long-term real estate investment properties in Dallas Texas.* Feel free to use that or change it up. Whatever you intend to do in your partnership, you will list in your partnership agreement as the purpose of the company.

Your partnership should address **OWNERSHIP**. In this section of your agreement, you will decide which party owns what and what the entitlements are for each one involved. You should address the distribution of equity and cash flow.

There will be a section on **CAPITAL CONTRIBUTIONS** that outline what each party is bringing to the table initially. If you are an investor bringing cash, then you will list the dollar amount of your investment. If you are providing an asset such as land or distressed property, then you would list the property details and the value of the asset as your capital contribution. An appraisal may be required to know what your investment is worth.

Another important segment of your partnership agreement is **MANAGEMENT**. You will need to discuss with your partner and outline in the agreement the expectation and obligation of management for the venture. If you would like to retain management control, you will be considered the general partner

and the obligation and duty to manage the day-to-day operations of the business. Even if you put a property manager in place, the general manager will still manage that outside manager and be responsible for their outcomes.
As a passive investor, you do not want management control. Your primary goal is to invest passively without being involved in the daily business.

It's important that this management section of the partnership agreement lists the duties of the manager and grants certain permissions that allow the manager to do their job freely without too many clearances and votes.
Consider whether the manager:
- Can borrow and spend without approval and up to what limits can they do so without your involvement.
- Have sole access to the bank accounts and can deposit and withdraw.
- Will possess signing authority. Will the general manager guarantee loans and personally in debt themselves to the liabilities of the business or will both parties be obligated to new debt? If you own more than 20% you may be required to sign, even as a limited partner.

Another section of the agreement will discuss **CONTROL**. Will you all decide matters through a vote? Will you require a consensus before important decisions are agreed to? Will one partner have the sole authority to make business decisions? In this case you can set a threshold for spending or loans made in the name of the business up to a certain amount that could limit the authority of one partner. Generally, the partner that holds the greatest membership percentages will have the greatest authority in a vote. Keep this in mind if you are seeking control of your business partnership.

Another section of your partnership agreement should involve **TAXATION**. It's important to consult your tax advisor regarding how your business will be taxed and which partner will be responsible for carrying profits and losses on their tax return.

Who will be responsible for creating accounting records? Who will be designated the *tax matters partner* with the IRS?

When it comes to **DISSOLUTION** or ending the partnership, think ahead. If you go into partnership with someone and you acquire assets together under the name of this partnership agreement, what happens to those assets when the business is dissolved? You can insert a *right of first refusal* to have the right for either party to purchase the asset from the other if you want to go your separate ways. If you would like for your assets to transfer to your heirs or spouse, then write that within the original partnership agreement.

Since so many varying terms and conditions could be placed within a partnership agreement, I encourage you to consult an attorney to draft your agreement before signing. If someone presents you with the partnership agreement to sign, then have your own attorney review that agreement and provide you with legal counsel before making a commitment.

In the event of a dispute, list in your partnership agreement how such matters will be legally settled. If you prefer *arbitration* or *mediation* over an actual lawsuit, put that in your agreement. It is always best to have clear terms of agreement up front so that issues do not have to be decided by a judge in a court of law. There is no perfect partnership and there will be no perfect agreement. If you can come to the table and come to terms that are agreeable by all parties, then your partnership can work. And if you cannot, then walk away. Period.

Step 3 – Commence Business and Manage the Partnership

Once you sign the partnership agreement, you are ready to move forward with getting down to business. Not only will you have to manage the actual real estate investment, but it is also important to think about how you will manage your business relationship with your partner. You should have already discussed with your partner the level of engagement and communication expected regarding the investment. Some partners want to be included in transactional information and some partners only want to talk once a year. Set expectations regarding the frequency, method, and location of all communication. Does your partner prefer in person or virtual meetings? Does your partner want email reports or texts? Does your partner like casual dinners or golf course updates? Because you are operating a business, provide financial reports to both parties on a monthly, quarterly, or annual basis. Within your partnership agreement you will have already decided the frequency of financial reports and to whom they will be distributed. As partners, all parties will have access to the books and records of the company and will expect to know financially where they stand at all times.

Another management practice will be the distribution of earnings. Likewise, you will live according to decisions outlined in your partnership agreement as to the frequency of distributions and whether they will be monthly, quarterly, annually or any other stipulated time frame. Sometimes partnership distributions are left up to the managing partner to decide. Of course, all businesses operating in the United States are required to file tax reports. The frequency of those reports will be determined by the type of business and the type of operations as defined by the Internal Revenue Service.

Another factor of managing the partnership is property updates and tours. Clarify if your partners expect to come onsite to see the property construction in process. Consider what liability could be assumed if random parties are coming on an active construction site unexpectedly without your notice. These are all things that should have been discussed and clarified in your partnership agreement. If not, simply have a conversation between all individuals in the partnership. I frequently see excited buyers and investors bringing family and friends to dangerous construction sites without giving proper notice. This is not a good business practice. However, it is important to schedule property tours, provide photos, and progress reports to keep investors excited and updated about what is happening with their dollars.

Personally, in one of my partnerships, we scheduled quarterly financial reviews, quarterly distributions, monthly financial reports prepared by a CPA. We conducted discussions by email as needed when important activities arise. Since my business partner is not local to our market area of investment, he makes a point to visit Dallas periodically to put eyes on our investments and ensure our partnership agreement is being executed as written.

There is no wrong or right strategy for managing your partnership. However, if you are a capital partner investing from a distance, you will want to see what is going on every now and then and be involved to the extent that you know how your capital is being spent. I discourage blind trust and long periods of absence because these are prime situations of which people are most often taken advantage of, even by people they trust. Even if your partner is honest, they may steer the company in a different direction than what you hoped or expected. Likewise, they may benefit from your input and advice to help the company grow to a more profitable and efficient position. Regular conversations are great ways to stay on track and keep everyone on the same page throughout the process of the real estate investment.

How You Earn

Formula to Determine Joint Venture/Partnership Profit:

```
        Profits of Business
   x    % of Net cash flows or Equity
   _____
        Your Share of cash flows or Equity
   -    Initial Investment
   _____
        Earnings
```

Crowd Funded Investment Strategy

To crowdfund is to raise money from a large number of people who invest lesser amounts of capital, typically through a website or internet-based platform. Crowdfunding is relevant as a passive investment strategy through which to invest your excess cash in real estate related investment offerings managed by others. It is alternatively a fundraising method where you can sponsor an investment raising substantial amounts of capital through a web-based intermediary platform.

As an active deal sponsor, you can envision a real estate deal, prepare the offering details, create your development plan, create architectural renderings, and upload all this information onto a crowdfunding web-portal. Crowdfunding has been called the democratizing of public offerings, making real estate offerings available to many who may have previously been demographically, economically, or geographically restricted.

In 2012 the United States Congress passed the JOBS Act, which allowed entrepreneurs and small businesses including real estate sponsors to use crowdfunding platforms as a method for real estate and other business fundraising. In 2016, the SEC adopted Regulation Crowdfunding which featured less restrictive barriers for raising capital from large groups of investors for early-stage investments or start-ups including real estate offerings. Prior to this, real estate investment trusts (REITs) were the primary method for pooling capital to invest in commercial real estate.

Since the inception of this legislation, several new crowdfunded trading platforms have been introduced to the markets that allow individuals to own a slice of the pie. Current crowdfunding platforms in existence include – Crowdstreet, Diversyfund, Equity Multiple, Yieldstreet, Realtymogul, and Modiv. *I am not directly promoting these investment platforms but only stating their availability so that you can research possible optional modes of investment.* The equity crowdfunding market was estimated at $12 billion in 2019 and anticipated to explode into $25 billion by 2026, according to a Valuates report.

According to the SEC, ***Regulation Crowdfunding*** enables eligible companies to offer and sell securities through crowdfunding. Based on the SEC rules, all transactions under REG Crowdfunding must take place online through an SEC registered intermediary, which is either a broker dealer or a funding portal such as the ones stated above. Regulation crowdfunding permits a company to raise a maximum of $5 million through crowdfunding offerings within a twelve-month period. Because of this limitation, crowdfunding platforms are smaller than real estate investment trusts (REITs) and have a cap on the deal size.

Regulation Crowdfunding limits the amount of individual non-accredited investors who can invest across all of the offerings on the platform within a twelve-month period. According to the SEC definition, non-accredited investors are individuals who earn under $200,000 a year as a single individual or $300,000 as a married couple for the prior two years, have a net worth of less than $1,000,000, and have assets equivalent to $5 million or less. Accredited investors meet or exceed these minimum requirements.

These regulations limit who can invest based on personal worth and limit the average American household from building wealth through real estate investments. According to the U.S. Census, the median household income was **$67,521 in 2020** and median individual net worth is **$121,760**. I am obviously not a fan of this accreditation rule because I know how it has restricted me from fundraising among ready and eager investors. However, I am grateful that this crowdfunding regulation creates an exemption allowing more non-accredited investors to access the real estate markets than in the past. To compute your net worth, add up the value of your assets (houses, cars, property) and deduct all of your debts (loans, mortgages, credit card balances).

SEC Investment Limitations

Individual investors are limited in the amounts they are allowed to invest in all Regulation Crowdfunding offerings over the course of a twelve-month period:

- If either of an investor's annual income or net worth is <u>less than $107,000</u>, then the investor's investment limit is the greater of:
    - $2,200 or
    - Five percent of the lesser of the investor's annual income or net worth.
- If both annual income and net worth are equal to or more than $107,000, then the investor's limit is ten percent of the lesser of their annual income or net worth.

During the twelve-month period, the aggregate number of securities sold to an investor through all Regulation Crowdfunding offerings may not exceed $107,000, regardless of the investor's annual income or net worth. Spouses are allowed to calculate their net worth and annual income jointly. This chart illustrates a few examples of the investment limits:

Investor Annual Income	Investor Net Worth	Calculation	Investment Limit[4]
$30,000	$105,000	Greater of $2,200 or 5% of $30,000 ($1,500)	$2,200
$150,000	$80,000	Greater of $2,200 or 5% of $80,000 ($4,000)	$4,000
$150,000	$107,000	10% of $107,000 ($10,700)	$10,700
$200,000	$900,000	10% of $200,000 ($20,000)	$20,000
$1,200,000	$2,000,000	10% of $1,200,000 ($120,000), subject to $107,000 cap	$107,000

Securities purchased in a crowdfunding transaction cannot be resold for one year according to the U.S. Security Exchange Commission website, unless the securities are transferred:

- to the issuer of the securities
- to an "accredited investor"
- as part of an offering registered with the Commission; or
- to a member of the family of the purchaser or the equivalent, to a trust controlled by the purchaser, to a trust created for the benefit of a member of the family of the purchaser or the equivalent, or in connection with the death or divorce of the purchaser or other similar circumstance.

Be aware that you may be limited in the ability to resell your securities and may have to hold them for indefinite periods of time unless transferred to people fitting the above listed categories.

Regulation crowdfunding also requires disclosure of information and filings with both the SEC and the investors and intermediary facilitating the offering. The benefit of using a crowdfunding platform is that the sponsor would be able to prepare these very costly documents using the intermediaries' staff attorneys for a lower fee than paying as an individual sponsor. I paid upward of $25,000 in legal fees to prepare disclosures in order to crowdfund with a group of non-accredited investors only to be told it was against the law. Now sponsors can upload their deals into funding portals, save the hassle, and lower the legal cost by obtaining exemptions through these intermediary platforms that are registered and comply with the SEC and FINRA. According to the *Financial Industry Regulatory Authority (FINRA)*, the oversight body that regulates broker's and funding portals' compliance with SEC rules, companies that conduct offerings under Regulation Crowdfunding are required to disclose:

- A description of the business of the company and its anticipated plan of business, including its name, legal status, physical address and website address.
- A discussion of the material factors that make an investment in the company speculative or risky.
- A discussion of the company's financial condition.

- The names and positions of the directors and officers; the name of each person who is a beneficial owner of twenty percent or more of the company's outstanding voting equity securities; and additional information such as the business experience of the directors and officers over the past three years.
- The price of the securities or the method for determining the price.

Before you dive into a promising investment, be sure to read the offering materials presented by the broker-dealer or the intermediary funding portal. Ask direct questions, consult professional advisors, think about worst-case scenarios, check for fraud, and only invest what you can afford to lose completely. (This same advice goes for every other method I have described previously and is a general rule of thumb for investing.)

Real Estate Crowdfunding sites offer two categories of investments including debt and equity. A debt investment provides a fixed interest payment based on your investment into the mortgage note on a property. There is no upside if the investment performs well, but there are fixed reliable interest payments secured by a lien against the property.

Equity crowdfunding pays a return on the net profit of the investment leaving room for strong upside potential with uncapped gains in situations where the deal outperforms expectations. Conversely, there is also the ability to lose on deals gone bad. Some real estate crowdfunding sites offer investment into REITs. In this case, the funding is obtained on a funding portal and then passed through into a REIT, thus obligating a 90% payout of their earnings on an annual basis. Other sites allow investors to review various deal offerings and invest directly into specific properties that they choose. With these you may have direct communication with the sponsors and be able to ask questions directly to make informed decisions and feel more vested in a property's development.

Pros

- Creates access to capital for small businesses and entrepreneurs, sponsoring investment deals.
- Investors can participate in large deals with as little as $500 investment.
- No requirement for direct management or property owner responsibilities.
- Creates access to a wider variety of investment opportunities for individual investors and a limited number of non-accredited investors.
- Deal sponsors enjoy a SEC exemption that reduces cost and federal registration requirements.

Cons

- New investment type, lack of investment performance data and untested in economic downturns.
- Limits the investment amount for non-accredited investors to 10% of their income or $107,000 whichever is greater.
- Caps the offering for deal sponsors to a $5 million offering limit.
- Investors must beware of fraud and swindles that more easily happen online.
- Less liquid than other investment types with longer investment horizons before securities can be sold or transferred.
- Management fees.

Step 1 – Research the Platforms and Select the One for You

Crowdfunding investments as a category is in its infancy and still a new system that the industry is learning. No historical data exists on how the platforms perform in economic downturns or guarantee that they are prepared to weather a monetary crisis. At the time of this writing, researchers have limited empirical data on deal performance; investment horizons are four to seven years on average; and results on yields and investment returns can be evaluated only on a limited set of deals. For example, Crowdstreet closed 560 deals since 2014 but only 76 had confirmed realized gains by the close of 2021. Whether the other 484 deals have unrealized gains or failed altogether is undisclosed. Measuring performance off 13.5% of deals closed over a seven-year period is a gamble. With this stated, the burden of research falls on the investor, many who are working off a glittering marketing package and some fast facts. Hundreds of crowdfunding platforms exist with new ones popping up regularly, making it difficult to legitimize what is worth betting on.

Do your research. Consider the record of the platform. Though all are new, see what they have accomplished so far. Investigate the team behind the platform, review the collective expertise, total amount of funds raised, the time for a deal to fully fund and close, the number of successful offerings, and whatever performance data you can find. Consider which platform is most accessible to you based on your investable funds to meet the minimum investment the platform requires. Some funding portals are only accessible to accredited investors while others are open to anyone. Check the rules and see if your net worth, career, or income qualifies you.

Research the available deals and the market where the deal is located. What do you know about that location? What do you know about the overall asset class? Research the deal sponsors and their historical performance on past deals. Do these sponsors have a team capable of managing this project? Do a gut check. Are you investing based on hype? Because someone you know is investing and you have a fear of missing out (F.O.M.O.)? Because of an ad that popped up on your computer due to behavioral retargeting. Or are you confident in the promise of the deal at hand? Regardless of how you come to the table, be sure to do ample research and only invest what you can comfortably lose.

<u>Step 2 – Wait until Payout</u>

Real estate equity or debt investing through a crowdfunding portal is a passive investment strategy only requiring you to check in to review investment performance. CREs have different payout structures. Some pay annual distributions and others have long time horizons only paying out when a deal is sold or refinanced.

As a passive investor investing funds into a crowdfunding portal, your earnings will be based on actual performance of the offering rather than the targeted return in the offering documents. If you have invested in the debt on the development, your rate of return will be fixed interest based on the rate agreed within the note. Common equity owners are entitled to a percentage of the overall investment's profits. Earnings are derived from the rental income and the income from a profitable sale of the property, sometimes years in the future. Make sure to focus on Step 1, so when you get to Step 2 it will be worth the wait.

How You Earn

For Equity Investments:

		Total investment profits
x		Your % of Equity of the Total Deal
=		Your Share of the Profit
-		Initial Investment
=		Total Investment Yield

For Debt Investments:

		Amount of debt contributed to fund deal
x		Interest rate in note
=		Fixed Interest Annually
x		Number of Years Held
=		Total Interest Income

PROPERTY TYPES AND CLASSIFICATIONS

RESIDENTIAL PROPERTIES:

- Residential Land
- Single Family Residence
- Condominium
- Town House
- Multi Family (1 - 4 Units)
- Tiny House
- Manufactured House
- Modular House
- Mobile Home
- Shipping Container House

COMMERCIAL PROPERTIES:

- Commercial Land
- Apartment
- Retail
- Office
- Industrial
- Hotel
- Medical
- Church
- High-Rise

RESIDENTIAL PROPERTY TYPES

Residential Land - land owned or being developed for residential purposes or held for future development or sale for residential purposes including all Land Held for Development, Lots Under Development and Finished Lots.

Single Family Residence - a structure, other than a multi-family residential structure, maintained and used as a single dwelling unit, or any other dwelling unit that has direct access to a street and does not share heating facilities, hot water equipment, or any other essential facility or service with any other dwelling unit.

Condominium - a large property complex composed of individual units, and each unit is owned separately. Ownership usually includes a nonexclusive interest in "community property" or shared areas controlled by the condominium management such as recreation rooms, swimming pools, and gymnasiums. Condominium management is usually made up of a board of unit owners who oversees the daily operation of the complex, such as building maintenance.

Town House - an attached single-family dwelling unit on a shared lot.

Multifamily Residence - a housing development with two or more attached residential units.

Tiny Home - a detached single-family dwelling unit of more than 150 square feet and usually 600 square feet or less. Tiny houses are constructed or mounted on a foundation and have utility connections.

Manufactured Homes - factory-built permanent dwelling units under a federal building code administered by the *U.S. Department of Housing and Urban Development (HUD)*. Manufactured homes are a minimum size of 320 square feet. The construction is built on a permanent steel chassis to assure the initial and continued transportation ability of the home and are placed on-site on piers, with masonry crawl spaces or poured concrete foundations and remain in one place during their lifetime.

Modular Homes - factory built houses shipped in sections and assembled on-site. They are set in permanent foundations and rarely, if ever, moved again. Modular homes must conform to all other federal, state and local building codes as site-built homes but are not subject to HUD code regulations.

Mobile Homes - factory-built and designed for easy delivery to their site and set up for a temporary time. Recreational "trailers" also fall into the definition of mobile homes.

Shipping Container House - a housing structure made from recycled shipping containers like a storage container or cargo container. These modular steel boxes can be assembled to create a permanent or mobile living space that varies in design, square feet, and cost. A shipping container home can be one container by itself, or multiple containers combined to create a more traditional housing structure by removing walls. Containers typically come in two sizes: 20 feet by 8 feet or 40 feet by 8 feet.

COMMERCIAL PROPERTY TYPES

Commercial Land – land owned and held for development for industry or business purposes or for large residential structures held for rent.

Apartment – any building designed for use and used as two or more separate flats or apartments or any campus consisting of apartment dwelling units which share common services.

Retail – a property housing business facilities that are open to the general public or sell goods directly to consumers, including retail stores, restaurants, pharmacies, convenience and grocery stores, seasonal and temporary businesses.

Office – a property where the substantial use of the building area and/or revenue is office space, including mixed-use property.

Industrial – a building or structure suitable for use as a factory, mill, ship, processing plant, assembly plant, warehouse, fabricating plant, research and development facility, or other industrial uses.

Hotel – a building or structure which is designed for occupancy by transients for dwelling, lodging, or sleeping purposes and includes any hotel, inn, tourist camp, cabin, motel, or place in which rooms and accommodations are furnished to transients.

Medical Building – clinics or offices for doctors, dentists, chiropractors, laboratories, pharmacies, or similar practitioners having a medical purpose.

Church – building used or proposed to be used by a church or house of worship.

High-Rise Building - a building exceeding 75 feet or 23 meters in height from ground level according to the National Fire Protection Association. High-rise buildings may be used as a residential, office, hotel, retail, or for multiple uses. A mid-rise building is a structure that has between five to ten stories and a low-rise building has less than five.

UNDERSTANDING YOUR TARGET MARKET

DECIDING THE CORRECT MARKET

So now that you have evaluated the various investment strategies available to you and reviewed the different property types, the next discussion is *where* do you plan to invest? Everywhere there is land and property can be a potential place for investment, even if it looks like miles of nothing but dirt. The question is what target market have you decided to focus investing initially? Do you plan to invest in:

- The top growing markets in the United States?
- The city closest to where you live?
- A community within driving distance of your home?
- A new area that you read is promising?
- An existing company that is investing in emerging markets?
- Around entertainment and tourist attractions?

We've all heard the term location, location, location. But a suitable location means a different thing to everybody. Location is important in real estate because it defines the real estate prices, availability, and investment potential within a given boundary. Every market depends on the relationship between supply and demand. Housing supply is limited to the number of available properties for sale in each market area. Demand represents the available buyers or tenants that are willing to buy or lease at a given price within the same market area.

There is a finite amount of land and resources on the earth and an ever-expanding population. Land is one of those things that we cannot create so this establishes the overall market and then it's minimized as you focus more narrowly on individual markets . Due to supply and demand, property value and availability differ from location to location. The price of a property in a downtown area can be triple the price of a suburban home of the same size and quality, all because of proximity to places of work, retail, or entertainment.

Within every location there will be differing demographics, economic factors, government policies, and interest rates that may have a contributing factor on supply and demand. **Demographics** are the data that describes the composition of the age, race, gender, and income of the population at large. These statistics contribute significantly toward how each location's real estate is priced and the demand. It's important to analyze the demographics within the area you have targeted in order to understand the wants, needs, and potential changes of your targeted buyers, tenants, patrons, and stakeholders.

For example, a buyer in Boca Raton, Florida is a completely different demographic than a buyer in Orlando. A middle-aged retiree living in a beach-front golfing community in Boca might be much more prepared to weather economic downturns than young parents with a vacation home near Disney, thus stabilizing demand in one area more so than in the other.

When choosing your target **location,** here are a few things you should consider:
- Proximity to the center of the metroplex or to a main point of interest
- Scarcity of land within or surrounding the target area
- Economic or infrastructure development current or upcoming

- Existing market factors such as going rents and housing prices
- Neighborhood conditions such as school performance, crime rates, walkability
- Population demographics
- Your firsthand knowledge as a resident or patron of the community

HOW TARGETED SHOULD YOU BE?

Certain investments such as equity REITs are diversified in many locations so having a target market may not be quite as important; however, we will do a deep analysis of a target market so that you can be prepared to understand the market where you invest and become an expert in that market.

Before we get deep into the details let me just admit that **I only invest in two zip codes**. I'm a community builder. I believe in focused investment because when you concentrate your properties in a targeted area, you can have a greater impact. I have a plan and buy any property that fits my plan and that falls within two zip codes. Since I am a market expert for this narrow market area, I know what I want before it becomes available for sale.

When you know what you are looking for, you know it when you see it. Before I tour the property, I already know 95% of everything I need to know to make a smart investment decision. Walking the property is the last step because in an aggressive market many cash buyers buy properties sight unseen. In recent years I saw corporate buyers submitting offer letters stating that they will buy sight unseen any property, anywhere, at any amount, and waiving the due diligence or option period and appraisal. How can new investors with less buying power compete unless they are targeted and confident in the prospects of their market?

Aside from being nimble, let me impress upon you the impact of owning multiple properties in a concentrated market area. As a community builder I want to make impactful developments that will transform a distressed community into a restored and beautiful place of improving property values and overall neighborhood appeal. I understand the possibilities that can happen by one investor who redevelops multiple properties on a city block. Countless lives can be changed, jobs created, lifestyles improved, tax revenue generated, and schools and parks renewed – all if one focused investor builds an office building, restaurant, and grocery store on the same street.

A neighborhood turns for the better when multiple residential properties on a street are improved and sold at a higher price. When change begins, others come along and continue the effort, momentum builds, and transformation appears. This will not happen without the concerted efforts of the investor, the local government, and the community. And this takes trust, unity, and a whole lot of tearing away of dysfunctional social systems. Plus, here's a secret – people bring you deals when they see you consistently, passionately working within a particular location.

The more targeted your investments, the more control obtained within that market. Being a big fish in a small pond is a good thing when your pond is real estate. I once met a man who owns 91 properties in the same part of town and at least eight of them are on the same street. Can you imagine the level of influence you could have over market value when you own that many properties in the same area?

Every time you purchase a property you supply a private appraisal report from your portfolio to help establish the value of the market area. The more properties you own, the more comparables you create. As a property owner, the rental comps for one home justify the rent for all the others, and what you list can establish the going rate for the area. You are the market maker instead of simply responding to existing market conditions. Amassing property within a territory gives you a voice to influence what is developed around your properties and what zoning changes are approved. You have greater political weight to advocate for city resources for infrastructure development, policing, and amenities.

Alternatively, some may argue against concentrating too many assets in one market area and to limit your risk by spreading investments across different cities or states. The basis for this reasoning is that if one market tanks, then your diversified portfolio limits the downside risk to your total balance sheet. I will admit that is good advice, but other ways to hedge for risk exist, such as diversifying your investment strategies or your overall investment portfolio to include some cash flowing real estate, some stock, some digital currency, bonds, and land. I encourage you to consider the potential benefits of concentrated investment in a targeted location versus a scattered, less strategic approach.

MASTER YOUR AREA

Have you ever heard the saying, "I know it like the back of my hand?" Look at the back of your hand. That is your market. Whether you are an active, moderate, or passive investor, you must know the market. I drew a circle around a map to enclose the land area where I am willing to buy, and I focus exclusively on that area.

This benefited me in that I studied my market. Besides knowing what I want and what it will look like, I know this market's trends. I know the buyer profile. I know the renters' behaviors. I know their income. I know the rent standards. I know the future development that is approved. I know the city's economic development agenda for this area. I know what I want to create, and I know what the people want.

The smaller the market that you target, the greater the understanding you can develop. It is harder to hit your target when you are constantly shifting your focus. You need to decide where you want to place your faith for increase and master that.
Think about it - the Dallas-Ft. Worth Metroplex has 6.3 million residents, more than 513,000 households, 65,000 businesses and 117 suburbs of the main city. If I say that I am going to invest in Dallas what does that really mean? Is it possible to understand the economics of such a large land mass? Every few blocks the

demographics change. There may be large swings in income from zip code to zip code. Building architectural styles vary depending on which street you live on. Having a broader target market leaves more investment opportunities available to you but narrowing your target market helps you become agile to make smart and fast decisions when opportunities arise.

Countless public resources are available for you to access information. Not to mention that local real estate professionals are some of the most untapped resources for gathering market data. Long before you are ready, you can tap your neighborhood agent for information on pricing trends, property sales data, industry data, and general advice. Do so in exchange for giving this agent your business when the time is right. You do not have to get a real estate license to do any of the things I am sharing in this book. Just build the right team, and you will save yourself the headache of juggling unnecessary roles.

Here are some things to research to build market knowledge and grow your expertise. While you are at it, why not write a complete market study compiled with sales data and trends to keep right at your fingertips. Market studies help with fundraising with investors and convince lenders that you know enough to be successful.

Compile this Market Data:
- Location Features and Attractions
- National Real Estate Market Statistics
- Local Market Appreciation and Pricing Trends
- Historic Sales and Leases
- Comparable Properties, Photos and Sales Information
- Neighborhood Demographics
- Schools and Public Facilities
- Economic Development Statistics and Trends
- Recent and Upcoming Land / Infrastructure Development
- City Policy Incentives, Subsidies, and Restrictions
- Nearby Property Appraisal Reports (Ask Neighbors and Businesses to Share)

Section III:

PREPARING TO INVEST

FINANCING OPTIONS

This section is designed to help you position yourself to invest in real estate. Whether it is your first home, your first investment deal, or you are a seasoned investor, it is imperative to prepare your personal finances in advance so that you can successfully obtain funding for your next deal. You do not need to obtain a loan to pursue a real estate investment opportunity; however, since bank financing is the most prevalent method to fund deals, I will review this funding source thoroughly. Many new investors have many questions (and fears) regarding their personal finances.

FINANCIAL Q & A

Are personal finances considered when financing real estate investments?

Yes, in most cases when using bank financing for an investment loan, the investors owning 20% or more of the business entity will need to provide a personal guarantee for the loan. The financial strength of each owner will be considered. This is not always true for seasoned businesses with an established banking relationship and funds on deposit. However, in most scenarios, new investors will be required to make a personal guarantee for mortgages, business loans, and lines of credit. The guarantee protects the bank by placing a requirement to repay the debt in the event of project failure, bankruptcy, or losses.

Both banks and investors may evaluate personal credit and request a personal financial statement or net worth statement to prove credibility, fidelity, and capacity to guarantee the loan. Lenders will delve more deeply into your personal finances for owner occupant mortgage loans and investor mortgages underwritten in the personal name of the borrower. Commercial borrowers are not subject to quite as much scrutiny and requirements can be as little as signing a *loan guarantee agreement* at closing.

If commercial loans are taken in the name of the business entity borrowing the funds, why are personal finances considered?

Most real estate deals are acquired in the name of a limited liability company (LLC), partnership or corporation. To limit liability and create a corporate veil, it is common for investors to create new businesses for each property or series of properties. Given the short amount of time that these businesses have been established, banks cannot rely solely on the finances of the business because there is not enough credit history, tax filings, or banking history for the business to qualify independently of the owners.

The property may be titled or deeded into the name of the business at the time of closing the deal. However, the majority owners may also be required to sign the note and the deed of trust as the representatives and the ultimate responsible parties of the organization. Federal requirements dictate financial institutions to collect sensitive personal data for owners holding 25% or more shares in the entity. These forms are often called **Beneficial Ownership** Forms and will contain the name, address, and social security numbers, passport numbers or other identification for non-US persons.

Do I need to be well-off financially or have a certain credit score to be approved for investor financing?

The answer to this question is always answered the same way by bank loan officers... It is a case-by-case decision. Every borrower's financial situation and deal is different, and you should never disqualify yourself without first making the attempt and submitting the application. Regardless of your financial strength and creditworthiness, the good news is that the bank is primarily underwriting the deal presented and not the owner. If you have acquired a solid deal that meets the underwriting approval criteria, you are closer to funding than someone with strong finances and a bad deal. We will discuss more on deal financing later in this section.

Keep in mind, banks are not the only source of funding to finance your deals. If you have a strong will to do something, you can find a way. A must-do attitude, patience, and positioning yourself for success is the recipe to finance your deal, whether now or in the future.

What is the best time to pursue financing for my deal?

Prepare your personal finances now, but do not apply for financing until you have assembled your plan, your team, and your deal. The more prepared you are, the more confident the banks and potential investors will be in you and your project.

I'm terrified to borrow money and/or make a personal guarantee. What if my project fails and I ruin my personal credit or end up in debt I cannot repay?

If you are averse to debt, there are other ways to finance your deal. I'll explain those options for you in the next discussion. As part of your preparation to invest, you need to have a hard talk with yourself, your family, and those impacted by your financial investments and **DECIDE** to bet on your success or bet on your failure.

Do it now. Do not wait until the deal is on the line and then waste time in indecision. Real estate investing has inherent risk, and no one can take the risk for you. No one can make you a promise, and no one can guarantee an outcome. There is a risk/reward analysis that each investor should make prayerfully before jumping into a deal. But here is the hard truth: if you will not take a risk for your own project, others will not either.

That's why most deals require a certain amount of developer contribution in capital, services, or sweat equity. Taking a risk might mean putting up your own cash in the project, guaranteeing a loan in the event of default, or pledging your existing assets and savings as security for the loan. The potential of success must outweigh the likelihood of failure. Historically speaking, trends show real estate investments to be smart, safe, places to invest your money.

How do I ask for such substantial amounts of capital from banks and investors?

The sheer number of capital providers looking for good deals in which to invest will shock you. If you have a good deal, someone somewhere wants to invest in it. Banks are in the business of making loans, and they love to build relationships with clients so that they can lend repeatedly. Their favorite people are not the ones with the biggest savings balances, but the biggest credit accounts. Put the banks' money to work by bringing them deal after deal and keeping your financial commitments.

When I started pitching my development projects to equity funds and family offices, I was so nervous that I trembled, and my heart raced. I was terrified to ask for $11 million dollars at once when I had never done a deal that size and I was only a hard-working real estate professional making about $100,000 per year. I was astounded to find that most firms told me my deals were too small. One company said they only invest $20 million or more. Another private lender told me he prefers to do deals upward of $100 million and to call him back when I had something bigger. He said, anything less than that amount was not worth his time.

That statement made me recalculate the value I placed on my time and the value my skill for putting real estate deals together was worth. I had undervalued myself, and my fear soon evaporated. I found myself turning down money when the terms were poor, because I learned that I had what they needed and not the other way around.

How do I know if I'm ready financially?

By the end of this book, you will be in a much better position to evaluate your readiness to proceed with a real estate investment opportunity. Since everyone differs in their personal finances, investment goals, capital needs, target markets, you will need to get out there in your local market and start contacting professionals in the business.

Introduce yourself to bankers and funders and start building relationships. Walk into banks and investor networking meetings with a sharp outfit, a strong handshake, and your head held high and make connections confidently. Put your face in the business space and start asking questions. Consult loan officers and take notes of their underwriting criteria. If it all sounds foreign to you, do more research. Come back repeatedly as your plan is solidified to get their feedback. Get into credit programs, take courses, listen to blogs, and read books. Meet other investors, get tips, ask for their referrals and advice. Find trusted partners to share your progress. Such as in the Comma Club Community platform!

SOURCES OF CAPITAL

- Cash
- Assets
- Conventional Financing
- Credit Cards and Lines of Credit
- Commercial Financing
- Hard Money Financing
- Private Money Financing
- Private Equity Funds
- Private Grants, Federal and Municipal Grants
- Crowdfunding Platforms

There are multiple ways to finance investments beyond simply obtaining a loan from the bank. Consider where you can source funding to place into a higher yielding real estate investment. Let's explore!

Cash
Consider your current cash that could be earning a higher rate of return if it was invested in real estate. Do you have any of the following: savings accounts, 401k, retirement accounts, pension funds, mutual funds, lower performing investment accounts, or cash value insurance policies? Take some time and review the interest, yield, or growth that you have earned on these accounts compared to what you might earn by investing in real estate. Ask yourself if you could take this capital and invest it into a higher yielding real estate investment to finance your deal. If you have a savings account, the answer is definitely yes.

I frequently see homebuyers borrowing from their 401k to source funding for their down payment. Some 401K accounts allow borrowers to pull funding from their retirement account to purchase a home. There are also self-directed 401k's and IRAs that allow you to boost your investment potential by giving you control to direct your investment into deals that you personally decide. As of 2021, the IRS allows self-directed IRAs to invest in real estate, development land, cryptocurrency, LLC membership interest, mineral rights, precious metals, tax lien certificates, and more. Consult your financial advisors on how to strategically use your cash and investments to get ahead. Gains from real estate can be redirected into these accounts; it is like borrowing from yourself the same way you would from the bank.

Assets
Take an inventory of the assets that you own and consider whether these assets can be sold, leased, refinanced, pledged, or invested to finance your real estate investment dreams. The first most obvious source of funding is your primary residence. Consider a cash out refinance loan to pull out cash equity that has built in your home since you purchased it or last refinanced it. This might be the lowest cost of capital that you can find.

Home equity lines of credit (**HELOC**) can also be used in any way you choose and is a smart way to buy property. If you are on the monopoly board stop here, cash out, and go pick up more houses. If you currently hold a piece of land, you could partner with an investor or real estate developer to build a property on that land that is cash flowing and earns income long-term. Alternatively, you could sell the property after its completion and take a split of the profit which might be greater than selling the land outright.

If you own a distressed house or property, the concept is the same as with the land. You do not have to sell your property simply because you do not have the money to develop it. Go back and read about partnerships to explore all the ways to improve this asset and create an income source for you and your family.

I often see distressed apartment buildings and commercial properties that owners refuse to sell. It disheartens me. I often wish I could partner with these owners to help them turn their ugly properties into income generating assets that can benefit their family and create multi-generational wealth instead of holding onto an eyesore in fear of losing what their parents or grandparents worked so hard to keep. If this is you, find the right partner and make that property work for you the same way your family worked for it.

Complete a personal financial statement and list out all of your assets. Do not forget to include things like jewelry, fur, heirlooms, vehicles, electronics, and other valuable personal items. These are all potential sources of funds that might help you source the money you need to purchase a property or raise the down payment needed to qualify for a loan. Even if you do not want to sell these assets, stating that you own these things on your net worth statement increases your net worth and makes you look more favorable to funders.

Conventional Financing

Conventional financing is available to borrowers who plan to occupy their properties or take loans in their personal name. Conventional financing is the most affordable, most accessible form of debt to obtain. Conventional loans are originated by private lending institutions like banks and credit unions. Since owning a home is the American dream, conventional lenders have tried to make the process simple and easy for prospective home buyers to qualify. They may also offer FHA loans which are government-backed. However, these loans can only be used if the investor uses the property, including duplexes and properties up to four units, as their primary residence for at least a year.

Credit Cards and Personal Lines of Credit

As part of your preparation to invest, I encourage you to obtain several personal and business credit cards. You never know when you are going to need access to capital fast and having a stack of credit cards is a surefire way to get yourself out of a hitch when you do not have a rich uncle to bail you out. Just a forewarning, it is also a surefire way to get yourself in a hitch. Credit cards are often abused but using them as a method to build cash flowing investments or to make improvements on properties that can be resold profitably may be an appropriate option.

If you plan to use credit cards and lines of credit as a method for financing your investments, such as material purchases, furniture, supplies, contractor payments, appliances, and decor, then also create a budget to pay off the credit balances using the profit from the investment. I have a friend who used $100,000 in credit cards to purchase a multifamily building, and she's now a highly successful multi-property owner. Do what you have to do but be disciplined and thoughtful with your spending. When at all possible, use business credit cards that do not report to the personal credit bureaus. Trust me, too much credit spending can tank your score and make it harder to obtain financing on future deals.

Commercial Financing

Commercial financing is business financing typically used to fund major capital expenditures or business operations. Once you establish your business, obtain an employee identification number (EIN), register with your state as a legal entity, create incorporating documents and/or an operating agreement, you should be able to open a business banking account at any financial institution of your liking. Most financial institutions also offer commercial lending products such as term loans, commercial mortgage loans, business credit cards, lines of credit, and letters of credit. Sit down with your banker and explore all of the lending products that they offer and find out how you can qualify. You may have to give a personal guarantee and/or have your personal credit pulled before you can qualify for these products. Be sure to ask if these report to your personal credit account. Steer away from debt that reports personally if you can.

Hard Money Financing

Hard Money lenders are individuals or private companies that provide loans primarily to investors for the construction and renovation of real estate. Hard money loans are short-term bridge loans intended to fund improvements until the loan is refinanced into long-term financing or the property is sold.

These lenders typically have high interest rates (11-13% annually) and set maximum loan amounts as a percentage of the After Repair Value (ARV) or future value of the property after construction or repairs are completed. In certain situations where the future value is high enough, the lenders may fund up to 100% of acquisition costs, repair costs, and loan costs leaving no money out of pocket for the borrower.

Hard money lenders can approve loans in less than a week, thus helping investors to close deals quickly and offer competitive terms over conventional borrowers. In strong markets, hard money lenders may waive appraisals and inspections helping the investor to be as competitive as a cash buyer.

Private Equity (PE) Funds

A private equity fund is a partnership of institutional, accredited investors who pool capital for general, ongoing real estate investment without specific knowledge of each individual deal. The private equity fund invests in a series of deals with a standardized risk and reward structure for the overall fund, as opposed to traditional partnerships in which investments are made directly by the investor into the partnership and evaluated on a deal-by-deal basis.

Within a private equity fund a general partner, referred to as the sponsor or deal manager, creates the fund. Limited partners invest capital in the fund with the goal of investing in a series of commercial properties that will be developed and then sold to obtain a greater return than they could earn in the public equity market. Money raised by the sponsor will be used together with money borrowed from the banks or other private lenders and will be invested in real estate development or acquisitions.

The sponsor is responsible for identifying, evaluating, leasing, and managing the property and the group of investors. Most of the funds come from the limited partners who are passive investors.

High caliber real estate developers or sponsors with the pipeline of potential investment deals are attractive to private equity funds who have large dollars to deploy on behalf of their institutional funders. These institutional investors have billions of dollars to invest, but do not have the bandwidth to evaluate deals individually. Therefore, a private equity fund sponsor serves as the go-between to evaluate and identify potential deals on behalf of large institutional investors.

The sponsor collects an acquisition fee and a split of profits as the deal performs according to goal. As of 2021, United States Private Equity Funds had amassed a record $287.8 billion in capital to invest in commercial property deals, that is, more equity than there are deals available to spend it on. Though I do not have exact figures, PE Fund deals average around $100 million with a minimum investment of $20 million. In my personal experience, some smaller PE funds will consider deals with the minimum investment of $5 million.

Private equity funds evaluate deals based on the asset type and class, market location, risk, holding period, cap rate, and other performance measures such as *internal rate of return* (IRR), *cash on cash return,* and the *equity multiple.* If you seek to raise funding for larger projects from equity partners such as private equity funds, consider the cost of capital to obtain this funding versus other sources, and strategize the mix of equity and debt that will yield the greatest outcome for your project.

Syndication or Partnerships

A property syndication is an individual real estate deal where a sponsor is raising money for the purchase of a specific income producing commercial real estate property from multiple investors. As a deal maker, consider forming a syndication and presenting an investment opportunity where you may obtain capital from a group of individual investors who sit as silent, limited partners.

The equity investors invest cash in exchange for a specific return. Depending on deal size and number of investors, the partnership may require a ***Private Placement Memorandum (PPM)*** given to the investors which specifies information about the deal, returns, and the sponsor. This PPM may be costly and require a great deal of time to put together. According to Forbes Business Council, investors will seek syndication deals in developing markets with undervalued rents or in markets with rents on the rise. They look for an internal rate of return of 6% or greater with a ***preferred return*** of 10% or greater and the projected value of the property to increase 20% or more in the next five years.

Crowdfunding

In 2012 the Federal Government approved crowdfunding via a SEC-registered funding portal or broker-dealer to increase access to capital for small businesses and entrepreneurs, including real estate sponsors. This law allows companies to raise up to $5 million in one year through crowdfunding offerings but limits the maximum investment to a proportion of the investors' annual income or net worth. Securities purchased through crowdfunding transactions typically cannot be resold within the first twelve months.

This new fundraising method is growing in popularity and funding portals are available and accessible to real estate developers and sponsors to list their deals online for the public to invest. The SEC Crowdfunding Regulation is subject to "bad actor" disqualification which prohibits individuals with certain criminal convictions, court injunctions, restraining orders, or SEC disciplinary orders from being an issuer, manager, beneficial owner, promoter, or solicitor of crowdfunding. Consult a securities attorney specializing in SEC exemptions for more information regarding this method of fundraising.

PREPARING YOUR PERSONAL FINANCES

The Top Factors that Lenders Consider:

- Credit
- Income
- Assets
- Debt

CREDIT

Understanding Personal Credit

Credit is the most avoided topic of discussion in America. Since it is the hard one, I will put it first. Your credit matters. Credit is a measure of your financial credibility based on historical financial choices and outcomes. We all know there are extenuating circumstances that may lead to poor credit. Still your credit score impacts your access to capital and ability to secure financing for your deals.

Three credit bureaus report your credit: TransUnion, Equifax, and Experian. Each bureau keeps a separate record of your credit accounts and history and computes a score based on their scoring model and verified financial information. It is common for each bureau to compute a different score, which is why mortgage lenders usually use the mid-score for loan approval.

The credit score used for mortgage lending ranges from 300 to 850. It is important to note that mortgage lenders look at a different FICO (Fair Isaac Corporation) score than the one you may see on public credit reporting websites. Most Americans' credit score falls between 600 and 750. Borrowers with a credit score above 720 will obtain the best interest rates and will have the most access to deal financing options.

Before we dive into this section, it is important that each of you know where your credit stands so that you can be off to the races fast, or so that you can make adjustments to be approved for a loan in the future. If you have excellent credit, I applaud you. Congratulations on your diligence, consistency, and sacrifice to pay those bills on time and exhibit fiscal responsibility. Still, do not skip this section. Review and share the information with a friend who needs it.

Understanding Business Credit

According to the U.S. Small Business Administration (SBA), "Access to cash and credit is a business' lifeline. Business credit allows a company to borrow money that can be used to purchase products or services. It is based on the trust that payment will be made in the future."
Business credit is not only useful for operational expenses, but it can also be used to purchase fixed assets like vehicles, land and property, also known as PPE (property, plant, and equipment). To qualify for business

credit, you must have a separate legal entity that has a business credit profile with business credit reporting agencies such as Dun & Bradstreet (D&B), Equifax, or Experian. These three business credit bureaus measure and report how a business interacts with its suppliers and vendors. They capture payment trends, credit limits, outstanding balances, financial stability, delinquencies, and likelihood of the business to fail.

When creating a new business, it is important to register the business with Dun & Bradstreet and to obtain an account number called a DUNS number (Data Universal Numbering System). Go a step further and be sure that your company has a PAYDEX score. This 100-point PAYDEX score reflects your company's credibility and will be checked as part of most credit decisions. To receive a PAYDEX score, your company must have at least two vendor relationships that have reported at least three trade events. Upload up-to-date financial statements and self-report trade lines for all vendors and suppliers with whom you are in good standing regarding payments.

Many suppliers do not report automatically, but you are allowed to provide your supplier's contact information that will be independently verified by Dun & Bradstreet and then added to your business to create a profile. These vendors may include your office supply purchases, technology, accounting, legal, company car, cell phone, office rent, equipment rentals, construction vendors, or any other suppliers of your business who you pay on an ongoing basis.

Having a PAYDEX score above 80 represents a minimal risk of default or delinquent payment. In order to find out your PAYDEX score, call Dun & Bradstreet, provide them with your DUNS number, and ask them to tell you your score. If you do not have a score reporting, then your next step will be to submit supplier or vendor contacts to report credit accounts to generate your score. This may be done for a fee. Or research suppliers that automatically report to the business credit bureaus and submit credit applications there. Uline and NAV are two companies with easy approval odds. They provide *Net 30 accounts,* which allows you up to 30 days to pay a bill in full. These companies automatically report tradelines to the bureaus, which is helpful in building business credit with commonly needed supplies and services.

Equifax takes data collected by the small business finance exchange, or the SBA, and translates that data into a report which is based on payment data from U.S. small business lenders who are part of their small business customers. Equifax pulls data from public records to record liens, bankruptcies, judgments, payment trends, and presents a score that ranges from 101 to 992. The lower the score the higher the risk, and the higher the score the lower the risk. Equifax also presents a prediction of business failure and computes a score that ranges from 1000 to 1610. Likewise, the lower the score the higher the risk.

Experian collects credit information from suppliers and lenders and also from public records. The Experian business credit score ranges from zero to one hundred similar to the PAYDEX score with an 80 to 100 representing excellent business credit. Some lenders only pull reports from Experian or Equifax depending on the type of credit application they are evaluating. Experian collects both trade data and bank data, which is a convergence of how D&B and Equifax measure creditworthiness.

While positive credit opens access to capital for your business, negative personal and business credit can potentially harm your approval odds. See the chart below to determine how long information remains on your credit report:

Personal Credit	Time on Credit	Business Credit	Time on Credit
Positive Accounts	Indefinitely	Trade Data	3 years
Chapter 7 Bankruptcy	10 years from filing	Bankruptcies	9 years, 9 months
Chapter 13 Bankruptcy	7 years from filing	Tax Liens	6 years, 9 months
Judgements	7 years from filing	Judgments	6 years, 9 months
Closed Accounts	10 years from closing	Bank and Government	3 years
Late Payments	7 years	Leasing Data	3 years
Collections	7 years	Collections	6 years, 9 months
Missed Payments	7 years	UCC filings	5 years

Credit Q & A

How Important Is Credit in Obtaining Financing for My Deal?

Lenders look at your credit to evaluate your readiness to borrow funds, likelihood for repayment based on past payment history, and probability of default, which is used to determine the interest rate for your loan. Strong borrowers with good credit scores obtain lower interest rate loans and more favorable loan terms.

Credit is a qualifying factor for residential mortgage loans; however, for commercial mortgage lending, credit plays a lesser role in determining if borrowers qualify for a loan. Hard money loans and commercial loans typically have a minimum credit score of 620. I met an investor with a large portfolio of properties who told me that he has never had a credit score above 600. I obtained multiple loans at commercial banks and hard money lenders where my credit was never even reviewed. That is because I already had credibility in other areas and my deals were standard to those funders, so they did not factor in my actual credit score.

Every situation is different and will depend on the other financing criteria that we will discuss later in this section. Do not disqualify yourself from investing or obtaining financing because of your credit score. It is important to not only look at your credit score, but at your credit profile and the items that are listed on your credit report. Lenders look at the age of the credit profile, the number of credit accounts, payment history, the number of late or missed payments, the number, age, and amount of collections, the age of delinquent accounts, and the overall credit utilization ratio.

Borrowers with positive credit profiles and low scores can usually obtain loans. If you have totally thrown your credit to the wind and you know you have much work to do, then change your behaviors and get in a credit repair program NOW.

What can I do if I have poor credit?

Often borrowers disqualify themselves by not using credit. It is important to have multiple open lines of credit, such as credit cards and loans, and to maintain low, revolving balances below 30% of the available credit. Even if it is not being used at all, having open lines of credit lowers your credit utilization ratio, which is one of the factors contributing to your score. Having other credit before you apply for a mortgage demonstrates that other financial institutions at some time trusted you to use their money. Yes, I hear your argument that using credit is dangerous, but in the American financial system, debt is a good thing if you want a mortgage loan. Apply for credit cards, stick them in your dresser drawer, and forget about them.

Another factor that may cause your score to remain low is when more negative credit history exists than positive credit history. If you have negative credit history, it is important to begin creating positive line items that report to the credit bureaus such as unsecured or **secured credit cards**. Some websites report rent payments and other bills to the bureaus on your behalf, but generally those items do not automatically report (that's a shame). It may take time for negative items to be resolved before a creditor will lend to you again. However, every seven years your credit resets and negative items are removed from your credit score computation. So, if you wait long enough, your credit can improve as long as you stop making poor credit decisions now.

Look at your credit report and check the date of your most recent negative credit item. This includes past due payments, collection accounts, bankruptcies, and other missed payments. If your most recent delinquent item was three years ago, then in four years you can have stellar credit if you continue to build positive credit items and wait for the negative ones to be removed.

You can also call your creditors, make payment arrangements and begin to get those negative items into repayment. Keep the payment agreement by paying monthly and revise the agreement when you can't. As the balances are paid in full, use the excess money you have left over to pay extra on other accounts. You can settle old collection accounts and have them closed immediately by agreeing to pay a percent of the balance due.

Some companies buy debt packages for pennies on the dollar as a business and are willing to settle with you for 10% on the dollar. Try it. Call those nagging creditors and offer them $10 for every $100 that you owe and see if they take it. If they do, make sure they write you a letter showing that you have settled this debt and that the account will no longer report negatively on your credit. If the collection company continues to report after you made your settlement payment, then send a copy of the letter to the credit bureaus and have the negative remarks removed.

Lenders typically look back two years to ensure that no more than two late or missed payments and no large delinquencies within that period exist. Older accounts may be overlooked by lenders, and they can be justified by providing an explanation letter for the cause of the delinquency. Be sure the explanation letter includes the short-term situation that impacted you financially in the past. Explain that you have overcome it, and that it is not something ongoing at the time of the credit application. I have seen lenders accept job loss, divorce, medical issues, separation, and economic downturn as justification for past credit issues, so long as the borrower has exhibited strong recovery in the most recent two years.

How do I break the cycle of poor credit?

At one point in my life, I tanked my credit by living off my credit cards when I did not have any other means of income to pay the bills. That financial choice I made affected me for years. However, one day I took charge of my credit. I decided to write letters to the credit bureaus disputing items and making agreements at the smallest payment amount possible. Some were $25 a month, others were $10. I borrowed money from my mother to pay unpaid speeding tickets and to pay balances larger than what I could manage. (Thanks, Mom!)

Month-by-month, year-by-year negative items fell from my credit. One day I looked up and saw that my score had increased to 799, and I knew that God was real. I see this all the time with my clients. The early 20's is often the age when people ruin their credit. The late 20's to the early 30's is the time when they fret about it, regret their credit decisions, and try to get out of debt. Then by the late 30's to 40's these individuals are overcoming poor decisions and moving into the ease of low interest financing and access to capital.

We can break this cycle by telling every teenager and young adult we know about credit so that the same abuses will not occur in the next generation. Let's give youth a head start by teaching them financial literacy, so that their future does not look like our past. And while you're at it, put a credit lock on your children's credit until you know they are financially responsible enough to make their own financial decisions and to ensure that identity theft does not ruin their credit.

What credit items does a lender look for to approve a loan?

The mortgage lender will look at your credit score and credit history to qualify you for a mortgage. You do not need perfect credit, but you do need to show a positive history of on-time payments for the past two years. Many lenders disqualify borrowers for delinquent payments or missed payments. Collections from many years ago and medical bills do not seem to have the same impact.

There are many available first-time home buyer programs and down payment assistance programs for borrowers with credit scores above 620. Some programs set the minimum score at 660, so be sure to shop around if you get denied. In my experience, there is always a lender somewhere that can creatively approve a loan. The credit score and profile will contribute to the lender's decision for the interest rate offered for the loan. These typically are non-negotiable and set by the bank underwriting department.

If I have approvable credit, should I wait to improve my score before applying for credit?

A low interest rate is preferrable. However, if you are obtaining a mortgage loan for the purposes of purchasing an investment property, then waiting is not ideal. I must remind you that your primary goal is to receive a spread between the mortgage payment and the rent amount. Often slight differences in interest rate have a minor impact on the monthly payment.

I encourage you to consider the strategy in which you compute the difference between the amount of rent you can earn on the property and the mortgage payment at your qualifying interest rate. If the spread is acceptable to you, then move forward. The opportunity cost of lost rents and equity outweigh the interest savings, especially if your tenant's rent payment will be covering the mortgage on your behalf. *Buy the property and use the income to pay off debt that is causing your score to be low.* When your score improves, the market rates are good, and the property has appreciated in value, then refinance the debt. Check out the example below and consider the difference between obtaining financing at 4% rate with a 650 score versus 3% with a 700 score:

Cashflow Difference between 3% and 4% interest rate:

           $1500 Market Rent for Subject Property
     − $1000 Estimated Mortgage Payment for Subject Property at 3.0%

     = $500   Potential Monthly Cash Flow

OR

           $1500 Market Rent for Subject Property
     − $1122 Estimated Mortgage Payment for Subject Property at 4.0%

     = $378   Potential Monthly Cash Flow

Also, if you wait several months to improve your score, property values will generally continue to rise, and interest rates are subject to change with the market. Consequently, by the time you improve your credit score to the number where you feel you will earn the best interest rate, the increased market price may offset the savings and you end up paying more for the same property.

I understand this perspective may be contrary to popular opinion which will teach you to improve your score to get the best interest rate. My point of view is simply focus on improving your score to get approved in the first place. Once you purchase the property and rent it, your tenant will pay the mortgage and the interest while you keep the spread as profit. The more you use your credit and the more on-time payments you make, the higher your score will trend over time.

Focus on buying when the market is ideal because that can be more advantageous than having a peak score. I purchased my first home when my score was 799 and qualified for 4.125% interest rate with the top credit. Then a few years later market rates dropped to the mid 2%'s, and I saw buyers with 600 credit scores qualifying for 2.5% interest rates. I say these things to remove the limitations that may unnecessarily delay you.

If you have a positive payment history over the last two years with minor dings or only one to two missed payments, start your approval process now. If you have more extensive issues, enroll in credit repair and start that process. Consistent payments over the next one to two years will put you in position to invest when the time is right.

I want to invest, but my credit will surely disqualify me. Is it worth the wait?

Time is on your side. If you have a vision, credit improves with time. Start making changes now because time will pass whether you make changes or not. But why not allow your credit to rise as time goes on. A year from now you could qualify for a loan that may not be possible today. I have seen this happen repeatedly with property owners who set a goal and begin to be intentional about building credit.

This chapter is all about getting positioned to invest. There is nothing wrong with creating a game plan years before you are ready to execute. Think about this, wealthy families create a 100-year investment plan. That means they plan investment moves today that they may not implement until they are 80 years old.

As a REALTOR, many of my home buyer clients have come to me over a year before they were ready to buy their home in order to get the information needed to position themselves for approval. It is no different with investments and may even take longer because many first-generation investors are already generations behind in property ownership and wealth accumulation. Whatever you do, do something. If you need a referral for a credit repair specialist, please reach out to us at Referrals@CommaClubCommunity.com or check the website at CommaClubCommunity.com

What are the best investment methods for poor or average credit scores?

Here are some options in no particular order:

1. Go for a method that is not reliant upon obtaining a loan, unless you already have open credit lines.
2. Pull money from your savings, 401k, or other retirement sources, and buy raw land.
3. If you have cash, consider investing your available funds as a limited partner into a general partner or sponsor's deal and obtaining a return. If you do not have cash, become the sponsor, identify a real estate investment project, create a syndicate, and have a group of investors invest into your deal. While your credit score may not be brought into question, your credibility certainly will.
4. Find someone who is trustworthy and good at real estate flipping or remodeling and become their capital partner.

5. If you own a property, consider teaming up with a real estate developer or financier to convert that old property into an income producing property. Your credit will not matter in this equation, only the value of the property that you own will be considered.
6. You can also invest in publicly traded REITs or crowdfunding deals through web-based funding platforms where your income is factored, but your credit will not come into question. Investments can be as low as two hundred dollars.
7. If you want to be an independent fix and flipper, you can obtain a hard money loan and expect to pay a high interest rate. Hard money lenders collaborate with borrowers with average credit.

INCOME

Another factor that is considered in mortgage financing is income, both the amount and your sources. This income will be used to compute a measure of available income versus total debts including the new loan you are applying to obtain. You will need to show proof of income from a full-time job, social security or retirement income, child support, alimony, or some other long-term income source. Full time workers can qualify with a new job offer letter before they start working. Income from part-time work is only counted if the job has been sustained for more than two years. Likewise, overtime pay, and bonuses are only counted if you have a proven history of receiving them for at least two years.

Sources of Income:

- Employment Income
- Self-Employment and Contractor Income
- Business or Partnership Income
- Rental Property Income
- Investment Income and Interest Income
- Child Support, Social Security, and Retirement Income

Showing Proof of Income:

- Tax Returns
- Employment W2's
- Business Profit and Loss Statements
- Property Leases and Agreements
- Legal Documents, Court Orders, Government Award Letters
- Bank Statements

Make a list of documents that you need to gather to provide as supportive documentation to prove your income.

Income Q & A:

Is there a minimum amount of income needed to qualify for a mortgage loan?

No minimum income is required to qualify for financing. Your personal income and/or the income of the investment will be used to compute a measure of debt coverage. This is called the ***Debt-Coverage Ratio.*** Banks want to make sure that enough income exists to cover the mortgage loan and the expenses to operate the property. If you do not earn very much, consider buying less expensive properties or putting up more equity.

Depending on how you intend to exit the investment, lenders may pay more or less attention to your personal income. For example, if you intend to fix and flip a property, the lender may not require you to have as much income to support that loan, which will be a short-term bridge loan until you sell the property and repay the full amount of principal. If you are borrowing long-term and putting up a personal guarantee, lenders may want the combined owner's income to be sufficient to make the monthly debt service payments
I'm self-employed, so will it be difficult to obtain financing?

If you are self-employed, most lenders require tax filings for the prior two-year period to support the claimed business income. When you are a W2 employee, your mortgage lender will look at your gross income *before* taxes to qualify you for financing. When you are self-employed, underwriters will look at your **Adjusted Gross Income (AGI),** which is your income *after* business expenses are deducted.

Prior to filing your taxes as a self-employed person with a Schedule C, K-1 or another business return, beware that you should report the highest income possible and that the deductions you take reduce your taxable income. Since mortgage lenders look at Adjusted Gross Income to determine the amount of income to use for loan qualifications, business deductions can reduce your income to a disqualifying amount.

If your tax accountant creatively finds ways to write-off so many expenses that you do not owe taxes, then you may find it difficult to qualify for a mortgage. This is a common mistake many entrepreneurs make. You must show earned income to qualify for financing. Therefore, at some point you must face the situation and pay taxes to get approved for a home loan.

You should always file your taxes honestly and appropriately according to the IRS regulations and guidelines. Discuss your investment plans with your tax accountant. If you are self-employed, I highly dissuade you from using a simple online tax filing service unless you have consulted the guidance of a tax advisor. It cost me between $500-$1,000 to have my taxes professionally prepared by a tax expert.

Also, keep in mind that as a homeowner, you can deduct the closing costs, property taxes, and loan interest on your tax filings, which will be additional savings for you in the future. As an investor, there are also tax advantages and write-offs for operating your property, such as deducting depreciation and operating costs.

I'm so excited about the big money I'm going to earn in real estate that I'm going to quit my job! Should I?

Many investors get excited about the prospect of earning big dollars as a real estate investor and consider quitting their jobs too soon. If possible, use your day job as support to build your investment business. After you replace your salary with investment income, then leave the job. At minimum, you will need two years of self-employment income before the lenders will consider this as reliable income to qualify for a loan. This includes certain income filed on certain schedules of your federal tax return.

How do banks look at rental income of existing or potential properties?

Rental income from properties can be counted immediately but will be counted at 75% of the rent amount. The bank will evaluate your income together with the potential or current rental income generated by the property that you are purchasing. Borrowers who qualify for a certain amount when they are buying a single unit property are often shocked to learn that they can qualify for much more financing when buying a duplex or fourplex. That is because the lender will count the potential income of the property that you are acquiring together with your other income sources. The more units, the more income.

If you are pre-approved for a residential mortgage loan, have your lender run your pre-approval based on a multi-unit (less than five units). In my market, multi-family units are extremely competitive property types. They typically sell fast. If you can put your hands on one and your financing is approved, move your feet and do it!

What are the best investment methods for low income and fixed income investors?

There is a huge misunderstanding that should be addressed regarding low-income borrowers. This inaccuracy is that an income requirement is in place for investment. This is untrue! Having a lack of cash to put into the deal is a bigger issue than having low income. If you are on a fixed income, part-time income, or no income, you can still invest, particularly when you have access to capital.

I have applied for loans with banks that do not request any income documentation. This is particularly true with hard money lenders. I have closed several loans where my personal income was never reviewed, and the only income ever evaluated was the income on the property itself. What I find most unfortunate is the number of people who disqualify themselves from opportunities to invest because they do not believe they can be approved for financing without attempting to try and put a deal together. This limiting mindset causes people to live below the ceiling placed over them by their income when investment in real estate could be the very tool to shatter that ceiling and create a breakthrough to greater financial freedom.

You may not be able to start with a huge development project, but perhaps you could start with a piece of land and flip that into a property that you sell, and flip that into a duplex, and flip that into a fourplex, and flip that into an apartment building, and go on to endless wealth creation. Regardless of your income you could sponsor a deal and raise capital from outside investors; or you could invest property that you own into a partnership; or you could withdraw money from a pension or retirement account and become a capital partner to some energetic flipper that can rotate your money faster than your investment broker could blink. Bottom line, low income does not mean low potential.

ASSETS

When a lender is considering a borrower's financial position, one of the factors considered is the borrower's assets available to pay the down payment, closing costs, title fees, and reserves. Assets are defined as cash, cash equivalents, or property owned by a person or company. Assets are regarded as having value and are available to meet debts or other obligations.

To obtain financing to purchase an investment property, the lender will want to see verification of *liquid assets* necessary to close the transaction. Though you may own other land and properties, liquid assets are defined as any assets that can quickly be converted into cash with a minimal impact on the asset's value. Examples include stocks, government bonds, tax refunds, accounts receivable, certifications of deposit, and marketable securities. Non-liquid assets that are not considered include real property, such as rental houses or land.

Look at a list of your potential total assets that add to your financial position to qualify. There is no minimum net worth, and your assets will always be considered on a case-by-case basis. The borrower must simply have enough liquid assets to pay the cash due at closing and the minimum required reserves to meet the underwriter's guidelines. Do not just consider assets that you currently have, but also figure in assets that you expect to receive before the date of your deal closing.

Personal Assets

- Cash
- Personal Checking Accounts
- Personal Savings Accounts
- Stocks/Bonds
- 401k and Retirement Accounts
- Income Tax Refunds
- Bonus
- Life Insurance
- Properties
- Vehicles
- Ownership in Corporations or Partnerships

To understand your financial position, complete a Personal Financial Statement which will include a list of your Assets and Liabilities. The difference between your total assets and your total debts is your next worth. Since this personal financial statement is "as of" a certain date, it is okay if the value of each account fluctuates to some extent. Do not worry too much about stock values fluctuating or spending money from your checking account, so long as there are not wild swings in those assets from the time you apply to the time you close.

Remember, lenders look at your total net worth to measure your overall ability to repay the debt, but they will verify that you have the minimum liquid assets to bring your cash needed to the closing table.

Business Assets

- Cash
- Accounts Receivables
- Notes Receivables
- Inventory
- Equipment
- Buildings
- Furniture
- Computers
- Fixtures
- Vehicles
- Patents

Assets Q & A:

Will the business finances be considered?

For a business loan, the lender may consider your personal finances but will primarily focus on the assets of the business. The lender may require you to present a business financial statement showing the business assets and liabilities in addition to or instead of a personal financial statement. If the business is a start-up, the lender will then lean on the personal assets of the owners who own more than 20% of the business. If you are doing a deal with partners or other equity or debt providers, your approval will not rely solely on your own liquid assets but the total of the group. So long as the group can collectively raise the funding needed to close, the limitation of your individual personal finances will not disqualify you.

As stated, this information is regarding personal mortgage loans. Business financing is considered much differently than personal lending. Often, businesses are expected to take on debt and without existing trade lines a business can be viewed less credible and may receive higher interest rates. The lender typically reviews investment deals based on the property's ability to cover its own debt and operating expenses.

How do I compute how much cash will be needed to close?

Before applying for a mortgage loan, ask your loan officer for an estimate of the cash required to close. The cash required to close will be the sum of lender fees, title or attorney fees, escrows (if required), down payment, processing fees, credit report fees, government fees, attorney fees, third-party appraisal, survey, pre-payments of interest or insurance, and other potential fees that have been negotiated for the buyer to pay within the contract. Since many fees are set by law or are typical for most transactions, the lender should be able to inform you of a reasonable estimate for the cash required to close. This way you can provide documentation showing the amount of cash needed to qualify, and you would not necessarily need to disclose all your assets.

On the contrary, if you do not have the cash required, the estimate can give you an idea of how much you need to save or raise before submitting the application. Do not assume that you do not have the cash needed. Always complete your personal financial statement, consider all sources of funds that you may have, and then talk it over with your banker. Refer to the sources of funds in previous pages of this book. What is your Net Worth? What are your Total Assets? What are your Current Assets?

DEBT

Debt Q&A:

How does debt impact my loan?

The final consideration for loan approval is your current debt load. For the purposes of your loan application, your lender will review your total monthly debt as a proportion of the total monthly income, after considering all sources and all balances. This measure is called the debt-to-income ratio.

In simple terms, the debt-to-income ratio looks at your debt as a percentage of your gross income. Borrowers who earn a modest salary but have little to no personal debt more easily qualify than high income earners with lots of credit cards and car payments in their personal name. This is the positive aspect for all borrowers of every income level. It is also a hurdle for borrowers who have lots of personal debt.

I always encourage future investors to finance their cars *after* they purchase their home and keep credit card balances below 30% of the available credit limit. I've seen a high-income earning Vice-President of a company be denied a home loan because of too many store credit cards and poor spending choices. I have also seen a temporary worker earning less than $30,000 a year purchase multiple houses because they had zero debt and a hefty savings account.

I encourage you to make wise spending choices with a long-term wealth goal in mind. It's so much easier to qualify for a mortgage if you keep your personal debt at or below 20-30% of your income. Your total debt including your mortgages need to remain at or below 50% of your gross income. The less debt, the more financing you can obtain and leverage for your investments. Likewise, in the future, you will be able to make many lavish purchases if that's what you desire.

I have purchased many cars in my lifetime. I can tell you; it is quite easy to walk on a car lot and qualify for a car loan, and it is quite difficult to go to a lender once you have that new car and qualify for a mortgage loan. A few hundred dollars of monthly debt may seem like a small amount versus what you earn monthly, but I have seen insignificant amounts of debt disqualify people and insignificant amounts of added income boost people's approval odds. So, if it is possible, limit your large debts until after you acquire your real estate portfolio. Think long-term wealth versus short-term rewards.

Compute Your Debt-to-Income Ratio:

Add all your *monthly debts* that are *shown on your credit report or recorded in state records:*

      Estimated Mortgage Payment for Subject Property
+   Student loans
+   Personal loans
+   Medical Bills or Other Debts on Credit Report
+   Auto loans (Include all cars you have co-signed exclude cars to be paid off in < 10 months)
+   Credit Card (Minimum payment due for all personal and store cards)
+   Child Support (Amount owed monthly for all children)
+   Alimony or Restitution due monthly

=   **Total Monthly Debt**

Then, divide your Total Monthly Debt by your Gross Monthly Income to get your Debt-To-Income (DTI) Ratio:
DTI Ratio = Total Monthly Debt / Gross Monthly Income before Taxes

I'm self-employed, so how do lenders compute my DTI?

If you are self-employed, use the average Adjusted Gross Income (AGI) that was reported on your last two years tax returns instead of Gross Monthly Income before Taxes. Here is the formula to compute your Average Adjusted Gross Income:

Average Adjusted Gross Income (AGI)

	Last Year AGI
+	**This Year AGI**
=	**Sum of AGI for Both Years**
/	**2**
=	**Average Adjusted Gross Income**

Now recompute your Debt-to-Income Ratio using your Self-Employed Income:

Debt-to-Income Ratio = Total Monthly Debt / Average Adjusted Gross Income

What is the Debt-Coverage Ratio and why does the bank use this ratio?

Debt coverage ratio is a comparison of the annual income on your property to the total amount of mortgage payments due in a given year. This ratio is expressed as a number, not a percentage and reflects how many times more income you have than your debt. The higher the debt coverage ratio the more likely you will be able to repay your mortgage loan.

Lenders compute your debt coverage ratio by taking the actual or projected net operating income for your property and dividing it by the debt service. Most lenders have a minimum debt coverage ratio that your project must meet in order to be approved. The higher the cash flows and the lower the operating expenses, the greater your net operating income will be. Take these figures into account when submitting your deal information to the bank so that you can be approved.

If you have questions or are unsure about the qualifications regarding that coverage, ask your loan officer for a consultation before applying. You can consult with the loan officer before you even identify a deal that you want to pursue. If you are the capital provider for someone else's deal these are the questions that you want to ask them or even compute on your own. Look at what they project their project to produce in income and then compute the debt coverage ratio based on the amount of debt that the project is required to pay. As a general rule, you want a project to be able to have a debt coverage ratio of at least two times the debt.

Debt Coverage Ratio:

Net Operating Income / Debt Service = Debt Coverage Ratio

Is it necessary to pay off my debt?

The Debt-to-Income Ratio (DTI) is a qualifying measure for approval. Ask your lender what the maximum debt-to-income ratio is. If your DTI exceeds the number for approval, look at your list of debts and see how your monthly payments can be reduced. Consider paying off low balance credit cards or asking creditors to lower your minimum monthly payments. Student loans are usually areas that inhibit borrowers, so be sure to reduce high student loan payments to the lowest payment possible before applying. You can always pay more than the minimum payment required, but lenders compute DTI based on the minimum required payments.
For those seeking alternative ways to eliminate debt, consider moving as many expenses as possible to business credit. For existing business owners, utilize your business credit before using personal credit whenever applicable and possible. If you are not a business owner, you should still position yourself for business as a new investor. Even without owning properties, you can register as an LLC, obtain an EIN tax ID number, and open a business bank

account. Then you will be eligible for business credit. We will discuss this topic in more detail during the financing section. If you are seeking a referral for tax or financial advisory services or to submit a mortgage loan application email Referrals@CommaClubCommunity.com

Should I use a co-borrower?

Using a Co-borrower is always an alternative if you have someone that trusts you enough to participate in your loan and that is willing to be jointly responsible for the debt. If you are being asked to cosign a loan, do so soberly, fully understanding that you will be 100% responsible for the debt, even though you are cosigning the loan with another borrower.

In commercial financing, business owners who hold more than 20% interest in the property or in the business are automatically considered co-borrowers and usually sign documents at closing. Some banks use a 25% threshold, and some banks require all owners to sign.

Only use a co-borrower when absolutely necessary, even if you are married. Married couples should consider applying for debt individually to allow the debt to report on one spouse's credit report versus both. This allows the other spouse's credit to be freed up to purchase additional properties or take on additional debt. When both parties agree, this can be a great strategy to qualify for more loans and expand your portfolio. Marriage is supposed to be teamwork, right?

Restricted Access to Capital

I could write a lament about the woes of being a self-employed, black, bootstrapping, female start-up developer and the difficulty of getting access to capital. I have heard NO so many times, in so many ways that it's laughable. I personally experienced redlining where lenders refused to lend on deals in my target market. I have seen lowball appraisals and outrageous lender-mandated repairs so the bank could decline my loan in a *legal* way. I heard banks admit, "No, we do not lend in *that* part of town."

Listing brokers told me, "Your company is not the right fit for this space," when I knew I was suited to lease. Commercial building owners have said to me, "We do not want people like you in our development," and I watched properties for which I applied sit vacant for years after my offer was rejected. Someone even put in writing, "We don't know you, and we don't want to waste our time with you," and, of course, they never took the time to meet me. I had sellers hang up on me and tell me my pre-approval letter written by the bank president was bogus.

When I did raise $2 million in private financing from trusted partners without the bank, I was told by the SEC attorneys that I could not accept it because it came from non-accredited investors (non-wealthy people), and that I could not accept that much money from people who earn less than $200,000 a year or have less than $1M net worth. Apparently, it is illegal to accept money from working-class citizens so that they can participate in wealth generation. I have heard it all!

Being a no-nonsense, calculated, expert negotiator, deal broker, and successful business owner with an iron clad credit profile and experience, if I faced these barriers to entry, I could only imagine what you may face. It is tough, but I'm telling you up front, do not give up. What created the barriers for me in the beginning, opened the doors for me somewhere in the middle. Because of my unique set of attributes, my voice was heard at many tables; my community trusted me; and I received the support that every good project requires. Because of these traits, I was asked to join many teams and support other development ventures because as diversity initiatives became more pressing, they needed "someone like me" on the team.

Do not let a "no" scare you. Go back to the vision and remind yourself of why you started. Then when they say no, move on to "New Opportunities," as my wise mother once said. Things are changing; our voices are being heard; and progressive banks and funds are opening the coffers to a more diversified client base. Social equity initiatives are on the rise; blacks and browns are on trend; and corporations are filling their websites and press releases with fancy words about making capital more accessible and equitable in communities across America. Only time will tell if their money is where their publicists say it is.

Get yourself in position financially so that when the doors of opportunity open, you can rush in.

FORMING A BUSINESS ENTITY

As a real estate investor, it is imperative that you create a legal separation between your business and personal assets and liabilities to protect yourself from personal loss associated with business failure, bankruptcy, lawsuits, or litigation. This can be done by forming a business entity that you operate for the purposes of acquiring, constructing, and renovating property, making investments, buying materials and furnishings, managing operations, leasing, hiring staff and vendors, and borrowing funds. In your zeal to get started, do not skip this step and think that you can go back and do it later after you are in motion.

Businesses need to be registered with each state where you will be conducting business and also with the federal government through the *Internal Revenue Service (IRS)* by obtaining a 9-digit *Employer Identification Number (EIN)*. You will also be required to provide formation documents, operating agreements and/or business articles in order to establish a bank account or business credit. This simple registration process can be completed online through your state's Secretary of State websites without paying fees to third party registration companies.

Most business law is guided by the *Uniform Commercial Code (UCC)* which was established in 1952 as a way of harmonizing the laws of sales and commercial transactions across the United States. Currently all fifty states have adopted the UCC, and the various articles cover topics such as the sales and leases of goods, promissory notes, banks and banking process, money transfers, letters of credit, auctions and liquidation of assets, storage of goods, securities and financial assets, and transactions secured by security interests. Local law has further modified these rules to conform with local customs.

Uniform Commercial Code filings allow creditors to notify other creditors about a debtor's assets that have been pledged as collateral for a secured transaction. You will see UCC liens filed with the Secretary of State for your business entity whenever you borrow secured funds. A UCC search will be completed as part of your title process to acquire property in this country.

Local law may require that you file registration documents, obtain a business license to operate or permits depending on the nature of your business and the requirements in your city. For example, in the city of Dallas where I live, a new law requires proprietors to register their properties annually and pay a rental registration fee. These rules will vary widely from place to place, so check with your local government for rules specific to your investment market.

Each entity type impacts bank financing and taxation of profits. If you are uncertain of the appropriate business type to select, seek legal and tax advice for greater understanding of the legal and tax implications of the various business types before making your selection, particularly regarding entity types that include partners. If you need a referral for business formation services, please reach out to us at Referrals@CommaClubCommunity.com for a connection to one of our affiliate partners.

Let's review the various business types:

Sole Proprietorship – a sole proprietorship is an unincorporated, unregistered business type that has a sole owner with profit that passes through to the personal taxes of the owner. Sole proprietorships usually start as hobbies and involve negligible risk activities and low profits (not real estate investing). A sole proprietor may operate a business in their personal name, using a personal bank account and social security number instead of an EIN number. The profits and debts of the sole proprietorship become the profits and debts of the owner, as does the liability associated with business loss, failure, errors and omissions, damage, personal injury, and an innumerable list of other potential risks.

The income from the business flows directly to the personal income tax return of the owner and is filed on a Schedule C, Schedule E, or Schedule F of the proprietor's 1040 tax return. For example, if you purchased a rental property in your personal name, rental income or loss would then be filed on a Schedule E as an attachment to your personal income tax return. No business return would be required.

While this type of business is easy and inexpensive to establish and has little oversight, it offers unlimited liability between the owner and the business and poses greater risk than a legal entity like an LLC or LLP. I discourage readers from doing investment business as a sole proprietor (unless you are in the business of knitting potholders for real estate agents as closing gifts and your only investment is yarn.)

Partnerships – a partnership is a business type with multiple business owners, where like a sole proprietorship the profit also passes through to the personal tax return of the owners. A general partnership is the most basic form of a business partnership and, like a sole proprietorship, does not need to be registered with the state government. Ownership, management responsibility, and profits are split between partners and liability is shared as well.

A *Limited Partnership (LP)* is structured where there is at least one general partner who controls the operations and decision making for the business and one or more limited partners who invest for a financial return but have no active management of the business. The limited partners are shielded from the liabilities and debts of the business, while the general partner is responsible.

A *Limited Liability Partnership (LLP)* operates similar to a general partnership except the individual general partners are shielded from liability from the errors of their partners. They all hold personal liability for the debt and liabilities of the business.

Finally, there is a *Limited Liability Limited Partnership (LLLP)* (seriously, couldn't they find a less confusing name) which operates like a limited partnership with one or more general partners and one or more limited partners. In an LLLP, the general partner also receives liability protection with the other limited partners. This type of business is only allowable in some states.

After deciding which type of partnership is most suitable for your company, the next step is to prepare a partnership agreement signed by all partners. Refer to the previous section on partnerships and joint ventures for more information on partnership agreements. Name your business, register it with the state where you plan to do business, collect the partners' investment funds, and commence business.

My current partnership took about thirty days to form with the state of Delaware, register as a foreign entity in the state of Texas, have an attorney draft and revise several iterations of our partnership agreement, negotiate, and sign. Funds were wired the day we signed, and business has been rolling ever since. Do not overcomplicate it. If the partnership is hectic from the start, take this into consideration before moving forward. Partnerships are like marriages... they work best on unity, agreement, teamwork, communication, and compromise. If you or your partner has commitment issues, communication issues, control issues, or you fight over money, the partnership could become a nightmare.

Limited Liability Companies (LLC)

According to the SBA, "your business type affects how much you pay in taxes, your ability to raise money, the paperwork you need to file, and your personal liability." A *Limited Liability Company*

(LLC) is a highly popular form of a business entity that combines the flexibility of a general partnership with the liability protection of a corporation.

LLCs consist of members, managers, and employees, and require filing a Certificate of Formation or Certificate of Organization with the state of operation. These documents are simple to submit online and do not require the assistance of third-party registration companies, although some new business owners elect to pay additional fees to have representatives prepare and submit documents on their behalf.

Owners of an LLC are considered "members" and can be an individual, corporation, LLC, or other foreign entity. In some states, a single member LLC is allowable which consists of one member only. The LLC is guided by the company operating agreement which specifies member roles, ownership, distribution of profit, and tax elections and outlines the rules of how the company will operate. It is important to include rules for changes in ownership if a member dies, transfer of assets or income to heirs, dissolution and other topics that might outlive the members or company itself. This document is private and can be amended as membership or operating rules change throughout the evolution of the company.

Since businesses have inherent risk, a Limited Liability Company is a common choice that allows owners, or members, to enjoy the benefits of a corporation with the limitation of risk. The personal assets of the member are shielded from claims against the business, their risk is limited to what was invested into the business, and only the business is held liable in the event the company is sued or fails to pay its debts as agreed. As a side note, it is a common requirement for owners of LLCs to give a personal guarantee of debt, ensuring that the banking institutions can make personal claims in the event of default of a business debt.

The LLC is not required to have annual member meetings, allows members to have greater management control than limited partners, and no member is jointly and severally liable as is true with general partners. One downside of an LLC is that members must pay a self-employment tax on reported profits. Consult your tax accountant to understand if the LLC is the right business model for you and the implications on your tax liability for profits earned.

S Corps

An S Corp is another pass-through entity type that is popular for small to mid-sized privately held companies. As a pass-through the owner passes the business income to their personal tax return in proportion to their share of ownership of the company. For example, if the business profited $100,000 per year and there are four owners with equal ownership, then each owner reports $25,000 of S-Corp income on their personal taxes and pay taxes, respectively.

The losses of the S-Corp that can be deducted from the personal tax return may be limited. As a Corporation, the owners receive limited liability protection, and their personal assets are shielded from claims against the business. While the S-Corp status requires the owner to pay themselves a wage subject to FICA tax, all other earnings above the annual wages are no longer subject to FICA taxes which can amount to a large tax savings for the owners. This is the primary reason that business owners would elect to become an S-Corp or designate their LLC to have S-Corp federal tax status. S-Corps are corporations and are subject to the formalities of a corporation such as keeping minutes and following state corporate requirements. Owners must be an individual, unlike LLCs which can be owned by partnerships, LLCs, or other entity types. There is a maximum of one hundred shareholders that must be United States citizens or residents, estates, trusts and certain tax-exempt organizations. Only one class of stock is allowed, meaning that some investors or venture capitalists that seek "preferred stock" typically would not invest in this type of business.

Some states do not recognize S-Corps so check with your local Secretary of State to see if S-corps are a recognized business type.

As a real estate professional reporting self-employment income on a Schedule C for many years, electing S-Corp status has had a tremendous impact on my tax savings and is a highly recommended tax strategy. Engage a tax accountant or attorney to properly structure your business prior to filing IRS form 2553 to make the Small Business S Corp Election.

C Corps

The most prevalent of corporations are C corps, the preferred entity type for large-scale businesses with greater income, shareholders, and number of employees. C-Corps have perpetual existence, even if the ownership changes. Another key feature is that C-Corps allow the sale of stock, thus creating unlimited growth potential.

A C corporation legally separates the assets and liabilities of the business from its owners and provides limited liability for the directors, officers, shareholders, and employees. Unlike an S-Corp which can have a maximum of one hundred members, a C Corporation can host an unlimited number of shareholders and those owners can be individuals, LLC's, partnerships, other corporations or foreign entities. Once the company has $10 million in assets and five hundred shareholders, the company must register with the Securities Exchange Commission.
There is a requirement to hold at least one shareholder meeting annually in addition to keeping record of meeting minutes, voting records, and a directory of owner's names and ownership percentages. When obtaining financing or investment, C Corps have more credibility and are more respected by suppliers and banks.

Profits of the business are taxed at both the corporate and personal level which is known as ***double taxation.*** This can be seen as a disadvantage of a C Corporation. The business pays corporate tax on all income before dividends are paid to the owners. Then each owner individually is required to pay taxes on their dividend income. C Corps are also expensive to start, have much more intricate regulations, and do not allow deductions of corporate losses. An S-Corp can be changed to C-Corp status after growing to a point necessitating the change in tax status.

BUILDING YOUR TEAM

This is the exciting part! We covered much in this book to prepare you to invest wisely. Now we are going to discuss the practical steps to build your team. Television shows that air real estate projects cannot nearly reflect just how many people participate in a project from beginning to end. As a real estate investor and developer, I have over twenty-five people that support my business as part of my team, including attorneys, accountants, financial advisors, tax professionals, title agents, insurance agents, lenders, and my construction crews. The team makes it all happen, so it is critical to build your team in advance. Your team can make or break you (emphasis on break). So, who do you need to get it all done? I put together a quick list to point you in the right direction for gathering your go-to people.

BUILDING YOUR TEAM:
- Real Estate Agent
- General Contractor/Day Laborers
- Real Estate Attorney
- Title Agent
- Insurance Broker
- Material Suppliers
- Banks and Lenders
- Home Inspector
- Property Manager
- Financial / Tax Professionals

Real Estate Agent

As a real estate broker, I must advocate that you hire a real estate professional who is an expert in the industry. This should be your first step. A real estate agent is licensed and trained with competency to assist you in your real estate transaction and market knowledge. If you want to get to know your market and see what is out there, have your local real estate agent show you listed properties in your target market area.

Real estate agents have access to tour properties on demand. When you are just getting started you need all the in-person research that you can get. You need to know what is in your market before you pull the trigger. Tour neighborhood properties, look at completed remodels, see properties above your price range, and even look at different property types. It will be difficult to access this much real estate in person without the help of a real estate professional. Additionally, your real estate agent or broker will know more about the market than you do. If they do not, you need a different agent. Find someone who was homebred in that city or community and knows the intricacies of every corner. A great agent can tell you about the best entrée at the local diner and knows upcoming development before a foundation is laid.

Also, real estate agents know when properties come to market first before other secondary services that feed from the MLS. Have your real estate agent set you up on market reports and lists so that you can see trends in the market and know when properties become available. These lists can be automated so you receive them daily or even as soon as the property becomes active because in real estate investing, speed is everything.

If you do not buy properties that are publicly listed but prefer to buy properties off market, real estate agents are a reliable source for off market deals. Many properties that agents sell get sold as *pocket listings*, meaning they are sold privately to people within the agent's network. When agents come across properties that are in poor condition, they often contact investors and give private tours, meaning that these deals sell without ever being listed. If you make friends with active agents and they know you are a serious investor, they will call you when they get deals before they list them. As a real estate agent, I keep a handful of investors in my network so if I ever get a tough-to-sell property or a home that my seller is not willing to fix up before listing, I can get them a cash offer as is. When you buy a deal from an agent, tell them to call you if they ever get another deal and continue to follow up with those agents on a regular basis as a primary source for properties.

Buyer's agent's services are usually FREE and that includes investors who are purchasing property. In most states real estate buyer's agents work for free until closing when you have secured your investment and they are paid at the closing table. Their fees can be negotiated to be paid by the property seller. In the state of Texas commissions are usually paid by the seller so you may not have to come out of pocket for all this great guidance that a real estate agent will give you.

Because agents are typically not paid until the closing table, most will not collaborate with you without you signing an exclusive agreement stating that if they help you find a property then they will earn a commission. However, many investors do not like to sign exclusive representation agreements because they like to put a handful of agents to work on their behalf without committing to give the business to any one person. This may work for you in the short run but eventually if you get a dedicated agent on your team, with a fixed commission agreement, that one agent is more likely to hunt down deals for you. I can tell you from personal experience that representing an investor is ten times more work than representing a traditional buyer so cut your real estate agent some slack. Unless you are paying for their time or putting them on your staff, give them ample time to find and evaluate your deals. If you need a referral for a licensed real estate professional in your area, send an email to Referrals@CommaClubCommunity.com.

General Contractor

Your general contractor is a construction manager hired to coordinate a real estate development project and is responsible for providing all the material, labor, tools, equipment, and services necessary to complete the construction work. The general contractor will first assess the project's scope of work by reviewing architectural drawings, engineering reports, property inspection reports, city code compliance rules and/or their client's requested scope of work and will prepare a bid for construction services. The contractor will consider the timeframe, overhead, labor, materials, equipment, insurance, and other contingent factors that drive the cost of the project and will provide a bid to you, including their markup for managing the project.

General contractors will not perform the work for an amount equal to what the job costs because they factor in their profit for time spent overseeing the project. Some contractors may mark up the bid 10-20% on the average from the cost of materials, overhead, and labor. The general contractor may hire and oversee a network of subcontractors and are responsible for the quality, safety, and performance of the work of the trade workers that they subcontract.

With the construction labor force shrinking and demand so high, having a GC with a network of dependable subcontractors and daily laborers helps accelerate your construction timeline. The general contractor will provide liability and workers compensation insurance for their contractors and should set worksite safety regulations to ensure their workers are working according to standard practices and construction code requirements.

As an investor, you will need a trustworthy, honest, and reliable general contractor in your "favorites" on your contact list. In some states, it is required that general contractors be licensed. Beware that in some states, like Texas, it is not. If you are investing in real estate that requires construction, improvement, or renovation of the property, you will need to add a good GC to your team. You should identify your GC prior to starting work and ask for references, insurance, license information and photos of their past construction projects.

Request a construction estimate upfront and use this as the baseline for your repairs. To get an accurate quote, it is important to provide your general contractor with detailed plans including a site plan, framing plan, foundation plan, floor plan, exterior elevation, window schedule, electrical plan, concrete plan with specifications for fencing, interior design, and stormwater drainage. To get a rough estimate for remodeling work, have your general contractor walk the property with you and provide you with a quick estimate to make an investment decision; and then come back later to provide a firm bid.

A smart move is to keep construction estimates on file to negotiate future bids and be sure to ask for tasks to be itemized between material cost and labor. Compute price/ft for your project to help you anticipate future construction costs and to make deal evaluations easier. If your contractor quotes you $170,000 to build a 1700 square foot home, you can estimate your construction costs at $100/square foot. Knowing the cost per square foot will allow you to predict construction costs and make quick investment decisions when your contractor is not available.

The more detail in your contractor's construction bid, the more you as the property owner can control your pricing. Bargain shop for materials to save on project costs, and purchase materials in bulk to help with economies of scale. The benefit of using a General Contractor is that they typically receive wholesale discounts on materials due to relationships and scale of business with vendors more than what you could achieve as a one-off purchase. Be sure to keep all invoices and material receipts to submit to your appraiser to prove value and in case of insurance claims.

Once you have reviewed the bid with your general contractor, you will sign a formal contract that obligates you to pay your general contractor for work performed. Be sure to review your general contractor agreement to discuss important terms including up front deposit, payment schedule, scope of work with exhibits showing design and material selections, indemnification, insurance and permit requirements, warranty, dispute resolution procedures, construction schedule, expected work hours, and project completion date.

Contractors may require you to put a lump sum deposit to start construction; however, it is possible to pay incrementally or in phases or even after work is completed, if you negotiate these terms. I suggest limiting upfront payments to 50% deposit with a 50% holdback for each task until it is completed, especially if you are collaborating with a new vendor. Construction is a highly litigious industry with many contractors facing lawsuits for incomplete projects, poor workmanship, property damage, construction site injuries, and comingling of funds amongst other disputes.

Also beware that contractors can file their own suits over nonpayment and even file a mechanic's lien against your property if you stop payment. Always have a contract and keep detailed records of change orders, dates that a task started and completed, delays, supplier issues, contractor concerns, inspection notes, conversations, and most importantly payments. Send all important communication to your general contractor in writing, preferably via email, and separate your property payments by property address so that funds cannot be mixed between various projects with the same contractor. Hire an accountant or bookkeeper to keep your records intact and create processes so that you can identify where you are in your project and spending at all times.
With a skilled general contractor on your team, you do not have to know how to build or have any construction related skill sets personally. As a novice investor, that should allow you to breathe a huge sigh of relief. You do not have to be present at your construction site because your general contractor is the responsible manager of your construction project. This allows you to invest and develop projects that may not be within your local area or frees you to focus on your career if you are not a full-time investor.

It is crucial, however, to regularly visit your construction site to inspect the work being performed. This will hold your general contractor accountable. Show up at unscheduled times to see if your work crew is present and doing what is outlined in the contract. A good GC will be present at the jobsite or will have a superintendent or other person in charge watching over the work when they are absent. They will also communicate progress and keep you up to date on the construction process. Regular meetings can be scheduled to keep communication flowing.

The General Contractor will use construction drawings to guide their work according to the dimensions and measurements listed on the plans. Plans that you provide your GC must be accurate. Plans may need to be submitted for official permit approval, and small errors in permit documents can cause lengthy delays, reinspection fees, or other setbacks.

Walk your construction site at each phase of construction and communicate changes or adjustments quickly. It is always easier to adjust the plan before a task is started or while the work is in process. It is more costly to make changes after completion. I learned this the hard way when the color of green cabinets was unveiled to me after the cabinets were installed and the paint was dry. It cost $1000 to tell the contractor I wanted mint green and not emerald one day after the cabinets were installed -- a cost that could have easily been avoided.

Room size and layout look different in person than they do on paper and in photos, so I highly encourage you to visit your construction sites during framing as well to make changes as needed. Finally, make material selections in person whenever possible. Do not allow your contractor to make material and paint selections unless you want to be surprised to find your contractor is color blind and thinks peach and tan are the same color.

Having a general contractor on your team is an absolute must to be successful in many of the investment strategies reviewed in this book. Your GC will walk with you through many deals helping you build a portfolio of properties while you provide them with ongoing business. GCs love investors who provide a consistent pipeline of work to keep their crews busy, investors that are easy to work with and pay on time, and those who provide repeated business or referrals. Remember all relationships are a two-way street. If you drill your contractor into the ground on pricing, do not expect loyalty when a higher paying client comes along.

Real Estate Attorney

A Real Estate attorney specializes in all aspects of real estate law, including the purchase and sale of real property (land and structures), legal issues, zoning, property taxes, estate planning, and chain of title. They can also ensure the proper procedures are followed in property acquisition and sales. Some states referred to as *"attorney closing states"* require that a real estate attorney be present at closing, while others allow title companies to prepare and notarize closing documents. Attorney closing states include:

- Connecticut
- Delaware
- Georgia
- Rhode Island
- South Carolina
- North Carolina
- Massachusetts
- Vermont
- West Virginia

All others are *"Title Closing States,"* also known as Escrow Closing States or Attorney Opinion States, in which an attorney is not required to supervise transactions or be present at closing but must review title documents. Illinois, Ohio, New Jersey, and New York do not require real estate attorneys at all. These states are subject to change depending on a new legislature that may modify requirements in the future. As prep work, be sure to check the rules and know the requirements for an attorney in your state.

International law would govern these rules for transactions outside of the United States.

When bank financing is used in a transaction, the lender hires a real estate attorney to prepare the loan closing documents. The title company may also utilize a real estate attorney to prepare the title insurance and review the chain of title. In cases where third parties use the services of real estate attorneys, this will be disclosed, and an acknowledgement will be signed at closing. Often these fees are charged to the buyer at closing, even though the attorney does not directly represent the buyer or provide them direct counsel or advice.

A real estate attorney is also equipped to litigate or resolve disputes over chain of title, property line encroachment, estate disputes, or other issues involving contracts. The attorney is required to be licensed in the state in which they are managing the real estate transaction and versed in the local laws that affect the transaction or suit. Real estate attorneys may work on an hourly fee. I have personally paid in excess of $500/hour for a real estate attorney. Oftentimes it is better to utilize an alternative method of dispute resolution, especially when the dispute is less than $10,000 - $15,000. This amount could be your bill just to engage an attorney and would go higher if litigation and court appearances are required.

There are other attorneys with specialties that may be relevant for your investment journey. When fundraising for an investment, it may be necessary to engage an attorney specializing in SEC exemptions and filing requirements. For preparing a will, a trust, or generational wealth plan you may want to consult an estate attorney and when overseeing the distribution of property of the deceased, you may be required or want to engage a probate attorney. To establish a business partnership or write a company operating agreement, you may consult a business formation attorney. When dealing with mineral rights, royalty disputes, or environmental law, you may want an energy, oil and gas attorney.

I imagine there are numerous specialties that could be applicable in various investment situations. While attorneys are not always required (or desired), having the contact of a good attorney on hand is good prep work in the event you find that you need to use it. It is possible to keep an attorney on retainer by paying an upfront fee and then utilizing their services as needed. Most large legal firms require a screening process that can take weeks before accepting your business.

Insurance Broker

An insurance broker is a professional who represents property owners in their search for the best insurance policy for their needs. The insurance broker acts as intermediary between the consumer and the insurance company, and their job is to assist in identifying the absolute best policy to protect your investment. As a real estate owner and investor, various insurance policies are necessary to protect you, your property, your renters, your business, your contractors, and your personal belongings. An insurance broker is like an insurance agent except they provide information on multiple insurance carriers offering insight into the best rates and conditions for the most unbiased cost-effective policy recommendations.

Request the insurance policy documents from your insurance broker and read them before choosing a policy. Pay attention to exclusions, such as mold and water damage, and know what is not covered. Ask about insurance riders that can be added for additional protection. Consider the amount of coverage that your policy provides and adjust as needed.
Research your insurance company's likelihood to pay out in the event of a claim and research the law regarding when you may be responsible for damage versus your neighbors. If a tree branch falls from your neighbor's tree and hits your fence, make sure you know whose insurance policy is responsible to pay for repairs. You might want to understand in advance of a windstorm if your insurance policy says they are responsible but will not pay if you fail to have the tree limbs trimmed on your side of the fence.

Unfortunately, I often find my real estate clients purchase insurance without really understanding what their policy covers and under what conditions the coverage will be paid. Then when an unforeseen situation happens, they learn how good their policy really is or isn't. I am guilty as well and have learned the hard and expensive way, so do the research and get a great insurance broker on your team.

Here are a few types of insurance policies you may need depending on your investment type, amount, and the level of protection desired.

Liability Insurance: Liability insurance covers accidents that happen at the property that may involve tenants, people who visit the property, or construction workers making repairs to the property. The liability insurance will provide benefits to someone who has been hurt on the property, such as a mail carrier who slips and falls on an icy patch while walking to your mailbox, God forbid. The insurance will cover hospital and rehabilitation bills of the injured party and financially protect the property owner from being responsible for events that happened even if the owner was not present.

Such accidents may seem unlikely, but I know a woman that visited a friend in her home. When she went to walk down a staircase, the woman did not notice that a shirt was hanging on the handrail and as she grabbed the handrail to support herself, she went sliding down the staircase, injuring her shoulder, and resulting in a surgery. Although this woman was visiting her friend, she was able to file a claim against her friend's insurance and request reimbursement for medical bills related to her doctor's visits, surgery, pain, and suffering. If the friend had not voluntarily allowed her to file a claim on her insurance, the injured woman could have filed a lawsuit against the property owner. Liability insurance also covers lawsuits where property owners are ordered to pay damages to the injured or harmed person. The insurance policy would cover those damages on your behalf.

Finally, if you hire a repair person to fix something on your property and there is an injury or theft, your liability insurance may provide you with coverage. Though it may already be obvious, it is especially important to maintain liability insurance for your properties and your business. Be sure to review your insurance coverage to make sure you have enough liability insurance to cover claims that could be made against you.

Hazard and Fire Insurance: Hazard insurance typically covers things like structural damage from storms, fire, or theft. Hazard and fire insurance is typically included in a basic insurance policy, but it is important to understand if the insurance covers the replacement cost of the property or just the cash value of the damage. This could be a significant difference in the amount that the policy pays out. Pay attention also to the deductible which is the owner's portion of the damage that they are responsible to cover.

In the event of roof damage from a hailstorm, for example, the insurance adjuster may estimate the cost of roof replacement is $10,000. If your deductible is $4,000, the insurance will only pay you $6,000, and you will be responsible for paying the difference out of pocket. The lower the deductible the higher the premium, and the higher the deductible the lower the premium. If you take a higher deductible, you may save money on your annual premium, but in the event of a claim, you may be out of pocket more money than you desire.

Landlord Insurance: Landlord insurance is a common form of insurance that real estate investors need and is often bundled with other insurance types like hazard insurance and loss of income coverage. This type of policy covers property owners who have tenants within their property but does not cover the actual belongings of the tenant. The tenant will need their own renter's insurance policy.

Flood Insurance: Flood insurance is a separately administered insurance program from the National Flood Insurance Program

(NFIP) and is administered by the Federal Emergency Management Agency (FEMA). Flood insurance is required by mortgage lenders if your property falls in a FEMA map area designated with an "A" or "V" meaning it is a coastal area, near a river or creek, protected by a levy, or in a low elevation and has greater probability of flooding. You can review the FEMA flood maps to determine if your property is in a flood zone which predicts the risk of your property flooding from a naturally occurring weather event where water comes from outside of the property at https://msc.fema.gov/

If you purchase a property with cash and without bank financing, then you will not be *required* to purchase flood insurance; however, it is highly recommended to have flood insurance. A flood could create a total loss of property that your hazard insurance would not cover. Note also that a standard hazard insurance policy does not cover water damage as a result of plumbing issues unless it is a sudden, unexpected intrusion of water from inside the property, such as a water heater bursting. *It is important to report major water leaks immediately to your insurance company.* Otherwise, an ongoing plumbing leak will not be covered even if it has led to severe damage, mildew, or mold.

Builder's Risk Insurance: A builder's risk policy covers the cost of repairs on unfinished structures or the cost of replacement for building materials as a result of damage caused by weather, fire, vandalism, or if there is theft to a construction site. If you are remodeling a property or building new construction, having a builder's risk policy will be crucial. Construction sites are hotspots for thieves. So, in addition to having proper lighting and security of your site, it is also important to have the appropriate coverage to protect stolen materials and construction supplies. Also, in the event of a fire that is started by construction, such as an electrical fire, having a builder's risk policy will protect you for losses that could destroy your property or cause considerable damage.

General Contractor Insurance: Construction work is high risk and contains many potential hazards such as falls, accidents, equipment and machinery malfunctions, or personal injuries. General contractors take on a great deal of responsibility and liability for equipment defects, accidents, injuries, and potential lawsuits from their workers and subcontractors. The insurance for general contractors may include coverage for bodily injury, property damage, errors and omissions, and completed product claims if someone is injured from the use of completed services or products installed by a contractor.

Workers Compensation Insurance: Workers compensation insurance helps with paying medical bills or lost wages when an employee is injured on the job. Worker's Compensation may also kick in when an employee is injured in a company vehicle on the way to a job-related location. If a person sustains long term injuries, it will be important to have workers compensation to ensure the employees are covered for their ongoing medical bills and lost wages due to their inability to return to work.

Sewer and Water Line Backup: Typical homeowner and hazard insurance does not cover replacement or repairs to the sewer water line. These expenses can be costly and shut down your ability to use your plumbing altogether. The sewer and water line backup coverage covers the cost of a range of services including unclogging blockages, digging up the pipe to locate the issue and then backfill in the area, appearing pavement, identifying the source of the water issue, pipe cutting and welding, replacing broken or leaking pipes and valves, landscaping and yard repair. Ask about previous repairs or replacements to the sewer and water lines to understand your need for this insurance and the likelihood of future repairs.

Umbrella Insurance: Umbrella insurance covers injuries, damage to property, lawsuits, and personal liability beyond the existing liability or auto insurance that the policy holder already holds. This additional insurance creates an umbrella over all other policies and starts once those policies have been exhausted. It also covers claims that may have been excluded from other liability policies such as false arrest, slander, and liability on rental property. This insurance is inexpensive compared to the potential protection to your net worth. A million dollars of umbrella insurance typically costs about $150 to $300 annually.

Loss of Income Insurance: Loss of income or rent coverage provides insurance when an income-producing property can no longer be rented due to a covered damage to the property even if the property was not rented at the time of the loss. For example, if there is a fire in the property which takes three months to repair, the lost rate for those three months would be paid by this policy in addition to the cost for repairing the fire damage. This is important for landlords and commercial property owners because if there are interruptions in your business, this policy will protect you from taking unnecessary losses.

Tenant Rent Default Insurance: Rent default insurance provides property owners protection from monetary loss due to unpaid rent. The annual premium can cost about $300 per unit per year or $25 a month. The insurance covers single family homes, townhomes, condominiums, multifamily dwellings, and apartments. This insurance would be considered a risk management solution to protect the landlord's income and hedge against losses if the tenant stops making payments.

The eviction process is often time consuming, and it takes time to get the property vacated and prepared for new tenants to lease the unit. This type of insurance covers those costs for lost rents during that time frame but be sure to read the fine print in the policy and understand under what conditions the insurance would not pay. Under these policies they will want the property owner to pre-screen the tenants to make sure they meet minimum income or credit score requirements and have no obvious threat of delinquency at the time the lease is signed. It may be possible for the property owner to pass off the additional cost of insurance on the renter, especially if they believe the tenant is at a higher risk of defaulting on their lease or has a past eviction, broken lease, or troubled rental history.

Renter's Insurance: Renter's insurance is an insurance policy that renters obtain to protect their personal property in a rented apartment, condominium, or house from unexpected circumstances such as a burglary, theft, fire, or natural disaster. The renter's insurance will protect the renter's personal belongings and will also protect them from liability if someone is hurt inside their residence. Additionally, the renter's insurance policy covers the cost to replace stolen belongings. If the property is not habitable for a covered reason, the renter's insurance will also pay for a temporary residence.

Many proprietors require that their renters obtain renters insurance as part of their lease agreement because the renter's personal items are not covered in the homeowner or landlord's policy. One of my rental properties was burglarized while the tenants were traveling. The home was ransacked, their medication and food were compromised, and their personal belongings stolen. Although my insurance policy would not cover any loss to the tenants' personal property, their rental policy covered them during this crisis. Their insurance company relocated them temporarily to a hotel while the police processed their report, and the insurance agency took inventory of the losses. This unfortunate incident could have ended worse had they not had renter's insurance to cover this unforeseen crime.

As a proprietor, my company requires all tenants to obtain renter's insurance at lease signing and thankfully the renter kept their policy in full force so that they received financial help in their time of need. While the burglar was caught and arrested, the damage the burglar caused to their personal property would only be repaid by the renter's insurance policy.

Renters need to understand their policy limits because most policies will only pay to replace or repair items up to a certain dollar limit. Valuable items can be listed by serial number or documented with photos and receipts to prove the value of the item. Many credit cards will also provide insurance on computers, electronics, and jewelry if you purchase the item using the credit card. In an incident where my computer was accidentally damaged, I was able to file a claim on my credit card insurance policy and receive a complete reimbursement for the full amount of the computer.

Pet Insurance: Pet liability coverage is included in the personal liability coverage of a renter's insurance policy. If the tenant has a pet, then adding a pet liability provision in their coverage would be a wonderful way for the tenant to cover their legal risk in the case that the pet causes damage to the property or injuries to other people. The proprietor may require a pet rider on their landlord policy to protect themselves from financial responsibility if their tenant's pet causes harm to others. This would be particularly needed when the pet is considered an aggressive breed.

Commercial Auto Insurance: Commercial auto insurance policies provide coverage for vehicles that are used for work related purposes. Coverage includes liability damages, collision, or comprehensive physical damage, damages sustained to occupants due to negligence by uninsured motorists, bodily injury coverage for accident-related injuries to others, and or accident-related damage to someone else's property such as a car or house. Commercial auto insurance will be important if you transport clients or crew in your vehicle, or you or your staff or contractors pick up or deliver materials or use a company-owned vehicle to do business.

Vendors and Suppliers

During the course of building your business, you will have many vendors through which you source materials, supplies, furniture, or appliances for your properties or business. If you are making a construction or renovation related investment, it is extremely important to select material suppliers who are dependable, have products in stock, carefully ship products without damage, and provide preferential pricing or discounts for regular customers.

Some vendors that you work with consistently will provide a greater discount based on the scale of business that you do with them. Establishing these vendors early in the process enables you to create cost savings for your business, which in turn creates greater profitability for your investments. In the construction industry, material prices fluctuate constantly, which results in unpredictability with budgeting construction costs. Doing steady business with a supplier makes them more likely to honor past prices for you versus a one-off purchaser.

Create personal relationships with salespeople so that they will notify you when items go on sale. Salespeople who know you will go out of their way to give you great service, and help you make material choices so that you do not have to hire a designer. Many suppliers will offer you payment terms allowing you to take your materials and supplies and pay in 30, 60 or 90 days to give you time to turn a profit before payment is due. These sorts of payment terms are sometimes only available when you have an established relationship and are on good payment terms with your vendors.

Some larger retailers like Home Depot or Lowe's offer credit cards, coupons, and easy return policies, and even allow you to track purchases by the project so that you can keep good accounting of the material costs for each job. As prep work for your investment, head out to some material supplier stores and grab the business cards of salespeople, apply for a vendor account, and make a wish list of materials that you would pick if you had a property to design. This preparation will allow you to know your selections and pricing so that you can properly budget when the time comes.

Banks and Lenders

All banks are not created equal, and all loan officers are certainly not created equal. Every bank has its own underwriting criteria and perspective on varying amounts of risk. I've walked into banks and been told no at the front door and walked into other banks and been invited into a cozy seat with the bank President. Just because one bank declines your loan application or refuses you financing does not mean that you are not approvable. This investment business is all about relationships so start developing them.

Your banker should be your best friend. Know your banker and make sure your banker knows you by name. Know if they are married, whether they have kids, and when and where they went on vacation. Keep them up to date on your vision and your plans; tell them your progress, and when you are in the lobby to make a deposit, wave to them to let them see you are doing business at their bank. Always be polite. Set appointments to have one-on-one conversations with the loan officer to understand the loan criteria and process for approval.

In commercial financing, many loan decisions are made by a loan committee. Weekly or monthly, the loan committee meets to approve or deny loans. If you have a banking relationship with the bank, or a personal relationship with someone on the loan committee, you have a higher probability of being approved for the loan simply because you already have a relationship with the bank. Be sure you have a *positive* relationship with the bank and that all your accounts are in good standing, even if balances are low.

I love community banks, credit unions, and banks with **Community Reinvestment Act (CRA)** products because they intentionally make loans to minorities or in minority or low-income communities as are incentivized to do so. If you are afraid to apply for a loan or have a general fear of going into a bank or talking to a banker, address this fear now. Banks are in business to make money by making loans and extending credit to their customers. Far too many of us only know banks as depository institutions to hold our money and charge us banking fees, without ever expecting the bank to do anything for us in return.

Having a checking account and a debit card means nothing to you regarding your wealth building potential. If you have a checking or savings account at a bank, then at a minimum expect that same bank to provide you with a credit card, a line of credit, or a loan so that you can build your business and build wealth. If your bank will not extend you that credit, remove your money from that bank and go to a bank that will. Change your mindset so that you can use banks to build wealth.

Home Inspector

During your investment process, you will need to engage a home inspector to evaluate the condition of the home including the structure, roof, foundation, electrical systems, plumbing systems, HVAC, landscape grading, and appliances. It is especially critical to have a home inspector to evaluate areas you cannot see such as crawlspaces, attics, rooftops, waste systems, and other areas that are not easily viewed. Inspectors are licensed professionals that are trained to identify deficiencies in property that could be hazardous or costly to repair.

As a new real estate agent, I built a relationship with an expert home inspector named Ed Paramo. He shared his invaluable expertise teaching me how to tour properties and look for issues so that my buyers could avoid contracting homes that might give them serious issues in the future. I carried these lessons and experiences into my career as a real estate investor. Knowing how to identify and price repairs in my construction budget became a gem to me. I spent years reviewing inspection reports on behalf of my buyer clients, adding city property code requirements into my knowledge base. I cannot encourage you enough to identify and add a home inspector to your team and to evaluate your properties during the option or feasibility period. In an aggressive market where you cannot negotiate a termination option, having this knowledge base from past experience will serve you well.

Lastly, I always bring my construction crew to tour property before the purchase so that I understand the cost of the renovations and have their viewpoint of repairs needed that I may have overlooked. Even distressed properties have varying degrees of work needed, and these may create wide swings in your construction budget. For example, a foundation that needs to be fully replaced is significantly more expensive than a foundation that just needs a few piers adjusted. A plumbing leak in a PVC pipe is a whole different issue than a slab leak. Your crew can inspect the property to give you an estimate of cost so that you can make a fast decision to purchase a deal or throw it back. If you hire a construction crew to do repair work, have an inspector come behind them and check their work so that they can fix mistakes before the property is rented or sold.

Property Manager

Upon closing your deal, hire a reliable property manager to collect rent and to manage maintenance schedules and repair requests. If you manage a handful of units, you may be capable of being your own property manager. Tenants keep their properties in better condition when they know their landlord is making visits and checking in regularly versus being managed by an impersonal company that only sends letters. There is one caveat to managing your property yourself: tenants may play your heart strings when difficult times arise. If you have a personal relationship with your tenants, it can make it hard to evict for non-payment, impose fines or late fees, and/or increase the rent annually. A property manager has a business relationship with the tenant and easily enforces these rules. The full scope of the property manager's duties should be outlined in a property management agreement to inform the PM of the requirements and limitations of their role. Some duties include setting, billing and collecting rents, attracting and screening tenants, preparing lease agreements, property maintenance, keeping records, making routine inspections, managing the operating budget and expenses, and communicating with tenants. The property manager should be well versed in federal, state, and local tenancy law and will represent the property owner's legal interests while providing a duty of care to the tenants. Property managers are often paid a percent of gross rent and may also be paid a fee for new leases that they secure.

Set aside reserves in your operating budget for maintenance and unexpected repairs. Deferred maintenance leads to asset impairment, increased repairs, and higher cost long term. Inspect your property on a quarterly basis to check for damage, infestations, or hazards, and take photos for records. If the pet agreement says no pets and you find a new dog, be sure to enforce the lease violation penalty or you may not be able to enforce at a later date. If the lease says non-smoking and you identify evidence of smoking in the unit, be sure to address the violation in writing and inform the tenants if deposits will be lost due to their violation.

Financial / Tax Professionals

There are many types of financial professionals that you may engage as part of your investment journey to build wealth and create a multi-generational legacy of financial success. It is important to rely on the expertise of those who are in the profession of wealth management, such as investment brokers, financial advisors, wealth planners, tax advisors, accountants, bookkeepers, transaction managers, project managers, and life insurance agents. As a small business owner with the mindset to create a dynasty for future generations to enjoy, I have engaged each of these professionals and meet with them at least once annually to track progress toward my goals. I meet with my accountants weekly in addition to having a bookkeeping software that manages my transactions daily. The accounting team creates financial reports on a monthly and annual basis which provide security for my investors to know that the money management is under an unbiased third party's constant review. I also hired a project manager to keep track of the construction financing to ensure that my contractors are paid according to our payment schedules and that bank draws are submitted for reimbursement of completed work. This keeps the money flowing in and out of the project, keeping my general contractor and their subcontractor's happy and up to date. My life insurance agent doubles as my financial advisor and wealth planner, in addition to holding monthly wealth planning meetings hosted by an investor who became a self-made millionaire. I have my tax advisor in the "favorite contacts" of my phone because tax questions are endless.

HOW TO KNOW WHEN YOU ARE READY TO INVEST

Analyze the Pros and Cons

Evaluate the advantages and disadvantages of investing in real estate before moving forward with your decision to become a real estate investor. Real estate investing is a function of risk and reward, and it is important to consider both the risks and the rewards from an objective perspective prior to having a hot deal in your hands. Investing is a matter of decisiveness, timing, faith, optimism, and preparedness. Investing is **not** a matter of certainty, fantasy, lottery, guarantee, indecision, or impulsivity.

In working with new investors, most people get stuck on simply being sure that they want to invest. When an opportunity comes along, they waste time asking everyone on their team to convince them that investing is a promising idea. Investing is a personal decision. Weigh the pros and cons now and once you decide, you will be equipped with the mindset to move on to the next steps of this book and grasp hold of your goal.

Benefits of real estate investing may include passive income streams, property ownership, building equity, increasing net worth, community impact, profitability, creating a legacy, building generational wealth, maximizing savings or investment returns, supporting affordable housing needs, creating jobs, stimulating the economy, reducing homelessness, obtaining tax savings, working in a desired career field, designing beautiful spaces and so forth. The disadvantages could be the exact opposite.

YOU ARE READY TO INVEST WHEN:

1. You have a solid vision of why you want to invest, what you plan to own, and the personal and communal impact of your ownership and wealth generation.

2. You have decided your investment strategy and understand the process to execute this strategy.

3. You have decided your property classification and understand the process to evaluate, acquire, inspect, manage, and divest this property type and/or you have hired the appropriate professionals to execute these tasks.

4. You have decided your target market for investment and have a solid working knowledge of your market with third party data to support your conclusions.

5. You have identified a funding source for your investment.

6. You qualify for bank financing and have been pre-approved. (If applicable).

7. You have formed a business entity and registered it with your state and/or local business registration departments.

8. You have identified and properly vetted your team/partners/vendors.

9. You evaluated the risks, and the Pros outweigh the Cons.

Section IV:

CLOSING AND MANAGING YOUR INVESTMENT

Congratulations! If you have made it this far, then you are ready to get started as a real estate investor and learn the steps to close your deal.

Take a deep breath. Yes, you are a real estate investor. I like to say, "success happens in the mind first." Soon you will be hunting your first deal (or second or tenth) and putting these lessons into practice. When I did it, I did not have a guidebook, so use these resources as support for your journey to fulfill your ownership dreams.

In this section, I will cover topics such as identifying your property, negotiating the deal, securing a contract to purchase the property, inspecting, and planning repairs, creating a profitable investment plan, closing the deal, and then activating your plan to start building wealth. Keep this guide handy so every time you are ready to buy an investment property, you can use this section of the book as your step-by-step guide to execute the deal. If you are investing in passive investments that don't directly involve purchase or management of property, this section may not apply. However, I encourage you to know what the people who are actively buying properties on behalf of passive investors are doing with their money.

PROPERTY SELECTION

Look around. Everywhere in your footsteps somebody owns that land. What do you mean somebody owns that? Even the mountains? What about the lakes? The sidewalks? The shiny floor inside the mall? The church? The schools? Yes. I am trying to make a point. Whether it's public ownership such as a city or municipality, corporate ownership, or it is private ownership such as a hedge fund or an individual ... someone owns every piece of dirt on the planet (and under the ground, and the airways, and the waters, and the virtual universe). Ok, I am sure an exception exists somewhere with some unclaimed property somewhere on earth or some territory that has not been discovered. But you get my point.

Properties are everywhere. How do you know which one is the right one for you? How do you make a property selection that has a higher probability of producing a positive investment return? What are the necessary considerations to buying wisely? What repairs are best to avoid? What if you have an eye on a property that is not for sale? Where do you find good deals?

I'll discuss these questions and more to help you identify a property that fits your investment goals, but you will make the call about what a good deal is for you. Every investment is different and unique, although your strategy often remains the same. The end result to keep in mind is that you want a property that appreciates in value, is worth more in the future than it is today, in a location that is beneficial to your investment goals, and where the income from the property produces enough cash flow to cover the property's expenses.

WHAT TO BUY?

In Section 2 you reviewed the investment strategies and the property types available. During this section you were asked to choose the investment property types you would like to own. Both commercial and residential property types exist. You can focus on multiple types of residential properties, such as single family and duplex properties since these types are the same and call for the same investment strategy to be executed. However, focusing on commercial and residential property types might have a steeper learning curve, leave more room for error, and pose greater risk.

Refer to Section 2 of this book and then list your property selection in the chart. If you chose more than one property type, rank them in order of where you would like to start. Let's focus on your top 2. Although you have the freedom to choose from unlimited possibilities, I encourage mastery of one investment strategy and one type of property before moving on to multiple investment strategies and property types. My advice is not meant to limit you. However, investing is not gambling. It takes intention, education, mastery, and planning. Taking a focused approach which will allow you to develop an expertise more quickly is a wise one.

After deciding what you want to purchase as your investment, review and reference all the information that follows based on the specific property type and investment strategy you selected. Because it is impossible for me to specify every unique possibility suited to each option available, I will teach what is most applicable to all property types.

WHAT IS YOUR BUDGET?

Besides the property type and how you intend to use that property as an investment source, another important question to narrow the decision of what to buy is "What is your budget?" REALTORs love to ask people this question, but they often do not know how to answer.

If you make your investment purchase with cash and do not plan to use outside financing, this question is easily answered because you know how much cash you intend to invest. That amount of cash is your budget. However, it is especially difficult to determine your investment budget when you use a mix of cash and financing or are acquiring distressed properties that need improvement. In these instances, the budget question can be answered by understanding answers to the following questions.

How much has the bank approved you for?

When seeking a residential home loan, hard money loan or investor loan, banks pre-qualify you for a maximum loan amount based on the information reviewed in section 3 of this book. At the end of the pre-approval process, your lender should provide you with a pre-approval letter that states your buying power or your maximum purchase price. This number enables you to identify properties within a price-range where you as the borrower can successfully obtain a loan.

If you are in receipt of a letter, simply provide this letter to your real estate professional or property seller as proof that you qualify to contract a property up to that purchase price. If you have not been provided a pre-approval letter, go back to section 3 and apply and request a pre-approval letter that gives you a defined budget to work within before you begin looking.

Remember, if you are looking for a property to occupy as part of the RRR strategy, you will apply for a home loan as the primary occupant. Your interest rates, down payment, required reserves will be lower and your buying power will typically be higher. If you do not plan to occupy the property, you apply for an investor loan which will allow you to immediately rent the property and earn income. These loans are rated as higher risk. As a result, they come with higher interest rates, stricter lending requirements, and less buyer power.

For commercial loans, lenders may or may not issue pre-approvals since the underwriting criteria is based more on the property than the borrower. Factors such as the property type, purchase price, term of loan, use of property, projected cash flow, interest rate, equity, and relationship history with the bank all impact the approval or denial of your loan.

In commercial lending, a loan package is submitted to an approval committee who reviews all the project specific data and then approves on a case-by-case basis; therefore, it is difficult for a lender to pre-determine a maximum loan amount before you identify a subject property and provide the necessary details about your property and investment plan. In this situation, you have approached the bank to determine your maximum loan amount, but they will not provide you with a specific number until you identify your property, then move to the next question to determine your budget.

How much cash can you access for your down payment?

When obtaining financing, commercial or residential investor loans have a required percentage of equity that you are responsible to invest. For example, if you plan to obtain funding from a bank, the banker may inform you that they will fund 75% LTC which is **Loan to Cost**. This means you need to bring or raise a minimum of 25% of the property's purchase price plus renovation cost to qualify for this deal.

To work backwards to compute a maximum budget for a project, you divide the amount of capital you have access to by the required equity. That amount gives you your project budget. If you have access to $50,000 capital and your bank requires you to bring 25% of the total project budget, then you can have a maximum project cost of $200,000. For example:

Do the Math:

$50,000 Cash available/25% Required Equity = $200,000 Budget

$150,000	Purchase Price
+40,000	Renovation Budget
$190,000	Total Project Cost

This project is within your budget. In this example, you are under budget and still have $10,000 remaining to pay for construction contingencies, closing costs, title costs, and REALTOR fees.

The required equity can come from your own savings, from investment partner contributions, or from equity in land or existing property you use as part of the deal. If a real estate professional asks for your budget, you would respond that your budget is $200,000 all in for purchase and renovation costs and that you are seeking a property around $150,000 that needs no more than $40,000 to $45,000 in repairs.

This process gets a little trickier when the bank finances a deal based on the **Loan to Value or 75% of LTV**. In commercial lending, Loan to Value is the amount of loan compared to the expected completed value of the project. The bank estimates the project value based on market value of comparable projects of similar kind and recently improved construction. Gathering comparable properties in your market research to know how completed projects in your target market are being valued helps you guide the bank in the future completed value of your project, also known as ARV or *After Repair Value.*

When computing the budget for a project where you plan to make improvements, first estimate the project's ARV or completed value. The best way to compute ARV is to use real market data.

For residential properties, find at least six comparable projects similar in size, scope of work, and the same use as your subject property. Then compute their average market value.

Do not use comparable properties with different classifications. For example, if you are looking to buy a distressed single-family house, a new construction duplex is not the same thing, and values would not be measured the same. If you find projects of various sizes, you will need to compute the average *price/square foot* to estimate your subject properties value.

Do the Math for Residential Properties:

Step 1: Compute the Price/ sq. ft. of Each Comparable Property

For residential properties, appraisers use the sales comparison approach to value properties. In order to get a good estimation of your investment property's completed market value or ARV, take an average of the sales price of six or more comparable properties:

Comparable Property 1 – Sold for $500,000, duplex, 2500 sq. ft. = $200/ sf

Comparable Property 2 – Sold for $600,000, duplex, 3500 sq. ft. = $171/ sf

Comparable Property 3 – Sold for $459,000, duplex, 2000 sq. ft. = $230/ sf

Comparable Property 4 – Sold for $750,000, duplex, 4500 sq. ft. = $167/ sf

Comparable Property 5 – Sold for $1,000,000, duplex, 5500 sq. ft. = $182/ sf

Comparable Property 6 – Sold for $480,000, duplex, 2300 sq. ft. = $209/ sf

Step 2: Compute the Average Price / sq. ft.

Add all the prices/sq. ft. for all six comparable properties and then divide by six which is the total number of comparable properties that you found. If you have more than six, then use whatever total number of comparable properties you find. If you find less than six, your estimates will be unreliable, but you can use them to obtain a rough estimate.

($200 + $171 + $230 + $167 + $182 + $209) / 6

= $193/ sq. ft.

Step 3: Multiply the Average Price/sq. ft. by Your Subject Property sq. ft.

If your subject property that you plan to buy is 3000 sq. ft., you could estimate its future value by multiplying 3000 x the average price per square foot.

= $193/Sq. ft. x 3000 Sq. ft.

= $579,000

The estimated completed value or ARV of your subject property is $579,000

Step 4: Compute Loan to Value

Now compute the maximum LTV for your project. If your banker says the bank lends 75% LTV, compute your maximum loan. If your lender is willing to lend up to 75% of the ARV, then you will take $579,000 and multiply times 0.75.

= $579,000 x 0.75 = $434,250

Step 5: Work backwards to determine how much cash you will need:

Maximum Loan Amount	$434,250
- Property Cost	$350,000
- Renovation Cost	$120,000
Cash Needed to Close	**$35,750**

In this scenario, the same $50,000 cash that you have to invest can afford you a $350,000 property that will be worth $579,000 after completion, and your out-of-pocket cash costs are less than in the previous example where the lender funded based on Loan to Cost.

It becomes a more complex estimation of budget when banks use a mix of LTC and LTV to determine their maximum loan amount. For example, some banks, such as hard money lenders will lend the lesser of 100% of Loan to Cost or 70% of Loan to Value. In these cases, you compute both loan to cost and loan to value, and then take the lesser number as your loan amount. You can always ask your lender to compute these numbers and provide you with a maximum purchase price based on your cash available. I highly recommend this approach because the numbers get complicated, and you do not want to waste time pursuing deals you cannot afford based on your current cash available.

COMPUTING BUDGET FOR COMMERCIAL DEALS

In commercial deals, appraisers value a property based on its income using the *cap rate* and *net operating income*. Dividing the net operating income of a comparable property by its cap rate will tell you its market value based on the *income approach* to appraisals. It is highly likely you will need to get this data from your local commercial real estate agent.

Comparable Property 1 – Sold for $500,000, retail, projected NOI = $50,000

Comparable Property 2 – Sold for $600,000, retail, projected NOI = $70,000

Comparable Property 3 – Sold for $459,000, retail, projected NOI = $40,000

Comparable Property 4 – Sold for $750,000, retail, projected NOI = $80,000

Comparable Property 5 – Sold for $1,000,000, retail, projected NOI = $100,000

Comparable Property 6 – Sold for $480,000, retail, projected NOI = $40,000

If we assume the cap rate in your target market is 8%, then we can estimate the average market value of your property, or you can use the sales comps to find your cap rate.

Step 1: Compute Cap Rate of your comparable commercial properties:

Comparable Property 1 - projected income $50,000/ $500,000 = 10% cap rate

Comparable Property 2 – projected income $70,000/ $600,000 = 11.7% cap rate

Comparable Property 3 – projected income $40,000/ $459,000 = 8.7% cap rate

Comparable Property 4 – projected income $80,000/ $750,000 = 10.6% cap rate

Comparable Property 5 – projected income $100,000/$1,000,000 = 10% cap rate

Comparable Property 6 – projected income $40,000/$480,000 = 8.3% cap rate

Step 2: Compute the Average Cap Rate of your nearby commercial properties:

Add all the various cap rates of the comparable properties and divide by the total number of properties.

= (10% + 11.7% + 8.7% + 10.6% + 10% + 8.3%)/6
= 9.88% average cap rate

Step 3: Compute Estimated Net Operating Income on Subject Property

Divide the projected Net Operating Income (Income less operating expenses) on your subject property by the average cap rate:

If your ideal commercial retail property has four units that rent at $2500/month each, then the annual income is computed as $2500 x 4 x 12 months.

$2500/unit x 4 units = $10,000 monthly

$10,000 monthly x 12 months = $120,000 annual gross income

If you project 5% vacancies, then your vacancies cost would be $6000. Subtract vacancies to get your effective gross rent. If you anticipate your operating expenses to be 30% of income, then deduct your operating expenses to compute your Net Operating Income. Refer to previous sections to compute operating expenses.

	Gross Rent	$120,000
-	5% Vacancies	$6,000
=	Effective Gross Rent	$114,000
-	30% Operating Expenses	$ 34,200
	Net Operating Income	**$ 79,800**

Step 4: Project the Estimated Completed Value of Your Property

Divide the Net Operating Income by the average cap rate.

= $79,800 / 9.88%

= **$807,869 Estimated Completed Value**

Step 5: Compute Maximum Loan Amount using Loan to Value (LTV)

If the bank is willing to lend up to 75% of the ARV or completed value, then multiply $807,869 x 75%.

= $807,869 x 75%

= $605,901 is the maximum loan amount

Step 6: Work Backwards to Determine Cash You Need:

You can use the same method to estimate how much cash you need to bring based on the sum of the purchase price and renovation cost of the property.

Using LTV:

Maximum Loan Amount	$605,901
- Property Cost	$450,000
- Renovation Cost	$200,000
Cash Needed to Close	**$44,099**

Using LTC:

- Property Cost	$450,000	
- Renovation Cost	$200,000	
= Total Project Cost	$650,000	
- Maximum LTC	x	.75
Maximum Loan	**$487,500**	
Cash Needed to Close	**$162,580**	

Again, banks may use the lesser of Loan to Value and Loan to Cost. These examples are meant to give you a fundamental understanding of how banks compute these values so that you can predict them in advance and be prepared to answer the question, "What is your budget?"

As you can see, a $50,000 budget can go far depending on how the bank finances your deal, the property value after completion, the asking purchase price, and the amount of renovation required. It is a difficult question to answer, but the best place to start is by figuring out how much capital you have to work with and work from that number.

WHERE TO FIND PROPERTIES?

For people who have access to capital and a desire to invest, their next big question is "Where do I find a good deal?" As a real estate broker running an office of agents, my phone blows up several times a day with corporate buyers seeking off market properties for sale. The same way that home buyers seek the perfect home that is suitable for their family needs, investors are always seeking the perfect investment property that is suitable for them to execute their investment strategy. Your property type and strategy will determine *where* to search for properties:

- Land, RRR & Turnkey Rental Properties – Real Estate Agents, MLS, REALTOR.com, Other Public Listing Sites
- Short-Term Rentals – Real Estate Agents, Apartments.com, On site meetings with apartment managers, Public Listings with Long Days on Market
- Commercial Properties – Commercial Real Estate Agents, CoStar, LoopNet and other Public Listings
- Wholesaling – Door Knocking, Mailers, Street Signs, Online Marketing for Off Market Deals
- BRR(R), Fix and Flips – Off Market Websites such as NewWestern.com, HudHomesUSA.org, or Public Listings with Long Days on Market, Pre-Foreclosure Lists, Tax Sales, or Following the Fire Truck

I said it before, and I'll say it again. Real estate agents are the best resource to identify properties. Agents have membership access to the most current listing data before other popular websites publish the data. Other sites that are available to the public and are filled with false, outdated, or incorrect data or with scammers listing properties they do not own. The MLS is a listing service that licensed REALTORs can view and send to their clients and this data is accurate, trusted, and beneficial especially for investors seeking turnkey properties for short-term and long-term rentals, new construction or the RRR strategy. For commercial property types, real estate agents are almost always necessary. Most properties that are listed by commercial agents are only accessible to other agents because these properties are marketed as pocket listings off the market or to people that have relationships with the owner's broker. Most commercial agents will not collaborate with a buyer who is unrepresented and certainly will not take the time to educate the buyer on the process or help them complete contracts.

Real estate agents also get access to off-market data because we are in the market constantly talking to sellers. We know before people sell their property; we see the condition of properties before they are listed; and whenever we find a property in need of repair or severely distressed, we often share it within our inner network of investors who pay cash or quick financing before we list.

Real estate agents often get a bad reputation in the investment industry because investors do not like to work with real estate agents. Why? Investors do not want to pay their commissions, sign exclusivity agreements, or wait for a REALTOR to provide market data if the agent is busy or responding slowly. I get this! As someone who works on both sides of the industry, I understand the need to be empowered to identify your own deals and close without being tied to an exclusivity agreement. I also understand some agents will allow their commission to break a deal.

Nevertheless, make friends with your local real estate agents. Let them know you are a buyer seeking a specific type of property and to call and let you know first if they come across a property. As an investor, I receive random calls at unexpected times from agents and other real estate professionals who know that I am a cash buyer for their properties. They offer me an opportunity to buy off market deals because we built a relationship. As a broker, when I come across a good investment opportunity outside of my target market, I share it with other investors because I know I can sell a deal quickly to a cash buyer in my network. I do not do this when a property is more suitable for a family, because I am considerate of the fact that families are the true buyers that need homes, and there is a very real erosion of corporations stealing the American Dream from families. However, when properties must be rehabilitated before a home can be sold to a family, I call my investor network.

Real estate inspectors, appraisers, and contractors are also great resources for properties that can be purchased off market before they are listed. Often before property is sold, a seller will complete an inspection or pre-appraisal or contact a general contractor to estimate repairs to ready it for a listing. Many sellers get sticker shock at the price that contractors quote for repairs and may take time to consider if they want to invest that much money into their property or sell it as is. If you catch an owner during the time period where they are considering the cost and hassle of selling their property and you make them a good offer, then you can snag a good deal without competition. Real estate professionals may be held to some confidentiality rules and cannot share the property owner's information or address; however, they can pass along your contact information to the potential sellers and the owner can call you directly.

My construction crews are often visited by neighbors who drive by the property and are interested in the cost of repairing their homes or rental properties as well. Sometimes if the cost of repair is too high, they decide they'd rather just sell. My construction crews then call me and let me know of homes in my neighborhood that I could potentially buy. It's interesting that the more work you do, the more deals become available to you.

One day, as I stood outside of a property that I visited regularly during the renovation process, a neighbor drove by and said, "Hey, do you want to buy my property that is just down the street?" I got in my car and followed them to a nearby home. They showed me that home and also offered me four other properties to buy. It was like an unreal moment! This is something investors dream about, and it has happened to me more than once. As a precaution, though, do not follow random strangers into their homes.

On another occasion, while I stood outside a recently remodeled home, a man drove by and said he had been watching the transformation of the property. He then offered me the opportunity to purchase his duplex. Another time, when I was cutting trees in front of a home, a code compliance officer drove by to write tickets on a neighboring property. I approached the officer and asked if it was okay to leave my trees on the curb. She then told me that she was condemning a property being foreclosed by the city. Wow! Off market property data was coming at me without my searching for it!

Start building relationships with real estate professionals such as real estate agents, property inspectors, repairmen, construction workers, code workers, trash and sanitation workers, and people who work in the market daily. Yes, you can find properties online or through auctions, but relationships are important to your business as an investor.

As you see in the list provided, "boots on the ground" strategies for finding properties are very real. Placing yard signs and posts throughout your target community can typically get you leads for home sellers looking to sell for cash. You have seen "We Buy Houses" signs on a busy intersection corner. Those are usually placed there by wholesalers hoping to get leads that they can resale to other investors for a markup.

Get out on a Saturday morning and go door knocking in neighborhoods where you see potential investment properties. Get involved in local politics and help share election poll information, voter registration sign-ups, get petitions signed for local legislation to be passed or some other community involvement that gives you a reason to be at people's door. Wear a shirt that discloses your company name, contact, and disarms people. While you are there, ask if they want to sell their home. Leave your contact information or flyer if they do not answer. This is a way to help the community while also allowing you an entry point to being received as a stranger knocking on doors. *NOTE: Only do this if this is legal in your community, and if people ask you to leave their property, follow their instructions immediately.* If you are carrying a weapon for safety, be very thoughtful about whether this strategy is the best approach for you to find properties. I live in Texas, and I have had law enforcement officers tell me that I can shoot anyone on my property that I feel is a threat. Stranger danger is real, so tread lightly.

Online websites for wholesale deals and foreclosure lists are also available for a monthly fee. I cannot advocate for these sites because I do not use them. I find foreclosure lists at my local title office, and these lists are made available to clients of the office. Every city host tax auctions for properties that are delinquent on property tax payments. These properties are posted in the newspaper prior to the auction to give interested buyers time to do their diligence and drive by the outside of the property. Since these properties were foreclosed on due to the owner's inability or refusal to pay taxes, it is important to also research other liens that may be against the property that would become your financial obligation as the new property owner. These can include code violations, mowing liens, mechanics liens, judgements, and other recorded liens against the property that you may inherit.

It is also important to complete a title search to ensure you would have a clear title to resell the property after your improvements and obtain a title policy. Check for flood zones; check the property for squatters; and physically go to the property to confirm that the address you think you are purchasing is the same as the auction listing. Tax properties are usually sold for cash, and the auction winner is required to bring a cashier's check upon winning the bid.

Research fire rescue incidents online. They typically list the address of properties with active structural fires. You can send a letter to those property owners offering to purchase their property at deep discounts. They may be inclined to sell their property and use their insurance proceeds to move elsewhere. Research any expired and canceled listings. Pursue for sale by owner listings. If you are in a hot, fast selling market, look for houses on the market for more than 60 days. Sellers are often willing to sell at a discount after a certain amount of time has passed. Look for abandoned and boarded properties, and research the owner's address on the local tax assessor's website. Leave fancy note cards on occupied properties and ask the owners to consider an offer. I had a home valued at almost a million dollars sell this way. These are just a few creative ideas for identifying your investment property, even if it is not actively for sale.

Never underestimate the power of vision. If you see a property that is not for sale, but you have a burning passion to own and transform it into a more useful purpose, then pursue it and don't give up on it. I have worked diligently for more than two years to own two apartment buildings in the neighborhood where I live, and they are not even for sale. Can you imagine working for two years to raise investment and bank funding, and build a financial plan, operating plan, construction plan, environmental plan, and property management plan, and even going as far as to pre-lease the renovated units to local non-profit organizations -- all for a building that is not for sale, and you do not own?

Yes, I did that. I meet next week to pitch two interested investors about raising $5 million to purchase those buildings. Why? Because God placed this unrelenting desire and vision in me to take possession of both properties that are being poorly managed in order to create a new environment on properties that can be stewarded for the community and give renters better living conditions. Also, simply because that corner of the block is an eyesore and I hate the way they look. I know if I own those buildings that corner will be transformed into a place of beauty reflective of God's perfect will for the earth. Every time I pass them, I pray and thank God for giving me that land and for transferring the deed into my name.

So, yes, go after your purpose projects and do not stop until you get what you want. I imagine myself like Caleb and Joshua overlooking the Promised Land, spying out the best parts and strategizing a plan to take it. The people who owned those lands had no idea that God's people were receiving divine help to possess their land. I can write a whole book on the topic of "Possessing the Land" because this is what we are called to do as Kingdom heirs, but I'll save that topic for my next book for those who want to understand the more spiritual aspects of real estate.

I know half of the people reading this section doubt everything I said because they lack the money to buy anything. I want to reassure you, money follows deals. You do not need to have all your funding before you start searching for properties. In many cases you cannot secure your funding until after you have identified an actual property and obtained site control through an option contract or purchase sale agreement.

Before you begin, know where you would go to obtain funding. Secure banking relationships, review approval criteria, gather your company or personal financial documents, and meet a few ready investors or capital providers. But do not think you need cash in hand to start. While it is great to be a cash buyer with a load of cash looking for a deal, it rarely works that way for many first-time investors. Avoid waiting until you have it all together; find a deal, and you will be surprised how much easier it is to find the money to pay for it.

THE PROPERTY INSPECTION PROCESS

After you identify a property of interest, you will need to do a walk-through inspection to visualize the layout, the condition, the age and performance of systems and structures, and to verify that the property is suitable for your needs. I highly discourage purchasing a property sight unseen. Photos are never sufficient to understand the condition, layout and spacing of a property. Photography is very deceptive and can even be doctored to cause spaces to appear larger, brighter, and better than reality.

The purpose of the inspection is to identify deficiencies in structure, or hazards on the land that could affect the property's current value, the repair cost, or the potential cash flows or resale value. Many of the potential problems with a property can be hidden behind walls and unseen without crawling into crawl spaces, attic spaces, looking into sewage systems, climbing onto the roof, having aerial footage, or walking every foot of land. Even if you do those things, without a trained eye to know what you are looking for you may overlook deficient items that are out of code, hazardous, inconvenient, or costly. Knowing the issues upfront can assist you in negotiating the price of the property or the necessary repairs before you take possession.

Your formal property inspection occurs during a feasibility period where you have an *option* or period of time to consider the home before pursuing a binding contract. It can be as limited as a visual walkthrough or as meticulous as numerous professional inspections with reports provided by licensed property inspectors, environmentalists, plumbers, electricians, foundation engineers, structural engineers, roofers, and/or general contractors. The extent of your property inspection will be determined by market conditions, length of option or feasibility period, property age and condition, and/or your intended use.

Check out these examples:

- If you are preparing to *tear down* a residential property for its land value and location and build a new single-family residence, you would have few, if any, inspections and would focus more on the design and construction of the future structure that you plan to build.

- If you are purchasing a 100-year-old *historic property* that needs to be preserved to its original architectural design, you would have extensive inspections including an asbestos survey, lead-based paint inspection, plumbing inspection, and a consultation with a historic conservationist who is fluent in the architectural features of that design period and the cost of modern materials to replace them.

- If you are purchasing an ***industrial building*** to convert to a new commercial use, you may be required to have several phases of costly environmental inspections to ensure the land and building aren't contaminated. The cost to clean the property and obtain a permit for use could be unfeasible and lead you to terminate your contract after doing your appropriate due diligence.

- If you are purchasing a ***distressed property*** to flip, you may focus on the main systems of the home such as the plumbing, roof, HVAC, and electrical and hire a structural engineer to tell you the number of piers needed to level the house so that you can more appropriately estimate the cost of your remodel. Cosmetic repairs, such as flooring and kitchen, might be less important anyway if you plan to remove those items for more updated finishes. Personally, I have my general contractor walk each property and quote the cost of repairs before I purchase a distressed property because I care less about what is wrong and more about whether it is financially feasible within my investment plan.

- If you are purchasing ***raw land*** or a ***ranch*** on 500 acres, you may hire an inspector to provide aerial photography to see the landscape and surrounding lakes, ponds, and creeks, sports areas, roadways, and structures. You may want to get out on a golf cart and drive the entire area to ensure you know what you are buying. Hire a farm and ranch inspector to inspect the barns, stables, workshops, barndominiums, wells, septic tanks, and the many other structures that could be present on a property of that size. You would inspect the livestock or horses, infrastructure, power sources, and water supply.

- If you are purchasing *farmland*, first inspect the soil, the floodplain, the topography, the fertility of the crop, the suitability of the land and climate, the orientation of the land to sun and the coverage of trees that provide shade, the sufficiency and usability of acreage, the location to markets, customers and labor and irrigation or water sources. Also consider environmental contamination, herbicides, and other contaminants. If you are farming cattle or animals, then inspect the access to water sources, the direction or amount of wind to cool livestock, vegetation, poisonous weeds, and fencing. Since farmland can abut other properties, research easements, access to the property, surveys showing borders, cell reception, and infrastructure. This type of property is such a specialty that it would most assuredly require a specialist.

- If you are purchasing *waterfront* property, you might need additional inspections beyond the home itself to inspect outdoor features that would be common with those property locations. These features requiring special inspection could include swimming pools and hot tubs and the equipment, outdoor kitchens, porches, decks, and pergolas, retaining walls, boat and jet ski lifts, docks, piers, bulkheads, sprinkler systems, gates and banisters which can be safety necessities, and lighting, especially around water area.

Let's Review a List of Systems to Inspect:

Structural Systems
a. Foundations
b. Grading and Drainage
c. Roof Covering and Materials
d. Roof Structures and Attics
e. Walls (interior and exterior)
f. Ceiling and Floors
g. Doors (interior and exterior)
h. Windows
i. Stairways (Interior and exterior)
j. Fireplaces and Chimneys
k. Porches, Balconies, Decks and Carports

Electrical Systems
a. Service Entrance
b. PANEL
c. Sub-Panel
d. Branch Circuits, Connected Devices and Fixtures

Heating, Ventilation, and Air Conditioning Systems
a. Heating System
b. Cooling System
c. Dust System, Chases and Vents

Plumbing Systems
a. Supply, Distribution systems and fixtures
b. Drains, Wastes, Vents
c. Water heating equipment
d. Hydro-Massage therapy equipment

Appliances
a. Dishwasher
b. Food Waste Disposers
c. Range Hood and exhaust systems
d. Ranges, Cooktops and ovens
e. Microwave Ovens
f. Mechanical Exhaust Vents and Bathroom Heaters
g. Garage Door Operators
h. Dryer Exhaust Systems
i. Other

Optional Systems
a. Landscape Irrigation (Sprinkler) Systems
b. Swimming Pools, Spas and Hot Tubs
c. Outbuildings
d. Private Water Wells
e. Private Sewage Disposal (septic) system

An inspection should include a comprehensive visual review and performance test of the various systems of the property, not limited to the list provided. A licensed inspector may also recommend additional specialized inspections to determine the condition or performance of a system that they may be incapable of accessing or unqualified to test. Again, this is not an exhaustive list and only provides an example of areas you should evaluate during your walkthrough. Leave the inspection to the experts.

ESTIMATING THE COST OF RENOVATION & REPAIRS

As part of your project planning, it is important to estimate the cost of your improvements before **_going hard_** on a deal. This step normally occurs during or immediately after you complete your walkthrough while you are within an option or due diligence period. If you are buying a property **_turnkey_**, you may not have renovations and can skip to the next step. However, if your property needs any amount of work, understanding your construction costs will be a necessary step to evaluate if your deal is **_feasible_**, affordable, and profitable.

A licensed general contractor (GC) or **_inspector_** knowledgeable about construction cost can assist in estimating the cost to repair deficient items found in an inspection report. Projects that require significant improvements or remodeling need a formal bid from the company(s) that you hire to complete your work before you proceed with your contract to purchase.

Verbal or back of the napkin quotes are not formal contracts and can lead to inaccuracies in your project budget. Ask for quotes in writing, itemized by category or task and subdivided into material cost and labor cost, if possible. Things spoken verbally can easily be lost in translation, such as the time when my contractor interpreted my verbal request for 'mint green' kitchen cabinets as "Crayola box, preschool classroom green," and I ended up with the most hideous cabinets in history. We now get paint samples and agree on the color in person.

Scope of Work

To get a reliable bid for work, your contractor or vendors will request a ***scope of work*** including measurements, material type and color, and details of all the work you desire them to perform. It is important to remember that general contractors and subcontractors follow the scope of work listed in their contract which typically includes renderings, floorplans, site plans, elevation plans, electrical lighting plans, and material schedules.

Improvements to an existing property may be referred to as a *remodel, renovation, reconstruction, redevelopment, restoration, rehabilitation*, or *rehab*, which are all acceptable terms meaning changes to an existing structure intended to enhance its value, restore, or improve the condition. Additions to existing properties' square footage, such as adding bedrooms, adding levels, or ground up construction, is considered *new construction*. Modifications to a property can range from changing paint color and replacing outdated finishes to pulling up floors and taking a property down to its studs, busting up concrete to lay new plumbing, and redesigning an entirely different floor plan.

The scope of work required is determined by a combination of the condition of the property at the time of acquisition, the end use of the property, and the investor's vision. What is common in the neighborhood where the property is located also regulates the extent of work. For example, if most houses in a neighborhood have a four-bedroom and two-bathroom layout, remodeling the investment property into a two bedroom and one bathroom layout might be less expensive, but riskier since it is out of line with the norm for the neighborhood. Having more spacious bedrooms and a more open floor plan would make that design choice an outlier and cause the property to sit on the market without an interested buyer or renter. That change may also devalue your property and yield a lower appraised value.

Still, design choice is within the investor's power to decide. If you acquire a piece of land, your scope of work will include the construction of a new structure from the foundation to the finishes. The vision for the build will be the investor's choice based on the property type allowed in the zoning, what is feasible with the available land and fits within the regulated *setbacks*, and what an architect models based on the desired floor plan and finishes requested by the investor.

Certain changes to a property may be required or limited by the local construction code, such as changes to structural walls, additions to an existing structure, fence heights, fire sprinkler systems, electrical systems, insulation types, clearances in hallways and doorways to meet accessibility and safety requirements. New construction and remodels are usually regulated by different construction codes with new construction having more extensive regulation and inspection than interior remodels.

Furthermore, commercial buildings and residential construction are also usually regulated by different codes and permitting requirements. Commercial projects require greater costs and inspections than residential work. If your property falls within a historic preservation district or is regulated by a property owners association, additional regulations may exist for exterior material selections, swimming pools, roofing, and even the placement and type of trees allowed.

The After Repair Value of the property will also constrain your scope of work. It is absolutely critical to improve your property without overspending and pushing the project cost beyond the values of the properties in the surrounding community. The scope of work allows your lender to estimate the loans they will make on your deal and assists your appraiser in valuing your property before the work is complete. Sometimes, the more extensive your scope of work, the more valuable your deal in the end. However, there are limits where too much improvement does yield the return you expect. Unless money is no object, the scope of work is also defined by your budget and how much capital you have available to make repairs.

Understanding project cost in advance of purchasing your property is essential to buying a good investment. With a good estimate of repairs in hand, you can renegotiate the purchase price if you feel that you are overpaying; you can revise your design plan to cut back on the renovation costs; or you can walk away from a bad deal if it just is not feasible. Without this information it will be difficult to predict the profitability of the project and make wise decisions.

Have a clear scope of work and estimate of the cost to complete that work **BEFORE** moving forward with your project. If possible, have multiple contractors bid on the work to see where you get better pricing, or subcontract parts of the project to save cost or get better quality. For example, one contractor specializing in post-framing work may give you a better deal on just that part of the work.

Ballpark Estimates

When time is limited to snag a deal, some investors use quick computations to model their estimated project cost to make a fast offer. Investors can do this because they have a good understanding of their cost based on knowledge of their market, experience, or historical data from past projects.

Since you are beginning, do research now to have a frame of reference to ballpark your construction costs when quick decisions are necessary. Keep in mind that your total project cost includes more expenses than the cost of repairs. However, for this section we are focusing on repair cost only. Having a general understanding of average costs in your local market helps you contract a hot deal and avoid missing potential deals while you wait for a contractor or inspector to show up.

I knew one investor who only bought deals that needed a cosmetic remodel, and they had their repair cost down to a science. This investor had done so many deals that they computed the average costs based on the cost per square foot ($ / sq. ft.). To make their analysis, they toured a potential property every time and estimated their repair costs based on their average $ / sq. ft. For example, if their average cost to make cosmetic improvements to a property (flooring, counters, paint, etc.) was $25/sq.ft. and the subject property was 1500 sq. ft., then they would quickly estimate their renovation cost as $37,500.

<u>Do the Math:</u>

Estimated cost of repairs is $25/ sq. ft.
Subject property size is 1500 sq. ft.

$25 x 1500 = $37,500

If they walked into a property a week later that was 2800 sq. ft., they would use that same cost per foot.

Estimated cost of repairs is $25/ sq. ft.
Subject property size is 2800 sq. ft.

$25 x 2800 = $70,000

Clearly, this formula does not itemize what necessary repairs, and the exact scope of work would vary project to project, but this simple estimation allowed him to make quick estimations to help guide his negotiations on the purchase price. If the repair cost were too high to make the deal worthwhile, the investor would push to get the price lower so that he could buy the deal, make necessary repairs, and still leave room for profit.

As a word of caution, your ballpark estimates can be off or dead wrong, and your general contractor is not obligated to meet you at your price. Be sure the assumptions you make are realistic or your deal can go wrong fast. It is best to use your ballpark estimates to make an initial offer and get your deal into an option contract. Then, make a formal bid during the due diligence period. Based on the formal bid, you can renegotiate your numbers with the property seller, or you can terminate your contract and walk away. A later section of this book will offer greater detail of how to make a financial model, including repair estimates.

Volatile Pricing

As much as I would love to provide an estimated cost of repairs, pricing varies widely across the country depending on your project location, scope of work, area demand, relationship with vendors, scale of business, material selection, etc. It is impossible to predict a reasonable cost list for everyone reading this book. Additionally, costs rose swiftly in recent years and construction material markets have been extremely volatile.

The cost of lumber jumped 288% from 2020 to 2021 sending the U.S. construction industry into a frenzy. New home builders did something I have never seen before and sold houses with variable pricing, because they could not foresee how much their materials would change over a 6-8 month build period. Any estimate I would give you for the purpose of making general assumptions would become wildly inaccurate with time.

For this section I will review the process to obtain estimates and in a later subsection of this chapter, I will show how to model your estimates into your overall project budget to measure project feasibility. Obtain your actual project cost from contractors who work in your local market. Use the following sample bids to see the type of construction tasks that may be quoted, but do not rely on the figures shown.

Gathering Your Construction Estimates:

As part of your due diligence to move forward with a project, **you need to obtain actual quotes from licensed professionals** to reliably model your investment plan. The more precise your estimates, the better you can predict your profit.

The provided sample construction budget shows various tasks that may be quoted within your project. Be sure your actual construction budget outlines the scope of work for your specific project in detail and that the pricing is within the normal range for your local market.

PROPERTY VALUATION & PROJECTING INCOME

Understanding Property Value

The term *Property Value* is often misunderstood because it encompasses multiple formulas and perspectives. In this topic we review Market Value, Assessed Value, Appraised Value, and Replacement Cost so that you can understand how to measure, grow, and predict future value. When trying to understand property value, it is important to know which type of value you are measuring so that you are using the right data points to compute the correct valuation.

Property Value is an "opinion of value" based on size, location, and condition of the property and land.

According to the Uniform Appraisal Standards for Federal Land Acquisitions (2016; 1.2.4),

> *Market Value is the amount in cash, or on terms reasonably equivalent to cash, for which in all probability the property would have sold on the effective date of value, after a reasonable exposure time on the open competitive market, from a willing and reasonably knowledgeable seller to a willing and reasonably knowledgeable buyer, with neither acting under any compulsion to buy or sell, giving due consideration to all available economic uses of the property.*

Market Value is defined differently by Black Law's Dictionary which states that it is,

> *The price that a seller is willing to accept, and a buyer is willing to pay on the open market and in an arm's length transaction; the point at which supply and demand intersect.*

Values are subject to change over time due to market appreciation or depreciation, increases and decreases in supply and demand, surrounding development or degeneration, improvement or wear to the property, and inflation/deflation in the overall economy.

Property value is also subject to change based on the decisions others have made and the prices paid to buy and sell properties neighboring the *subject property*.

Property value is also subject to the opinion of the person hired to determine the value, often an *appraiser,* who is a licensed professional enlisted to determine the *appraised value* of property. Because property value is often changing based on multiple factors in varying markets, banks typically require an *appraisal,* to determine the loan amount they are willing to lend. An *Appraisal Report* is a detailed document that outlines a property's value based on its quality, condition, location, and surrounding market conditions provided by an independent, third-party appraisal company.

When property value is misunderstood or misjudged, or intentionally suppressed, it results in a ripple effect on neighboring properties, and the entire community. Receiving a correct appraisal value of your property that most accurately matches the property's true market value is especially important. If you believe your property value has been devalued, stand up and fight for the correct value of your property and your overall community.

A study conducted by the Metropolitan Policy Program at Brookings.edu made an interesting case explaining the *Devaluation of Assets in Black Neighborhoods.* They found that "homes in neighborhoods where the population is 50% Black or greater are valued at roughly half the value of neighborhoods with no Black residents." They described an intrinsic bias in the appraisers' perception of value of the properties in a neighborhood because of the appraisers' biased perception of the people within that community based on race, ethnicity, age, and appearance. They made a claim that across all majority Black neighborhoods in the U.S., "**owner-occupied homes are undervalued by $48,000 per home on average, amounting to $156 billion in cumulative losses.**"

Whether this study is accurate or not, I have personally experienced bias in property appraisals and witnessed the suppression of values on many occasions. Recently, an appraiser undervalued my investment property by $30,000 because of its location in a primarily minority community. When the bank that ordered the appraisal report informed me that the value had come in 12% lower than predicted, I responded that I would like the bank to contest the appraisal. I was told in a very condescending tone that I should leave it alone and just move forward because "the appraiser would **never** change his opinion." I thought about it for a moment and told the banker, "If I don't fight for the values of my community, who will?" I rejected the appraisal.

I am armed with market data and keep detailed records of my improvements. I know my target market like the back of my hand and am extremely passionate about this issue. I immediately called the appraiser and began to advocate for the values in my community based on the data points shown in the appraisal report. After explaining to the appraiser why my property was valuable, and pinpointing the errors in his report, the appraiser admitted "I am not from this neighbor and honestly do not know much about it." He went on to admit, "The appraisal industry is made up of mostly older White men that are not in touch with the neighborhoods they are appraising. I wish more Black people would become licensed appraisers because they are more in touch with these communities than we are."

The appraiser apologized to me and reviewed the data that I sent to him. He agreed he had made an error due to an unconscious bias and increased the value of my appraisal report by $20,000. Now, this is the first time in my career history that an appraiser owned up to his mistake. It was worth putting up the fight because all future investment properties that I acquire in this same target market will be tied to that one appraiser's opinion of value. If I accepted the lower value, all subsequent values would have come in low as well with that property being a precedent to justify the others.

Many homeowners simply do not know the value of their home. They do not know how to measure value and settle for an erroneous appraisal before arguing the correct value. Ignorance has cost owners billions in value because they simply do not know the data. This same appraiser explained that uninformed property owners have undervalued their own properties by selling well below value. This happens when homeowners misconceive and use the *assessed value* listed on their tax records as an indication of market value.

Assessed value is a dollar amount assigned to a piece of property for tax purposes and is often a percentage (%) of its market value. To compute this value, the county tax assessor determines their opinion of the current market value using their own calculations, which is separate and unique from what may be shown on an appraisal report. They then take the market value and multiply it by an assessment rate to determine the assessed, or taxable, value of the property. The assessment rate is usually somewhere between 80 and 90%, though in some cases it is 100%, like in Texas.

The homeowner can mistakenly believe their home is worth the value listed on their tax bill, which can be just a fraction of what the property is worth. Tax assessors often deeply undervalue properties because they are not privy to off market sales, improvements, or differences in properties. And home buyers prefer lower assessments because it leads to lower tax bills. The point I am making is do not use assessed value to determine the market value of your property.

Another factor of confusion is *replacement cost.* Replacement cost is a figure used on insurance policies as a determination of the cost to rebuild a home of similar size and likeness should you experience a total loss of property. Replacement cost is different from market value. Replacement cost measures the construction material and labor costs to rebuild, which may be lower than the market value.

Another measure insurance companies use is ***Actual Cash Value,*** which is the replacement cost less depreciation. This value on insurance policy documents further misleads property owners as to the actual market value of their property. Although your home or building may be worth more, insurance carriers may not even insure your property for the full market value because they are subject to limitations. So, do not leave money on the table by selling your property based on its replacement cost or Actual Cash Value.

Now that you have a basic understanding of property value, estimate your property value at the time of acquisition, construction, and after all repairs are completed. Be the expert of your property's value ***before*** the appraiser, tax assessor, or insurance assessor show up to make their calculations. In my experience, owners have pushed and received valuations their real estate agents, lenders, and appraisers said they would never get.

Remember, property value is a price that a buyer is willing to pay, and a seller is willing to accept. In hot markets like what saw in Dallas over the last decade, sellers commanded prices so insane that they received cash offers over $100k above their ***asking price*** and far exceeding the appraised value. In some cases, because demand was so high and inventory so low, buyers waived the requirement to have appraisals, or they committed to pay the difference between appraised value and offer amount.

These are extraordinary circumstances and the exception and not the norm. Yet only owners who knew their value were able to capitalize in a market that allowed them to earn top dollar. Investors, flippers, and wholesalers did the same, pushing prices to an endless height in a market that appears to have no top. While economists know this trend will not last, an investor can ride the wave only if they are armed with the information necessary to surf the market heights.

So, how do you determine market value so that you invest wisely, get a good deal at acquisition, maximize your financing, contend over inaccurate appraisals, and set your resale price to maximize your profits? Good question. The accuracy of your prediction will impact your investment deal's profitability, so pay attention.

Predicting Value Before Acquisition

To make a wise investment or purchase decision about a property, you must understand the existing value of the property in its current condition. This is called ***As-Is Value,*** or the value before additional repairs or improvements are made to the property. Once you determine As-Is Value, you can make an offer that allows you to buy the property at a price lower than market value.

When buying property off market, these figures are commonly subjective and based on the valuations given to the property by the seller or the buyer. For example, if you buy a property that you plan to tear down and rebuild, you may value the structure on the property low because you are only interested in the land it sits on. However, the property owner may have a shed on the property grounds that holds lots of antiques and collectibles they have treasured for many years. They may have tinkered in their shed, listened to their favorite songs, and shared a six-pack of beer with their best friend for fifty years in that shed. Their valuation of the property may be based on the memories and nostalgia of what that property means to them.

Sellers and buyers commonly disagree on how value is measured. Buyers must be skilled in the art of negotiation so that both parties *believe* they are meeting at a fair value. Property sellers never want to feel like they are selling their property for a steal. In fact, most investors start with a low offer and raise their price as negotiations proceed, knowing the property is worth much more than their initial offer. In the end, this approach leaves the seller feeling like they won the negotiations, when in reality they still may be selling below value. You cannot force anyone to sell their property below value, but as long as both parties *agree* to the price, you have a fair deal.

You always want to buy a property for the minimum amount possible. To understand *As-Is Value*, study your market, assess recent sales data, and compute an average price/sq.ft. of six or more nearby properties that sold in a similar condition in the past six months. Having this data on hand can help you persuade a property owner to accept your offer. Obviously, if the average sales prices are higher than what you want to pay or can afford to make your deal work, then you may be relying on the owner not having seen the recent sales data. When buying an existing business, the property value may be based on its income and the contents of the business plus any goodwill from the company's reputation and existing customer list. When buying a commercial property, you may value it based on its cap rate and net operating income (NOI). I discussed how to determine your average sales price in a previous section which may be more or less than its As-Is Value. Do a quick review.

Do the Math for Residential Properties:

Step 1: Compute the As Is Value Based on Comparable Sales

For residential properties, appraisers use the sales comparison approach to value properties. To get a good estimation of your investment property's market or As-Is Value, take an average of the sales price of 6+ comparable properties that are within a quarter of a mile distance and within 500 sq ft of size:

Subject Property: Asking Price is $95,000, distressed SFR, 1500 sq ft

Comparable Property 1 – Sold for $50,000, distressed SFR, 1300 sf
Comparable Property 2 – Sold for $60,000, distressed SFR, 1350 sf
Comparable Property 3 – Sold for $75,000, distressed SFR, 1400 sf
Comparable Property 4 – Sold for $58,000, distressed SFR, 1350 sf
Comparable Property 5 – Sold for $90,000, distressed SFR, 1700 sf
Comparable Property 6 – Sold for $108,000, distressed SFR, 1800 sf

Step 2: Compute the Average of all 6 Properties

Compute the average sales price of similar homes in the same area:

Average Sales Price = ($50,000 + $60,000 + $75,000 + $58,000 + $90,000 + $108,000) / 6

Average Sales Price = $441,000 / 6

Average Sales Price = $73,500

Now compute the average size:

Average Square Feet = (1300+1350+1400+1350+1700+1800)/6

Average Square Feet = 8900/6

Average Square Feet = 1483

Average Sales Price/ Sq Ft = $73,500/1483

Average $/Sq Ft = $49.56/SqFt

Now Compute the Maximum Purchase Price

Subject Property Size * Average $/Sq Ft

1500 Sq Ft * 49.56 = $74,340

Step 3: Adjust for Differences Between Comps and Subject Property

As you can see, the six comparable sales all have different sizes but are within 500 sq.ft. of the subject property. If they had been larger or smaller than the subject property by more than 500 sq ft., the appraiser would likely consider it incomparable and exclude it from his evaluation.

In this scenario, if the average sales price is $73,500 for the comparable properties, but yours is slightly larger and has an additional bathroom, you may value the subject property slightly higher. While you want to purchase a property for as little amount as possible, you may be willing to pay up to $74,340 because you know the property is a bit above average. Just do not overpay.

Okay, let me cushion that last statement by admitting that valuation is such a subjective number that many times I pay more than a property is worth on paper because I believe it is worth more than the data reveals. This is only because I am privy to so much private off-market data that does not show up in the records. You must be confident and risk-tolerant to overpay for properties, which is why I encourage you to buy low so that you can have equity on the front end of the deal. This is the best approach.

Step 4: Compute Maximum Purchase Price Allowable

In some situations, you may be willing to pay much more than a property is worth. The location of the property or the expected cash flow from its end use may drive your decision more than the as-is value. For example, if a local developer is planning to build a casino near a waterfront downtown area that abuts a distressed neighborhood with low value homes, they may be willing to pay ten times more than a property is worth. She will do so because the income from the casino is projected to be higher in that area of town and location is essential to the success of the development plan. They are paying for the land value and not the actual home. Many situations exist where you may be willing to pay a premium for a property because you consider its future value more than its current value; however, still set a maximum threshold for your negotiations. I shared this formula in the Fix-and-Flip section, and I will restate it here for your review.

Compute the Maximum Price You Can Pay and Still Be Profitable:

> After Repair Value
> - Estimated Cost of Construction or Improvements
> - Estimated Closing Costs and Commissions at time of Purchase
> - Estimated Closing Costs and Commissions at time of Sale
> - Bank Interest during the Holding Period
> - Holding Costs during the Holding Period
> - Profit Investor Expects to Earn
> _____
> Maximum Price Paid for Property

Use this formula to determine the highest price that you are willing to offer to the property owner before the deal is no longer profitable. Once you know your maximum purchase price, you can negotiate to justify acquiring the property for the price needed to make your deal work. Remember to leave room for errors or miscalculations.

CREATING A FINANCIAL MODEL

A financial model is a spreadsheet built in software like Microsoft Excel that allows an investor to forecast the financial performance of an investment by looking into the future. When building a financial model, you are looking at an investment from the perspective of the equity investor or the bank and projecting when the property will return the investment and how the property will cash flow or profit overtime. Before participating in an investment opportunity, it is imperative to complete a financial analysis of the deal to understand if the deal meets your profit expectations. Understanding the metrics used in a model will enhance your ability to make swift and smart investment decisions and predict your return on investment. To evaluate a financial model, you must possess a solid understanding of the inputs that go into the financial model and scrutinize the assumptions that drive the model. Because it is easy to creatively manipulate inputs in a financial model to portray an outcome that is more optimistic than pragmatic, many capital providers adjust the assumptions to more conservative figures to see how much negative adjustment the investment can bear before the investment is poor. For example, if you are assuming construction will cost you $75/sq.ft. the bank's underwriter may push those cost assumptions to $100/sq.ft. to see if the deal would fail if the cost of construction increases. The more conservative your assumptions, the less risk of loss in a situation of rising construction pricing. Understanding how to build and analyze a financial model will provide greater confidence that you are making a wise, well informed investment decision. If you are the deal sponsor fundraising from others, it will give investors the confidence to partner with you because your numbers are strong, and your model is realistic.

If you are sponsoring a deal and seeking to raise capital, you will need to build a financial model to present to the bank or investors to convince them that your deal is a good one to fund. You will typically create a *Pro forma*, which is a real estate investing method to determine the property's projected income potential. The model should be able to formulate the project's *Cash Flow*, *Net Operating Income*, and several other financial metrics, but most importantly it should tell the investor when they can expect to receive their investment back and the *Return on their Investment* (ROI) or *Internal Rate of Return* (IRR). The actual inputs in the financial model will differ depending on what type of investment strategy and property type you have selected.

To build the model, you will need to first select what type of project you want to model:
- *Are you buying a property and renovating it?*
- *Are you building ground up construction?*
- *Are you developing land?*
- *Are you buying a turnkey rental property with existing tenants?*

You will need to know if your deal is operating for *commercial or residential use*. This use will drive the sources of income. If your property is residential, the income will be derived from a tenant paying rent or from the resale of the property. If the property is a commercial use, the income will be projected based on historical rents that existing tenants have paid or the market rents in your target area for the commercial use.

- *What is the end use of your ideal project?*
- *Will your property service business customers?*
- *Will there be a residence where people live?*
- *Will it be a mixed-use of both business and residential uses?*

You will need to know your asset class:
- *Single Family Housing*
- *Short-term rentals*
- *Multifamily Housing*
- *Condominiums*
- *Office*
- *Retail*
- *Etc. (refer to section 2)*

Refer back to the various asset classes reviewed in Section 2. If you are renting a single-family house on a single lease, you will have one source of income from the rent that your tenant would pay. If you have a multifamily apartment, you will forecast the income by computing the market rent times the number of units in your multifamily. If you are an office tenant, you would project the market rent for the various spaces x the number of office tenants and perhaps include a utility recapture or parking fee as additional income. The assumptions in your Pro Forma would also be adjusted based on the asset class. You may project higher vacancy rates for office tenants than you would for residential housing. *What is the asset class that you have decided to pursue?*

Since this book is providing a basic review of investment topics, I will only provide a limited review of financial models. I intend to discuss financial modeling in greater detail in more advanced course material provided by Comma Club Community because there is much greater depth of understanding required for you to truly master financial modeling. There is sophisticated financial modeling software available to support your investment analysis or you can build a simple spreadsheet on your own. Whatever your choice, the numbers that go into the model and the assumptions behind those numbers are more important than the method you used to create the model.

The sample financial model that we will review is showing a 50-unit multi-family apartment building that has an acquisition cost of $2,500,000 and will be renovated and held as a long-term rental property. Let's get started!

Property Assumptions:

The first section of your model will include a section that lists the inputs or assumptions that drive your formulas in your model. In this example the inputs would be based on information that can be obtained easily once you identify a subject property. Be as descriptive as possible and include a list of relevant property details including the following details:

- Property Sq. Ft. and size of each building
- Costs of Construction
- Number of units
- Number of parking spaces
- Age of property
- Utilities (separately or jointly metered)
- Roof type
- Foundation type
- Type of heating and cooling system

You will also have financial assumptions about the loan or equity such as the interest rates, term, and amortization schedule for the debt repayment. You may have to assume the year of repayment. In this model, I have also estimated the cost of construction per unit to renovate the property at $46,000 per unit.

Once you have detailed the general assumptions of your model, then you can create a *Unit mix and Rental Structure* section that details the current and future rents.

UNIT MIX AND RENTAL STRUCTURE									
Unit Type	Number Units	Unit Size SF	Current Rent	Monthly Income	Current Annual Rent	Rent/SF	Pro Forma Rents	Monthly Income	Pro Forma Annual Rent	Rent/SF
1BR/1BA	8	625	$800	$6,400	$76,800	$1.28	$1,100	$8,800	$105,600	$1.76
2BR/1BA	42	725	$1,000	$42,000	$504,000	$1.38	$1,300	$54,600	$655,200	$1.79
Total/Avg	50	675	$900	$48,400	$580,800	$1.33	$1,200	$63,400	$760,800	$1.78

This sample model shows the multifamily has 50 units, the average size of each unit is 675 sq.ft and the building comprises 1 and 2 bedroom apartments. The Pro Forma Rents show the future rent to be charged after the renovations are completed. The Total Pro Forma Annual Rent will be used later in the Income and Expense Statement as part of the Gross Potential Rent calculation.

Sources and Uses

Another section of the financial model is the *Sources and Uses*. You will need to detail the total cost of your project and how your funding will be structured to cover the costs. You may have a few sources of funding such as developer equity, senior debt, a 2nd loan called mezzanine debt, grants, or government incentives.

SOURCES AND USE OF FUND SCHEDULE

Sources of Funds

Senior Debt	61%	$3,500,000
Mezzanine Debt	17%	$1,000,000
Equity (Down Payment)	22%	$1,250,000
Total Sources		**$5,750,000**

Use of Funds

	Per Unit	
Purchase Price	$50,000	$2,500,000
Hard Costs	$46,000	$2,300,000
Soft Cost	$5,000	$250,000
Carrying Costs	$3,200	$160,000
Syndication Costs	$500	$25,000
Capitalization Reserve	$7,200	$360,000
Developer/Broker Fee	$3,100	$155,000
Total Uses		**$5,750,000**
Per Unit Acquisition Cost		**$115,000.00**

In this example, the total project cost is $5,750,000 of which $3,500,000 is financed by a bank that has 1st lien position on the debt to be secured by the property. The second source of funds, $1,000,000 comes from a second loan that will take a 2nd position in repayment after the first lender is paid. This is called mezzanine debt because it is subordinated to the first lender and in this case does not require repayment until year 3. Mezzanine debt typically does not require repayment during the term of the debt but becomes due at the end of the term. This allows a company to improve its cash flow. The remaining balance is sourced from equity investments or the deal sponsor's own funds. In this example the sponsor would need to invest 22% of the total development cost which would be $1,250,000. If the sponsor didn't have access to that amount of cash, they would need to raise equity from limited partners in exchange for shares of ownership in the deal, which is how deals are commonly funded.

The uses section of this sheet shows how the funds will be applied to the various project costs. The first use of the funding would be the purchase of the land or properties included in the investment deal. If you are planning to construct a new property or renovate an existing building, you may have other line items to show how the funds will be used. Some line items might include construction hard costs, soft costs, or carrying costs during construction. Finally, this model shows syndication costs, capital reserves, and developer and broker fees.

Hard Costs include the cost of construction and contingencies. These estimates can be obtained from contractors who provide construction quotes or bids for repair work. It can also be estimated as a price per Sq.Ft, but this will be a less reliable estimate.

Soft Costs might include the appraisal, architecture and engineering fees, survey, property testing and inspections, soils report and geological survey, environmental phase 1 or phase 2 study, lead, mold, and asbestos reports, permits, accounting, utility fees, construction management fees, relocation, closing fees, marketing or leasing fees, and security.

Carrying Costs may include property taxes and insurance during the construction period, or interest.

Syndication Costs would be included for deals where multiple investors were being brought together through a syndication and the fees might be syndication accounting or legal expenses.

Capital Reserves would be additional reserves the bank may require for principal or interest payments or even operational expenses. The bank may go as far as to escrow these funds at loan funding to ensure there is additional cash available for debt repayment and unexpected expenses.

Developer or Broker Fees includes fees paid to the developer managing the deal or the brokerage fees associated with the purchase of the property. These fees will range from 3%-15% of the total development cost. Include applicable line items in your uses of funds section. Whatever is not relevant to your project will not be included.

Pro Forma of Income and Expenses:

INCOME & EXPENSE ANALYSIS						
Number of Units	50	YR 1	YR 2	YR 3	YR 4	YR 5
Rentable Area	26,352 SF					
Income						
Gross Potential Rent		$760,800	$791,232	$814,969	$839,418	$864,601
Other Income-Fees/Laundry		$15,216	$15,825	$16,299	$16,788	$17,292
Credit/Lease Loss		-$15,216	-$15,825	-$16,299	-$16,788	-$17,292
Vacancy Loss		-$38,040	-$39,562	-$40,748	-$41,971	-$43,230
Utility Reimbursement		$67,058	$69,070	$71,142	$73,276	$75,474
Non-Revenue Unit		$0	$0	$0	$0	$0
Rent Concessions		-$7,608	-$3,956	-$4,075	-$4,197	-$4,323
Effective Gross Income (EGI)		$782,210	$816,784	$841,288	$866,526	$892,522
Operating Expenses						
Leasing & Advertising		$4,573	$4,756	$4,946	$5,144	$5,350
On-Site Payroll		$37,440	$38,938	$40,495	$42,115	$43,800
General & Administrative		$18,132	$18,857	$19,612	$20,396	$21,212
Management Fee		$58,666	$61,259	$63,097	$64,989	$66,939
Legal & Accounting		$5,800	$5,974	$6,153	$6,338	$6,528
Utilities		$74,509	$77,489	$80,589	$83,812	$87,165
Contract Services		$5,000	$5,200	$5,408	$5,624	$5,849
Repairs & Maintenance		$17,460	$18,158	$18,885	$19,640	$20,426
Payroll Taxes & Benefits		$8,467	$8,806	$9,158	$9,524	$9,905
Miscellaneous		$500	$520	$541	$562	$585
Real Estate Taxes		$42,207	$43,051	$43,912	$44,790	$45,686
Property Liability Insurance		$7,200	$7,344	$7,491	$7,641	$7,794
Operating Reserve		$15,644	$16,336	$16,826	$17,331	$17,850
Replacement Reserve		$15,000	$15,000	$15,000	$15,000	$15,000
Total Operating Expenses		$310,598	$321,688	$332,112	$342,907	$354,088
Net Operating Income (NOI)		$471,612	$495,096	$509,176	$523,619	$538,433
Debt Service		$210,000	$270,607	$270,607	$270,607	$270,607
Debt Service with Capitalized Interest for 2		$0	$0	$71,910	$71,910	$71,910
Preferred Return		$150,000	$150,000	$150,000	$150,000	$150,000
Asset Management		$11,733	$12,144	$12,569	$13,009	$13,464
Net Cash Flow After Debt Service		$99,879	$62,346	$4,091	$18,094	$32,453

Let's take this very large and detailed 5 Year Income and Expense Pro Forma and break it down in sections. The first section of the Income and Expense Section of the Pro Forma reviews the operating inputs that drive your projections of income for your project. It's very important to know how much income your project will generate to forecast your investment performance.

Number of Units Rentable Area	50 26,352 SF	YR 1	YR 2	YR 3	YR 4	YR 5
Income						
Gross Potential Rent		$760,800	$791,232	$814,969	$839,418	$864,601
Other Income-Fees/Laundry		$15,216	$15,825	$16,299	$16,788	$17,292
Credit/Lease Loss		-$15,216	-$15,825	-$16,299	-$16,788	-$17,292
Vacancy Loss		-$38,040	-$39,562	-$40,748	-$41,971	-$43,230
Utility Reimbursement		$67,058	$69,070	$71,142	$73,276	$75,474
Non-Revenue Unit		$0	$0	$0	$0	$0
Rent Concessions		-$7,608	-$3,956	-$4,075	-$4,197	-$4,323
Effective Gross Income (EGI)		$782,210	$816,784	$841,288	$866,526	$892,522

To estimate income, you have to start with the inputs that drive income. For a multi-family apartment, sources of income may include rental income, laundry or dry-cleaning services, mail services, valet, dog-walking, trash pickup services, utility reimbursements and/or parking. Other income may also include application and processing fees, late fees, pet fees, credit report fees, and other charges the property manager may charge for leasing requirements. The income shown in this model was pulled from the Unit Mix and Rental Structure tab of the spreadsheet. If the assumptions for the rent amount change, the rental income in the income statement will also change.

For other types of financial models, revenue would be based on the asset type which dictates the use of the property. A financial model of a hotel investment, for example, might have income streams from nightly room rentals, food and beverage room service, spa services, restaurant leases, valet parking, etc. A duplex investment would have income from two residential units and may have additional line income for landlord charges such as application fees, pet fees, lawn care, and fee for access to the neighborhood tennis courts. For your ideal investment, think about all the potential income sources and list them.

List potential income sources for your ideal investment.

Computing Income:

Let's look at the multi-family example again. The operating assumption in this model is that rent will be charged at $1.78 per rentable sq.ft. every month. This number is formulated in the model to multiply times the rentable sq.ft. to derive the expected monthly income and then multiplied times 12 months to arrive at the annual rental income. Another way to compute rental income is to simply multiply the monthly rent per unit times to total number of units. Since the model suggests that rent will be increased at a growth rate of 4% in the first year and then 3% in subsequent years, this increase is added into each year to automatically adjust rent higher annually.

The next source of income in this model is other income/laundry fees which was estimated at 2% of the gross potential rent. If there were definitive income sources such as a monthly parking fee or a fixed trash fee, that could be more easily computed times the number of units. There is a 2% reduction in rental income for credit/lease loss and then another deduction for vacancy loss. There will always be the risk of non-payment or vacancies, so the assumptions made in these line items are of importance by lenders and potential investors. In this example, the property is assumed to have a 5% vacancy rate due to turnover and renovations. This vacancy rate would more than likely be increased by the lender to test the model in the event that construction was delayed, or it took a longer period of time to market and rent the property. Lenders may use a 7-9% vacancy rate.

The next line refers to the assumption for *Utility Reimbursements* as a % of Utilities expense. Since this particular property is on a master utility meter with all utilities being billed to the landlord, then the utility reimbursements represent the amount of utilities expected to be reimbursed by the tenants. In this model, 90% of the total utility expenses for water, electric, gas, sewer, etc. will be collected from the tenants. Finally, the model shows that no units will be given to staff as non-Revenue units and there will be rent concessions (discounts) given in the first year of the property that are phased out over a 5-year period.

Computing Effective Gross Rent:

The first subtotal of the Income and Expense Analysis is the computation of the *Effective Gross Income.* In this example, the first section of the Pro Forma shows the various revenue line items that increase or decrease the income of the project to result in the Effective Gross Income. The Operating Assumption for market rent per sq.ft. per month drives the Base Rental Income. A formula has been entered to deduct rent discounts, credit losses (unpaid rent) and concessions, and add other income and utility reimbursements. When expected vacancies are accounted for the net is annualized Effective Gross Income (EGI).

Computing Expenses:

The next section of the model projects *Operating Expenses* that will be the ongoing expenses required to operate the property. Expenses decrease your income and can be fixed (a flat fee) or variable (based on units rented, hours worked, electric kw used, etc.) and often rise over time due to inflation.

Operating Expenses					
Leasing & Advertising	$4,573	$4,756	$4,946	$5,144	$5,350
On-Site Payroll	$37,440	$38,938	$40,495	$42,115	$43,800
General & Administrative	$18,132	$18,857	$19,612	$20,396	$21,212
Management Fee	$58,666	$61,259	$63,097	$64,989	$66,939
Legal & Accounting	$5,800	$5,974	$6,153	$6,338	$6,528
Utilities	$74,509	$77,489	$80,589	$83,812	$87,165
Contract Services	$5,000	$5,200	$5,408	$5,624	$5,849
Repairs & Maintenance	$17,460	$18,158	$18,885	$19,640	$20,426
Payroll Taxes & Benefits	$8,467	$8,806	$9,158	$9,524	$9,905
Miscellaneous	$500	$520	$541	$562	$585
Real Estate Taxes	$42,207	$43,051	$43,912	$44,790	$45,686
Property Liability Insurance	$7,200	$7,344	$7,491	$7,641	$7,794
Operating Reserve	$15,644	$16,336	$16,826	$17,331	$17,850
Replacement Reserve	$15,000	$15,000	$15,000	$15,000	$15,000
Total Operating Expenses	**$310,598**	**$321,688**	**$332,112**	**$342,907**	**$354,088**

Operating Expenses may include:

- Leasing & Advertising
- Office Salaries
- Supplies and Equipment
- Lease/Rental of Equipment
- Office Rent
- Management Fees
- Legal Expenses
- Accounting, Audit and Professional Fees
- Background Checks and Credit Reports
- Bank Charges
- Utility Fees such as Electricity, Gas, Internet, Stormwater, Sewer, Trash Removal
- Maintenance Staff
- Septic Tank Cleaning

- Pest Control
- Pool Maintenance
- Grounds Maintenance
- Repairs and Unit Maintenance
- Payroll Processing
- Payroll Taxes
- Health Insurance
- Workmen's Compensation
- License & Permits
- Security & Fire Safety
- Other Miscellaneous Expenses

The list of operating expenses has been aggregated into the line items shown in this section of the Income and Expense Analysis. You do not need to reveal all the details of every potential expense in your projections that you share with bankers and investors because that may open up far too many questions than what is necessary to obtain funding. The Operating Expenses you assume for your model should be based on the research you have performed and determined as common for your asset type. Some investors will take a percent of Effective Gross Income to make a quick estimation of operating expenses and then later detail these costs once they have a property under contract. The more detailed your operating expenses are in your model, the more reliable your predictions will be to those who review your model. Many of these expenses can be estimated by researching the standard prices in your market area. The various expenses shown in this financial model have been itemized and include various Sales, Administrative, and Marketing costs that are projected to increase between 3-4% annually. As someone analyzing this investment, it would be advisable to dig into the details of this estimation and determine the detailed line items in the budget that represent sales, administrative, and marketing. If you found salaries to be high, for example, you might point that out and then adjust your model downward.

The property tax % can be found by researching the local tax rate and the management fee can be found by researching average property management fees in your local area or by speaking with a property management group that you are considering contracting to manage the property.

Liability Insurance can be obtained by reaching out to an insurance broker for an annual price to insure the property.

The Operating Reserve is cash set aside from the cashflow as savings for unexpected expenses. This figure may be computed as a percent of Effective Gross Income or a dollar amount per unit. In this model it shows a 2% reserve set aside from EGI.

Replacement Reserves represent money that is set aside in a reserve account for eventual replacement of building components. Some states require a minimum replacement reserve per unit per year if the property is constructed or purchased using certain government funding. See the Texas Administrative Code rule 10.404 regarding reserves accounts. In the state of Texas, the minimum reserve is $300/unit for rehabilitated developments. This rule is required so that property owners do not neglect regular maintenance and to ensure housing remains in sanitary, safe, and decent condition, suitable for occupancy. It is important to adjust your expenses for inflation which is why you see the model increases each year.

The next Subtotal is *Total Operating Costs* which sums all the Operating expenses into a total.

Computing Net Operating Income:

Effective Gross Income (EGI)	$782,210	$816,784	$841,288	$866,526	$892,522
Operating Expenses					
Leasing & Advertising	$4,573	$4,756	$4,946	$5,144	$5,350
On-Site Payroll	$37,440	$38,938	$40,495	$42,115	$43,800
General & Administrative	$18,132	$18,857	$19,612	$20,396	$21,212
Management Fee	$58,666	$61,259	$63,097	$64,989	$66,939
Legal & Accounting	$5,800	$5,974	$6,153	$6,338	$6,528
Utilities	$74,509	$77,489	$80,589	$83,812	$87,165
Contract Services	$5,000	$5,200	$5,408	$5,624	$5,849
Repairs & Maintenance	$17,460	$18,158	$18,885	$19,640	$20,426
Payroll Taxes & Benefits	$8,467	$8,806	$9,158	$9,524	$9,905
Miscellaneous	$500	$520	$541	$562	$585
Real Estate Taxes	$42,207	$43,051	$43,912	$44,790	$45,686
Property Liability Insurance	$7,200	$7,344	$7,491	$7,641	$7,794
Operating Reserve	$15,644	$16,336	$16,826	$17,331	$17,850
Replacement Reserve	$15,000	$15,000	$15,000	$15,000	$15,000
Total Operating Expenses	$310,598	$321,688	$332,112	$342,907	$354,088
Net Operating Income (NOI)	$471,612	$495,096	$509,176	$523,619	$538,433

See the Formula:

NOI = Effective Gross Income − Operating Expenses

NOI Margin = Net Operating Income/ Effective Gross Income

Now that the income and expense assumptions have been entered into the operating section, the formulas of the spreadsheet will compute a 5-year proforma of projected revenue, expenses, and net operating income so that investors and banks can understand potential income available to repay debt or return capital that has been invested. You can forecast income for many years into the future such as 10-year, 15-year, 20-year, or 30 years depending on how long you plan to hold the investment. The proforma will also be used to compute financial ratios that determine financial performance of the investment. Net Operating Income is a financial measure of high importance.

To Compute NOI, the Operating Expenses are deducted from the Effective Gross Income. All expenses that are part of the normal operations and management of the property are considered Operating Expenses. Capital Expenditures or money paid for major improvements to the property should not be included in NOI calculation. NOI represents the income that remains to pay debt/investors and make property improvements after operating expenses have been covered. The higher the NOI, the stronger the investment performance.

Repayment of Debt & Equity and Capital Expenditures:

Net Operating Income (NOI)	$471,612	$495,096	$509,176	$523,619	$538,433
Debt Service	$210,000	$270,607	$270,607	$270,607	$270,607
Debt Service with Capitalized Interest for 2	$0	$0	$71,910	$71,910	$71,910
Preferred Return	$150,000	$150,000	$150,000	$150,000	$150,000
Asset Management	$11,733	$12,144	$12,569	$13,009	$13,464
Net Cash Flow After Debt Service	$99,879	$62,346	$4,091	$18,094	$32,453

Capital Expenditures are major improvements to assets such as roof replacements or bathroom remodels. In this example, the model suggests that $46,000 has been spent on major renovations to each unit in the existing year so that the following year there will only be $300 per unit required to be held in replacement reserves. There are no capital expenditures shown in the first 5 years because the model assumes that there will be none required. If your property does not have new construction or major renovations at the start of the project, you should assume capital expenditures will be necessary. As an investor, I would ask to see photos of the current property condition and records of improvements made to ensure the property will truly be able to operate long-term without any additional capital invested for major improvements.

Asset Management Fees are deducted and will usually be between 1-2%. The asset manager, also known as the deal sponsor, may charge an asset management fee for their responsibilities including creating and managing the budget, collaborating with lenders, managing cash flows, and managing the portfolio of properties.

The asset manager responsibility is different from the property manager who would manage the payment of bills, the tenants, and maintenance related responsibilities.

Debt Principal Repayment and Interest Expense are both deducted from NOI because *Debt Service* reduces cash flow. NOI net of these line items is shown as Net Cash Flow. Investors would be interested in this line item on the Pro Forma because the net cash flow represents if the deal is strong and there is sufficient cash flow to repay all the debts and have available funding for the investors to receive their investment back plus the expected return. It is also an important number for deal sponsors because it represents the available profit remaining from the investment income.

As the debt is repaid, the principal balance of the debt would be reduced each year. You could create a separate tab of your spreadsheet to model an amortization of debt which is reduced yearly by the amount of Principal Repayment until the debt is fully repaid at the end of the term. Lenders would analyze this number to compute the available cash flow to repay bank loans and interests and to understand the term in which debt can be repaid in full based on the property operations.

Computing Financial Ratios:

After the Cash Flow has been computed, the Pro Forma can be used to generate financial ratios. This chart shows how the figures from the Income and Expense Analysis can be used to formulate various performance ratios.

OPERATING RATIOS	YR 1	YR 2	YR 3	YR 4	YR 5
Break-even Ratio	62.64%	68.68%	76.53%	75.49%	74.49%
Debt Service Coverage:	2.25	1.83	1.48	1.52	1.57
Gross Rent Multiplier (GRM)	3.29	3.16	3.07	2.98	2.89
Income Growth	--	4.00%	3.00%	3.00%	3.00%
Expense Growth	--	4.08%	3.72%	3.72%	3.72%
Credit/Vacancy Loss as % of EGI	-6.81%	-6.78%	-6.78%	-6.78%	-6.78%
EGI Per Unit Per Month	$1,304	$1,361	$1,402	$1,444	$1,488
Total Expenses Per Unit	$6,212	$6,434	$6,642	$6,858	$7,082
Total Operating Expenses Ratio	39.71%	39.38%	39.48%	39.57%	39.67%

Here is a list of potential financial ratios that can be computed using the figures from the Income and Expense analysis:

- Break-even Ratio
- Debt Yield
- Interest Coverage Ratio
- Debt Service Coverage Ratio
- Gross Rent Multiplier (GRM)
- Income Growth
- Expense Growth
- Credit/Vacancy Loss as a % of EGI
- EGI per Unit per Month
- Total Expenses Per Unit
- Total Operating Expenses Ratio
- Cap Rate

Once the Pro Forma is complete, various financial ratios can be computed using the figures to determine if the investment opportunity is a good one. The metrics shown in this example are just a few of the many analytics that can be extrapolated.

The *Break-Even Ratio* will show you the occupancy required to cover the debt and operating expenses.

The *Debt Yield*, Interest Coverage Ratio, and Debt Service Coverage Ratio (DSCR) are measures the bank uses to estimate the borrower's ability to repay the loan. The Debt Yield Formula includes the Net Operating Income divided by the total loan amount, which in this example was $4,500,000.

The *Interest Coverage Ratio* takes NOI divided by Interest Expense to see how many times the interest can be paid after the operating expenses are covered. This higher the ratio, the higher probability the interest will be paid.

The *Debt Service Coverage Ratio (DSCR)* is a measure of the ability to cover both interest and principal payments combined, known as Debt Service. Each lender will have a minimum ratio for the underwriter to feel comfortable making the loan. Increases or decreases in income or expense assumptions can have a big impact on these ratios, so pay attention to assumptions in your spreadsheet that drive these formulas.

Gross Rent Multiplier is a measure that will allow investors to compare multiple available investment opportunities amongst others. It divides the price of the property by the potential gross income.

The *Income Growth* and *Expense Growth* allow people reviewing the spreadsheet to quickly determine how income and expenses are increasing annually.

The *Credit / Vacancy Loss* as a % of EGI shows approximately what portion of rental income is conservatively assumed to be bad debt due to non-payment of rents. Your investors may give additional scrutiny to this measure depending on the location or income mix of the tenants that would be renting in your market area. For example, if your project is located in a low-income area, your credit/vacancy loss may be higher due to missed rent payments and evictions that might be more frequent than in an area with a higher average median income.

Effective Gross Rent per unit per month conveys approximately the average rent collected per unit, without regard to the unit size or bedroom count.

Total Expenses per Unit takes the total expenses and divides that number by the total units in the multi-family. In this example there are 50 units and in YR 1 the average annual expense for each unit is $6,212.

The *Operating Expense Ratio* is also an important financial measure to reveal the cost to operate a piece of property versus the income generated by the property. It is often measured against the industry average to determine if the assumptions in the model are reasonable or underestimated. The operating expenses in this multi-family example are roughly 40% of EGI. The industry average for multifamily would fall between 35% and 45% so this pro forma is accurately predicting justifiable amounts of expenses.

Cap Rate is a financial metric to compare the returns of multiple commercial properties against the others. The cap rate, though not shown in this sample, can be computed as the Net Operating Income divided by the Property Asset Value. The going in cap rate will divide the YR 1 projected NOI by the purchase price. The exit cap rate also known as the ***terminal cap rate*** will take the NOI at the final year by the expected property value in the year you intend to sell the asset.

See the Formulas:

Break Even Ratio =(Total Operating Expenses + Annual Debt Service) / Annual Effective Gross Income

Debt Yield = NOI / Loan Amount

Interest Coverage Ratio = NOI / Interest Expense

Debt Service Coverage Ratio (DSCR) = NOI / Debt Service

Gross Rent Multiplier = Property Acquisition Cost / Annual Potential Gross Rent

Effective Gross Income = Rent + Other Income – Vacancies

Operating Expense Ratio = Total Operating Expenses/EGI

Net Operating Income = EGI – Total Operating Expenses

Cap Rate = NOI / Property Value

As an investor creating or analyzing property deals, it is necessary to create your own proforma for each investment property to predict its income potential, cost, profitability, and ability to repay debts and return the initial investment before making an investment decision. The complexity of your model may vary, but a review of the financial credibility of the investment is necessary. Whether you are a math whiz or struggle with understanding math and finance this is still an important topic that requires mastery. This short review of financial analysis and projection is not sufficient for you to accomplish mastery. There are pro forma templates that you can find online that will guide you in your modeling or you can enroll in a course for further instruction. I encourage further study on this topic, practice building a sample pro forma, and having experienced third parties analyze your data before presenting to potential investors or proceeding with an investment decision.

STEP-BY-STEP PROCESS FROM OFFER TO CLOSING

Now that you have identified your investment strategy, property type, target market, financing sources and you understand the investment process and how to choose an investment property, you are ready to select your property, complete your due diligence, inspections, financial modeling, and then close the deal! Once you close the deal, you will officially become an investor! I will discuss the steps of acquisition of an investment property which will be relevant regardless of your exit strategy. If you are investing indirectly and obtaining a security or membership interest in a real estate related company you may not be the one executing these steps, but it is still important to understand the process that others will perform on your behalf.

1. **SUBMIT AN OFFER**
2. **NEGOTIATE THE DEAL**
3. **OBTAIN TITLE INSURANCE**
4. **FINANCE THE DEAL**
5. **OBTAIN PROPERTY INSURANCE**
6. **CLOSE THE DEAL**
7. **AVOID PITFALLS AND SCAMS**

1 - SUBMIT AN OFFER

A real estate sales agreement or a ***Purchase Agreement*** is a legally binding contract that buyers and sellers use to spell out the terms of a real estate transaction. The sales agreement may be promulgated by the real estate commission in your state or may be drafted by an attorney representing the owner or buyer. The details of the contract will include the following terms:
- Parties to the contract (buyer and seller names and contact information)
- Legal description of the property (lot and block, metes and bounds, address)
- Sales price and financing terms
- Earnest money including the purchase price offer and the agreed terms of purchase.
- Feasibility or option period and termination options
- Title company, title commitment, title notices, escrow agent, responsible party for payment of title (if title is applicable in your state)
- Attorney details
- Survey requirement or waiver and responsible party to pay
- Property condition disclosures (examples: property is in a flood zone or mud district, has deficient structures or non-functioning furnace, etc.)
- Acceptance of property condition and/or required repairs
- Access for inspections and utilities availability
- Brokers' fees (% of sales price or flat fee)
- Closing date
- Possession (at closing or guided by a lease)
- Special provisions (unique terms between buyer and seller)
- Settlement expenses
- Prorations and rollback taxes
- Casualty loss and Indemnification
- Default and terms of conflict resolution
- Federal tax requirements
- Contract addendum and notices
- Signature pages

In the state of Texas, The Texas Real Estate Commission promulgates a blank contract that buyers and/or their real estate agents can fill in to complete an offer to purchase with all the pertinent legal language already pre-written. The blanks in the contract can be filled in with the specific offer terms and then presented to the property owner as an offer to purchase. Consult the real estate law for your state to determine if a promulgated form exists. As a part of your homework, review the real estate sales agreement for your state so that you are familiar with the terms that can be negotiated when you are ready to submit an offer. As a licensed real estate agent, I encourage you to engage a licensed agent or attorney to assist you in the process of identifying, negotiating, and closing your property. The purchase agreement is a legal agreement and having a licensed professional's help can spare you costly mishaps or oversights. In the state of Texas, it is standard for real estate commissions to be paid for by the seller; however, with off-market unlisted properties the commissions may be paid by either party. Either way, factor your commissions into your pro forma and ensure that you engage the appropriate council to execute your purchase agreement.

2 - NEGOTIATE THE DEAL

After you submit a Purchase Agreement, the property owner has the option to accept your offer, reject your offer, or counteroffer. Sometimes negotiations are verbal via in person meetings or phone calls, mostly they happen through email where a marked-up contract is returned to the buyer with different terms. For a contract to be binding, it must be executed in writing and signed by all parties. Verbal agreements do not hold up in court, so it is important that all negotiations and terms discussed verbally be put in writing. It is permissible to mark up the purchase agreement with newly agreed upon terms and initial where changes have been made. Every area of the contract is negotiable even the parts that are promulgated or drafted by your attorney. As the buyer, read the details of the purchase agreement and all addenda. Ask questions, revise terms, and negotiate the contract to a mutually beneficial agreement that all parties can agree to execute. Remember, contracts are only agreed to when the contract is beneficial to both buyer and seller in some way. Parties who are so firm in their position typically don't make a deal. Know your bottom before making an offer and do not negotiate beyond the limits of your pro forma. It is important to negotiate with a logical evaluation of the market and not based on idealism. There is no perfect deal so be willing to make concessions to get a deal done if the deal can be profitable.

In a seller's market, the property owner has more leverage to demand terms that are favorable to them. This is especially true when the subject property is unique or has a desirable location and/or there is limited inventory of like kind. When a property is off-market and you have approached the owner who is unmotivated to sell, this is even more a fact. In a buyer's market, investors have more leverage to negotiate purchase price and contract terms because they have many options and can implement a take it or leave it approach to negotiations.

Unfortunately, at the time of writing this book, the US real estate market is in a definite seller's market and investors are competing amongst each other to purchase property because *Months' Supply of Inventory*, which is a measure of market supply, is at an all-time low. Months' Supply of Inventory (MSI) is a calculation that quantifies the relationship between supply and demand in a housing market. If new homes stopped entering the market, months' supply computes how many months it would take to burn through all the inventory. A balanced market is somewhere between 4 to 6 months according to ShowingTime.com. As of March 2022, the months' supply was at 2 months across the country indicating a strong sellers' market. This limited inventory has driven bidding wars amongst homebuyers and investors with the average home in North Texas selling for 4% over the asking price. In some cases, buyers are paying more than $100,000 over the seller's asking price to get a winning bid. Conditions vary nationwide and will change as trends in the real estate market and the overall economy balance. However, reference Months' Supply of Inventory to have an assessment of supply and demand at the time of your purchase.

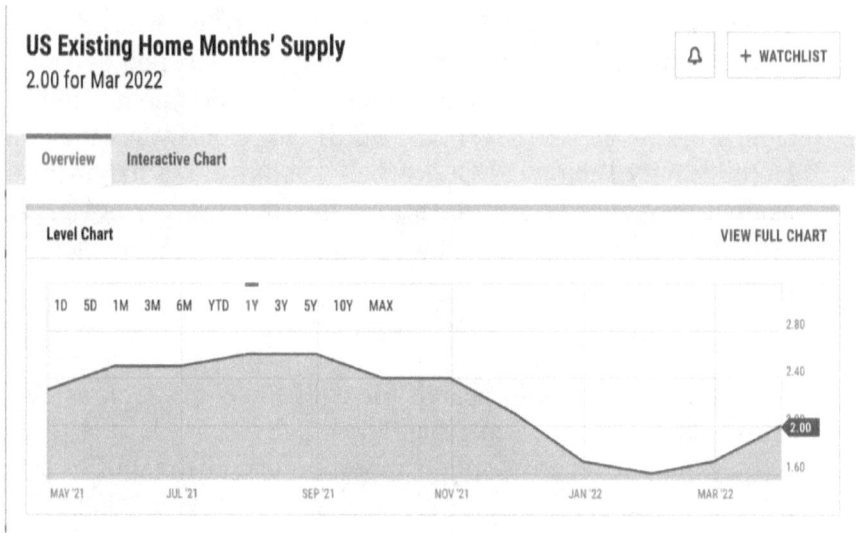

Chart Reference from Y-Charts.com

3 - OBTAIN TITLE INSURANCE

Title Policy
Once all parties sign the deal the next important step is to submit your contract to a title company to obtain a title insurance policy. Title Insurance is a form of indemnity insurance that protects lenders and buyers from financial loss due to defects in a title to a property. There are two types of title insurance: lender's title insurance and owner's title insurance. A lender's policy is almost always required in a transaction that involves a loan. The lender requires the borrower to purchase the lender's policy to protect them against loss because of defects in a title for which claims may arise at a future date from a third-party. The lender's policy only protects the lender against loss. An owner's title insurance policy is optional coverage that also protects the property owner and his/her heirs from financial and legal liability under the same circumstances and is available for additional cost. Title insurance

is sold through title agents who perform a title search, prepare a title commitment, and provide coverage through the issuance of a title policy. According to Florida's title insurance company, "coverage may include a fraudulent or forged prior deed, unpaid taxes, if an angry contractor filed a construction lien against the property, if someone's name is incorrect, if a past notary forgot to sign, a mortgage was never paid off, if the prior owners took out a Home Equity Line (HELOC) which was unpaid, a judgment lien against the seller was never paid, assessments were not paid, or any other such innumerable flaws that could impact your ownership."

Title Search
The title company will search for public records such as deeds, utility assessments, marriage and divorce decrees, court judgments, tax records, child support orders, abstract of titles and private records such as heirship affidavits and wills related to the contracted property to identify title defects such as liens, easements, incumbrances, or issues which might create a "cloud on the title." A lien is a burden on the title of a property resulting from an unpaid bill or judgment. An easement is the right for someone else to use the property such as the utility companies' easement for a gas meter in the backyard of a home or a neighbor's easement to use a shared access road to enter their property which is abutting yours. An encumbrance against your title might be things such as zoning laws, restrictive covenants, HOA rules, or other financial encumbrances placed upon the deed holder. The title search will identify clouds on the title which are problems and then attempt to resolve them before the deal closes. The title company will not insure a title that is defective until the clouds have been cured or the buyer has agreed to the exceptions placed on the title which limits coverage.

Title Commitment
"Title Commitment" is issued informing that the title company has *committed* to insuring the property. The title commitment spells out the terms and conditions upon which the title company will insure the title including any exclusions, exceptions, and

issues that must be addressed before closing. The title commitment will be provided to the lender and the buyer within the timeframe specified in the purchase agreement, and there will be contractual language that determines the length of time the owner and lender have allotted to review the title commitment and address the conditions or terminate the contract. For example, if the property has a restrictive covenant that prevents leasing, then the investor might terminate the contract if their intention of buying the property was to hold it for rent. If the buyer terminates because of a defective title or encumbrances that they do not agree to, then their earnest money would not be at risk and would more than likely be refunded based on the terms of the agreement. The title commitment is a lengthy document with many schedules. Be sure to read the title commitment immediately upon receipt, and the related schedules, and pay specific attention to name spellings, legal descriptions, coverage amounts, and encumbrances to the title. Look for conditions that must be cleared before closing which may impact the closing date or the ability to close altogether. Also, pay attention to any exclusions of coverage which may limit your protection. If you don't understand the title commitment, call the title agent, real estate agent or your attorney, and ask for clarity. Remember to do so in a timely manner as your response to the title commitment is time sensitive.

Title Fees

The rates that a title insurance company can charge will vary state to state. Some states regulate title insurance and set blanket rates across all carriers. In other states, the title insurance company may set their own rates and file them on record with the state insurance commissioner. A fee schedule can be shared upon request from your title insurance agent at the beginning of the transaction. It will also be provided at closing because of the **Real Estate Settlement Procedures Act (RESPA)** which provides consumers with improved disclosures of settlement costs to reduce the cost of closing by eliminating referral fees and kickbacks. Title fees can be paid by the seller or buyer of the property unless designated by the state to be paid by either party. In the state of Texas, it is customary for the seller to pay for title fees; however, in a sellers' market buyers make their offers stronger by offering to pay for their own title policy.

4 - FINANCE THE DEAL

Now that you have identified a property, contracted the property to purchase and are preparing to close, you must decide how you will pay for the property and any subsequent improvements, repairs or treatments to the property that will be required to operate the investment. If you have sufficient cash on hand or liquid assets in your investment, retirement, or insurance accounts you may be able to personally finance your project without the need of outside bank financing or private money debt or equity. Since 94% of home sales in 2021 used some type of financing and only 6% were purchased with cash, we will review the process of financing your deal with some form of debt. Even if you have cash on hand, you may find it wise to leverage the bank's financing in times when interest rates are lower than market yield.

We spent a great deal of time in Section 3 discussing the process of obtaining financing for your real estate investment deals. By now, you should have a good understanding of the process to apply for a loan and the criteria that the underwriter of a lending institution may consider as part of their approval process. You may have already had conversations with bankers to understand their underwriting guidelines and established a relationship with a particular banker or several bankers that you would like to consider financing your project. You should know your credit score, credit profile, personal net worth, annual and monthly income, sources of income, available assets, total debts, and your debt-to-income ratio. You should have already gathered the relevant documents that a bank may request as part of their application process including business formation documents, personal and/or business tax returns, business financial statements, personal and/or business bank statements, government identification, proof of income, court orders, judgements, or other applicable documents. See the complete list in *Section 3: Preparing to Obtain Financing for Your Deal.* In many cases, a banker will also require a pro forma, drawings, site plans and a construction budget if you are financing the construction or renovation of the project. Be prepared to provide those documents that pertain to your transaction. You may already be pre-approved or conditionally approved contingent upon final approval of the property. Some banks do not provide pre-approvals without having a formal loan application and the necessary project documents to consider; however, you may have received positive feedback from a loan officer outlining their process and giving you the greenlight to apply. If so, you have been following the guidance in this book and you are on track to proceed with financing your deal. You are ready to submit a formal application for a loan.

Obtain a Term Sheet

You can consider a bank application process as a two-way interview. The bank will review your personal and business financial documents and your property to ensure it is a lendable deal that makes sense for the bank. Likewise, you should be interviewing the bank to ensure their financing terms, closing timeline, loan servicing process, and customer service is sufficient to meet your needs. The most important of these to consider is the loan terms the bank has offered after review of your credit, income, assets, debt, and the loan request. This is usually presented on a term sheet. Since there are banks situated on major corners across the country and banks are competing with one another for business, you as the customer should expect a competitive offer to win your business. The bank should provide you with a written term sheet that specifies the interest rate, maturity date, amortization period, balloon payments, Loan to Value (LTV), required reserves, escrows, or other pertinent details of their offer. You should review these terms and apply with several banks so that you can leverage multiple offers to obtain the absolute best financing terms. Negotiate with your bank and push back if you do not agree with the terms of their offer. You do not have to finance your loan with the same bank that you have a checking or savings account with, nor do you have to be loyal to a bank you've had a longstanding relationship with if they are not offering you the best terms. If banks or their staff do not compete for your business or treat you like a valued customer, you do not owe them your business. Move on and find a bank that values you as the wealth creating investment mogul that you are in the process of becoming! Financing is relationship driven so build relationships with banking advocates that will fight for you in a loan committee and push for your approval.

Underwriting Process

After you have submitted your loan application, the loan officer will review your files to ensure you have a complete loan package and will then submit it to the underwriter. The underwriting process may take anywhere from 2 days to several months while the underwriter evaluates your credit history, assets, and overall financial health to determine the amount of risk the bank will assume by lending to you. The underwriter will also consider the size of your loan, the borrower's ability to repay the debt, the projected income, expenses, property value, and the guarantor's financial position. The underwriter will then submit a list of items required to be submitted and reviewed before the loan is approvable. The list may include but not be limited to:

- Appraisal Inspection & Report of Appraised Value – As Is
- Appraisal Inspection & Report of Appraised Value - Subject to Completion
- Property Condition Report
- Environmental Inspection, Phase I and/or Phase 2 Report
- Asbestos and/or Mold Inspection
- Survey
- Site Plans, Building Plans
- Scope of Work
- Construction Estimates
- Insurance Quotes and Policy Documents
- Flood Map Determination
- Financial Pro Forma and Cash Flow projections
- Development Budgets

- Resume of Developer, Investors, or Applicants
- Personal Net Worth Statements
- Title Commitment
- Review of Owner's Association Declaration of Covenant, Condition and Restriction Documents (CC&R's)
- Bank Statements, Investment Accounts or Sources of Capital
- Tax Transcripts

Equity or Cash Required

The bank may lend between 50-90% of the project cost, depending on the terms of their offer and the borrower or the borrowing entity will be required to bring the difference in cash, land, or property from existing real estate invested as part of the deal or pledged to secure the loan. Refer to Section 3 to identify the various sources where you could raise the required equity to close your loan. Many investors take on partners to invest capital into their deal for the required equity and then repay the investors out of the profits of their investment deal. For borrowers who intend to hold their property long-term, consider refinancing your project after the first 2-5 years to payback equity partners who want a shorter-term exit.

Loan Approval

Before closing your deal, you will need to obtain final loan approval and clearance to close. The process to get there may be an arduous journey and may even be a lengthy process taking several months; however, keep in mind the bank's intent is to ensure you have a solid investment project that can repay the debt and that the guarantors are financially positioned to repay the debt in the event the project does not actualize as presented. The loan officers, loan processors, underwriters, reviewers, and closers work as part of a team to pass your application through the various stages of the process to fund your loan. The banks do not earn your business unless your loan is approved, so lenders usually work diligently to clear objections and issues so that your loan can close. In a perfect situation, you will submit your loan application and be automatically approved. However, in situations where a loan is denied, it can be an indication that the project would not be successful in its current structure and can be taken as an additional layer of protection and prevention of a financial default. This is not always the case, sometimes denials are mechanically generated because some area of the project did not fit within the formulated approval ranges that a bank has established. Having a conversation with a decision maker may reveal the source of the denial and new information provided can lead to an approval.

If your loan is denied, ask detailed questions why the loan did not meet the requirements. Determine if the issue is the borrower, the property, or the investment structure. If the issue is found with the borrower, such as insufficient reserves, find out if you can add a guarantor or partner who has a greater net worth. Perhaps you did not provide the bank with all your savings, stock, and retirement account information and by doing so they will be informed about additional reserves that you have available. If the issue is with credit profile, find out if an explanation letter can be written to justify erroneous or out of date information that an underwriter may exclude from the credit review at their discretion. If the issue is with the borrower's income, perhaps you can provide greater transparency about other income sources such as bonuses, overtime pay, or raises that are approved but not yet funded. I had a client who entered their monthly income into an online application and was denied because she didn't realize she was supposed to enter her gross income before taxes were deducted. After the denial, I dug into the issue, corrected the mistake and her loan amount increased and she was automatically approved. I personally was denied for a loan because a review of historical tax returns showed a dip in income in the prior year which brought down my average income. I was heartbroken because my loan was denied just one day before I was contractually set to close. That evening while sleeping, God gave me wisdom in a dream to write a letter to the underwriter asking for an exception because I had been pregnant the prior year, suffered a difficult postpartum period and had taken off more than 6 months due to childbirth which resulted in a slump in my income. I woke up and quickly drafted my plea. After reading my letter, the underwriter met with their boss (who was a woman), they agreed to make an exception for me and changed their decision. By 10pm that same day I was closing my investment at my kitchen table with my one-year-old daughter there! I'm thankful I didn't accept their denial as final.

Sometimes a loan denial can be a result of an issue with the property such as a low appraisal. If so, find out if you can renegotiate the purchase price with the seller based on new information. If you can get the seller to agree to drop the price to the appraised value, your loan may be approvable. As an alternative, you may have access to additional assets that were not disclosed in your application that could be used to pay the additional funds needed to close or you may be able to contest the appraisal and get the value raised. If the issue is with the inspection report such as a deficient structure, roof, or environmental study, you may be able to get the seller to agree to make the necessary repairs prior to closing so that the lender will be appeased. I had a borrower recently help the seller clean their pool, clear their foliage in the yard and treat termite related issues so that the lender would approve their loan. This was all before closing because the lender had a condition for these repairs to be completed and the owner refused to make the necessary repairs. The borrower got the tools, got their hands dirty and did the work themselves to get their deal closed; all with the approval of the property owner, of course.

In some cases, the denial is a result of poor investment financials such as a weak Pro Forma that you have submitted. If the underwriting review shows that the project financial numbers do not support the loan or do not meet the minimum profitability and leverage ratios, then your loan might very well be denied. It is important to submit approvable financials upfront. Before submitting your pro forma, be sure to know the measures that your bank uses as their guidelines for approval. For example, if the debt coverage ratio is 1.5, you will want to be sure the NOI/Debt Service shown in the documents that you submit exceed these numbers. If it does not, for example, you may need to increase the rents or reduce the operating costs to increase the ratio. Have an advisor or an experienced investor review your financials before submitting them to the bank. Your loan officer may be willing to do a preliminary look to tell you if your project is approvable before officially submitting your application. There are also proforma classes that can be taken to increase your aptitude so that you can obtain the financing you need and ensure you are creating and/or investing in profitable deals.

Remember, each bank has different underwriting criteria and risk levels. It is good to shop your deal around so that you have options, regardless of the justification of the underwriter. Don't simply accept a denial and walk away until you have exhausted all your options. There are private money lenders that may be willing to take on more risk for a higher cost of capital. There may also be government incentives such as low-rate loans or grants that can strengthen your project and reduce the debt required. In a recent commercial development that I sponsored I was able to fund the deal using a capital structure that mixed several different funding sources. This caused the senior lender that was bringing most of the funds to become comfortable with the project and get on board quickly.

59%	Senior Debt from a Community Bank at 5.25% Rate
21%	2nd Note from Local Government at 1% Rate
5%	Equity Raised from Local Investors
8%	Local Government Grant
7%	Deal Sponsor's Investment from Company Assets
100%	Funded

Consider early on the ideal capital structure of your investment and have conversations with your lenders, business partners, and local advocates in ways that you may structure your deal to maximize profitability, reduce risk, and gain approval.

Special Financing for POC

Lending discrimination has suppressed the potential wealth of Blacks, Hispanics, and other racial & ethnic groups, and has contributed to the racial wealth gap in America. Studies have shown that Black and Hispanic applicants are often regularly denied for mortgages than white borrowers. According to a report from TheMarkUp.org, a 2018 study of Philadelphia mortgages showed that black applicants were almost 3 times as likely to be denied a mortgage. When looking at nationwide findings, Black people were 1.8 times as likely to be denied, Latinos were 1.4 times as likely to be denied, Native Americans were 1.7 times as likely to be denied, and Pacific Islanders were 1.5 times as likely to be denied. This systemic barrier to ownership has been directly correlated to racism and bias of the lawmakers, bankers, appraisers, or other persons involved in the lending decisions. It is unfortunate that historically Blacks and Hispanics have automatically been deemed a higher credit risk rating to lending institutions because of unspoken biases, hatred, and racism that has persisted even until today. Minorities have further been hindered from ownership by lower net worth, lower per capita income in minority neighborhoods on average, and disinvestment in some predominantly minority neighborhoods that reduced property values versus predominantly white neighborhoods. The Wealth Gap is a two-sided coin where on one side the disparity in wealth has made it more difficult for minorities to own, and on the other side of the coin, the inability to obtain property has further expanded the wealth gap pushing minorities further away from white counterparts. We must address these realities head on so that we can overcome them.

Lending discrimination occurs when a lender bases credit decisions on other factors beyond the borrower's credit worthiness. It includes the denial of financial services in neighborhoods due to race or ethnicity. Less than a century ago, redlining was approved by the federal government where maps of minority neighborhoods were marked with a red circle and lending institutions were encouraged to deny loans in these neighborhoods citing minority borrowers as a higher credit risk. The Fair Housing Act of 1968 was enacted to outlaw redlining; however, lending discrimination still exists as reflected by the gap in loans made in minority communities and disparities of ownership by race and ethnicity. I have reported to you that banks have told me outright, "we don't make loans in that neighborhood." So, I know redlining still exists. The Equal Credit Opportunity Act (ECOA) of 1974 was written to make it illegal for creditors to discriminate based on color, race, religion, national origin, sex, marital status, age, or because of public assistance. The Community Reinvestment Act of 1977 was enacted to address overt and persistent discrimination in the mortgage lending process. Because of this law, there is a record card that keeps score with regular evaluation of banks' performance in making loans in low-to-moderate income neighborhoods. I have spoken with enough bank managers personally to know that they struggle to get their CRA credits and are always seeking creative ways to find borrowers who meet CRA guidelines. This is a conundrum to me because all they have to do is simply look up to see all the black and brown people with their hands up eager to be financed.

Lending discrimination has been addressed through these laws that have been enacted to reduce systemic barriers to ownership but there is still more work to be done. The Comma Club Community is an investor community that aims to stimulate ownership and increase wealth opportunities through real estate and investment education, empowerment, advocacy, and awareness. It is important that each of you individually understand the barriers that exist and press against them with preparation, mastery, resilience, and hope. If one bank says no, there may be another bank that will fund your deal in its exact structure simply because the decision maker is empowered to approve the file changes.

There are community credit unions and Community Development Financial Institutions (CDFIs) that are sometimes able to use more flexible lending requirements such as higher LTV and DTI ratios, lower credit scores, and take on greater risk for people of color, women, or people who fall within disenfranchised investment areas or people groups. The Capital Impact is a good example of a national lending institution that is working hard to deliver capital to support investors and developers in underinvested communities. Visit www.CapitalImpact.org for more information about their loan programs.

The JPMorgan Chase & Co has committed to lend $30 Billion by 2025 to advance economic growth and opportunity for Black, Hispanic, and Latino communities. According to their Black and Hispanic Wealth Summit, JPMorgan Chase & Co is committed to helping close the racial wealth gap and driving economic inclusion by providing more opportunities for homeownership, access to affordable housing, entrepreneurship and bolstering financial health. Take advantage of their programs that aim to support minority buyers, investors, and business owners. Learn more at https://www.jpmorganchase.com/impact/racialequity.

For small businesses start-ups, the Small Business Association (SBA) is a great place to start for financing. The SBA will guarantee debt up to 80-90% giving conventional lenders the confidence to take risks on new borrowers. https://www.sba.gov

For properties located in a majority minority neighborhood or low-to-moderate income tract, your bank may offer a CRA product with special financing terms. This is not often publicized as a CRA product so be sure to ask your bankers if they offer CRA loans or special financing for loans made in these areas.

Loan Funding

Upon approval of your loan, your bank will wire the funds needed to close your investment purchase to your escrow agent, such as a title officer, who will hold the funds until the note, the deed of trust, title work and other property documents are notarized and executed by all parties involved in the transaction. Loans typically fund within a few hours of signing the documents. The escrow agent will then disburse the loan to the appropriate parties as dictated by the contract.

5 - OBTAIN PROPERTY INSURANCE

As soon as you contract a property to purchase, it is imperative to evaluate the insurability of the property and the cost to insure the property. Any lender will require the property be properly insured and that the mortgagee clause be added to the policy. You will want to know immediately what types of property insurance are required to purchase, construct, or make renovations and to protect your investment. In an earlier topic about ***Building Your Team,*** we did an expansive review of the various types of insurance that are available and sometimes necessary for your company and your team. Your insurance broker should be able to take an application and collect information including the insured party's contact information, the property address, the property value, condition of property, and other questions they may have and then they will provide you with a quote for their recommended insurance. The insurance broker should also be able to run a report that will determine if there have been prior claims made on the property which may reveal hidden issues that you were not aware about such as flooding, fire damage, structural damage, or other hazards. If the insurance broker's report reveals the property falls within a low elevation or near a body of water, you may be required or encouraged to purchase flood insurance which would be a separate policy. Your lender may mandate amounts of insurance and/or certain types of policies based on the specifics of your project or property. It is important to be as informed as possible about your insurance requirements within your due diligence period. I had one client who learned that a property they were purchasing required a $6,000 annual flood policy because of a creek that was situated behind the home which placed half the property in a flood plain. They were not prepared to pay this additional fee; therefore, they were able to terminate the purchase contract within their allotted due diligence period and received a refund of their earnest money.

As you prepare to hire a general contractor or any construction teams to perform work on your property after closing, start the conversation about their insurance to cover property damage, injuries, or other unforeseen problems. Your general contractors should have workers compensation insurance for their subcontractors or workers, auto insurance for any vehicles they will be using to transport their workers, general liability insurance, and in some cases insurance bonding to protect you against incomplete work.

Your lender may require that you pay for annual policies directly with your insurance company, or they may escrow the funds on your behalf to ensure the policies are always in effect and do not lapse. Either way, you should keep your properties insured starting immediately the day of closing. Be sure to set your policy effective date for the day of closing, even if you will not take possession of the property until a future date.

Annually, re-evaluate your coverage, shop around if your rates have changed, and keep your lenders informed about changes in policies.

6 - CLOSE THE DEAL

We have arrived at an exciting part of the journey, **CLOSING**! Closing means you have completed innumerable steps and made it the full distance to become an owner and you can officially call yourself an investor! Closing means you have obtained the approval from your banks, equity investors, partners, family and/or friends to take possession of the property that you have worked diligently to possess. Closing means you have signed the deed which is a legal record transferring property ownership to you or a company that you have invested in. Closing means that you have taken on the responsibility to manage, improve, operate, and/or build your project with the vision & faith that it will be an investment that is profitable, impactful and worth the effort.

Congratulations are in order! Whether you are reading this section for the first time and imagining yourself on Closing Day, walking through this guidebook as you close your first deal, or adding to your portfolio and expanding your empire, I am proud of you for your accomplishment.

Here is a list of what to expect on **Closing Day:**

Final Inspection: Before signing, visit the property to inspect for vacancy, damage or changes in condition, completion of all required repairs, removal of seller's possessions, or simply to verify that the property is still standing. If you cannot physically be present, send a representative to tour the property on your behalf or hire an inspector to reinspect prior to closing.

Final Credit Pull: Many lenders will pull a credit report just before closing to see if the borrower's credit profile has changed. The closer will check for new negative items such as late payments, missed payments, or collections and will verify that the borrower still meets the underwriting guidelines for debt-to-income ratio and credit score. The review will look to see if borrowers or guarantors have taken on new debt, opened new credit lines, or balances of existing accounts have increased. This is a forewarning: do not open new credit card accounts; do not borrow funds; do not spend using your credit cards; do not make vehicle, furniture or other large purchases using credit; do not borrow your cash to close using personal accounts. Slight changes to your credit profile or debt balances can cause the lender to reverse their loan decision.

Cash Due at Closing: Your escrow agent will provide you with a settlement statement that shows the breakdown of your closing costs and the amount of cash you will need to bring to the closing table. The escrow agent will also inform you of using acceptable payment methods such as a bank wire or a cashier's check. The escrow agent will provide the wire instructions and due to wire fraud, be certain to call and verify the account numbers before sending funds via wire. The bank may verify and trace the source of your funds before closing so be prepared to provide documentation for the accounts that you will use to withdraw the funds. Check wire cutoff times in advance to ensure you have access to the funds needed by the date of closing.

Sign Closing Documents: The Buyer and Seller will be required to sign the closing packet of documents that may include loan documents, title documents, government documents, disclosures, and statements. Read the documents thoroughly before signing and ask questions to your real estate agent, loan officer, or title officer if you are unsure about something written in the documents. Errors are often found in closing documents, including names, addresses, figures, terms, and rates even after review by various parties prior to signing. All errors will need to be amended to validate the change, do not sign until you are totally in agreement to what is written in the documents. You will be legally bound to what is written, not what is verbally stated. As a tip, ask to receive the loan documents 24 hours before closing day to give ample time for you to read them without rushing and have errors changed so that closing will not be delayed. Some of the documents will be notarized by a licensed notary at the closing.

Verify Insurance: Be sure to verify effective dates of your insurance policies and update them to the day of close if closing is delayed or moved earlier.

Connect Utilities: Connect utilities or transfer service into the new owner's name and be sure important utilities like water, power, trash, gas, and sewage are on. Breaks in power and water can be hazardous to the property especially in extreme heat and cold where pipes may freeze over, or mold can grow in dark warm areas.

Document Review: The lender's closing department will review all the signed documents and approve the loan for funding. If there are missing or illegible signatures, or errors in the documents, the lender will require the documents to be resigned. Upon completion of the review and approval, the bank will wire their loan to the escrow agent who will then receive approval to disburse.

Funding Disbursement: Even after signing your loan documents, you will not receive the keys and the permission to occupy the property until the loan is funded and disbursed. Sometimes when parties sign later in the day, funding and disbursement can carry over to the next day or if it is a weekend, it can carry over to the following Monday. If the Monday is a bank holiday, disbursement can carry over to the Tuesday of the following week. For this reason, attempt to close earlier in the day so that the lender can review documents, fund the loan, and the escrow agent can disburse to all parties before the wire cut-off time. Upon disbursement, funds will be paid to the various parties shown on the settlement statement including the seller, real estate brokers, title agents, attorneys, government entities, taxing authorities, and others that may be due payment. All liens against the property and debts will be settled at closing.

Get the Keys!!! If you are buying a property with a structure, you will receive the keys at closing or sometime after funding. Congratulations. Keys represent access, authority, and the right of possession. There is nothing like holding the keys in your hands for the first time! Your contract will specify if you have the right to immediate possession at closing or if your right to access the property is subject to an existing lease agreement.

Deed Recording: Your deed will be e-recorded in the county where your property is located and may be filed in person if the electronic submission is not accepted. You will receive a copy of the recorded deed and the title policy in the mail approximately 30 days after closing.

Notate Important Dates: Your loan documents will include important information such as your loan payment due date, amount, and payment address. Be sure to note this information on the day of closing so that you can schedule for payments to be automatically drafted from your bank accounts.

7 - AVOID PITFALLS AND SCAMS

In your zeal to pursue a new, exciting path toward wealth don't fall victim to pitfalls and scams that incredulous deal makers may deal you. Promises and guarantees should be your first red flag to watch out for because in the investment game there is always risk of failure or loss to consider. I find it common for new inexperienced investors to rush into deals without doing the work to investigate, evaluate, or test the assumptions that drive the deal. Many investors make hasty decisions that are ill-informed. Rather than asking questions and taking the time to do proper research, they follow the promise of a perfect opportunity and are bated into a bad deal. In the Comma Club Community, there is no room for ignorance or laziness! Read everything that is presented to you, ask in-depth questions, and if you don't understand the answer, ask twice. Rely on professional advisors such as real estate brokers, attorneys, experienced investors, financial advisors, wealth managers, accountants, and trusted friends. My desire is that the Comma Club Community will become a repertoire of real estate investor resources, case studies, and a database of trusted industry providers that you can call upon for further guidance. Until we grow to that scale, you will have to proceed with caution.

As a new and very enthusiastic investor, I once raised $2 million from within my network to invest into a multi-million-dollar development project, led by a dubious deal sponsor, that I'm now convinced was a scam. The deal sponsor may or may not have been a con artist, but something about his perfect deal did not add up. On the phone, his pitches to the investor group seemed perfect. Tours of the land proved to be promising and the excitement of our investment group was over the top! I felt a complete block every time I prayed about the deal. Counselors cautioned me to withhold my investment until after I had peace. At a sit-down dinner at the finest restaurant in town, I berated the deal sponsor with questions until his demeanor revealed an inner secret. He was hiding something. I thank God that he surrounded me with wise and discerning pastors, counselors, attorneys, and friends to advise me to walk away despite what it would cost me. I forfeited millions in potential profits, tens of thousands in legal expenses, and even risked my reputation as a businesswoman. By doing so, I protected 50 people from losing their hard-earned money and I avoided a pitfall early in my investment career. That lesson has stuck with me years later as a guiding principle of thought. Now, I am led by the peace of God in all my investment decisions. I don't care what the numbers say or how good the opportunity sounds, if I don't have peace, I won't do it. I encourage you to pray about every opportunity and wait until you have peace with your decision before you proceed. Some people refer to this as a gut feeling, others hear clearly from God in very individual ways and know when they have the green light to move. However, you choose, just accept this advice as your forewarning that scammers do exist.

ANSWER THESE PRECAUTIONARY QUESTIONS:

I encourage you to ask these questions as you evaluate every investment opportunity that you have within reach:

1. What is it that I don't know that I don't know? Where are my blind spots?

2. Have I read all the deal information and I do understand it all? Have I highlighted questions and returned to ask further questions?

3. What are my primary concerns? If I have no concerns, what is it that gives me such confidence?

4. Am I being driven toward this opportunity by the promise of a perfect deal or am I cautiously evaluating the risks and making a calculated decision on my own?

5. What is the character of the person that is leading this opportunity? What is their performance history? What do other trusted individuals say about their character?

6. Am I looking at what the deal sponsor has financially or am I truly considering the merit of this deal on its own?

7. After reading the proforma, what happens if the assumptions change? Market fluctuations? Costs change?

What is driving profits and what happens if those drivers change?

8. Who have I consulted that is unbiased in their counsel and wise enough to help me evaluate this deal?

9. Do I have peace about the decision to move forward, and if I don't, why?

10. Does this investment line up with my investment plan, target market, area of expertise, and budget?

11. Am I investing an amount that I can lose and continue with life normally?

WHAT HAPPENS WHEN THE DEAL FALLS APART?

Deals sometimes fall apart in the process of evaluating, inspecting, financing, and closing the property. Every deal that seems great at first isn't suitable for investment and that's okay. It is better to evaluate a deal with a clear head and walk away before closing day than to force a bad deal to work. In your process of working through the steps from contract to closing, you may learn new information that indicates the title may not be clear, there could be unexpected repairs needed, the bank may not be willing to finance the deal, the investment may not be as profitable as you projected, or a slew of other issues. Depending upon the contingencies allowable in your purchase agreement, you *may* have the right to terminate your contract and recoup the initial deposit that was paid. There are some contingencies such as the option period, due diligence or feasibility period or financing period that allow you to gather information about the property, renegotiate the deal based on new information and/or terminate without penalty if you no longer want to purchase the property. It is important to review the dates and contingencies allowed in your contract *before* signing so that you can avoid losing money on bad deals that do not make it to the closing table. Knowing these dates *in advance* of signing can position you to utilize your contingency periods to complete the necessary due diligence to ensure you are making a wise investment decision. During these periods where the contract permits an exit and refund of your initial deposit, you may research the property condition, title, repair cost, financing terms, and obtain approval within a timely manner as to not pass the cutoffs times within your contingency agreement.

Smart investors expect for some deals to go bad, and some even play a numbers game making offers on multiple properties then closing only the deals that are a good fit. Like catching some fish to cook and some to throw back in the water. Whether you take this approach or not, understand that not every deal will be a homerun and be willing to terminate if your better judgment, training, and advisors say so.

If your promising deal falls apart before you make it to the closing table, stop and evaluate the lessons before you start again.

GENERATING INCOME ON INVESTMENTS

Everyone reading this book is interested in one topic: how to generate income and build wealth through real estate investments. You may have other goals to achieve as part of your real estate investment journey, but to be an effective investor and developer, you must be profitable and earn income.

Depending on your investment approach, you may not be immediately profitable. There may be a holding period that takes months to several years to recoup your initial investment and see a return on your investment. Let's discuss how to generate income with the various investment approaches and recap the earnings formulas in section 2.

ACTIVE INVESTMENT STRATEGIES

BRR(R) Strategy

The Buy, Rehab, Rent (Refinance) strategy allows investors to profit from ongoing cash flow generated from the rental income and the equity earned from long-term property appreciation as values rise over time. Using the BRR(R) strategy, the investor purchases property, makes the necessary renovations, and rents the property to tenants for an amount that is high enough to cover the mortgage (if financed) and all expenses to maintain and manage the property.

The investor receives cash flow which is computed as the rental income less the mortgage and property taxes, capital expenditures, and operating expenses. This formula can be applied to residential or commercial properties that are rented to others including single-family homes, duplexes, apartments, retail strips, office complexes, medical buildings, salon suites or any other property classification where you rent space to a tenant. The property classification may require additional operating expenses that are not shown in the example below. Checkout the formula to compute your potential cash flow on your investment property.

Example to Compute BRR(R) Rental Income Profit:

	$3,000 monthly rent x 12 months	= $36,000 annual rental income
-	$1,200 monthly mortgage x 12 months	= $14,400 annual mortgage cost
-	$36,000 annual rent x 8% management fee	= $ 2,880 annual property mgmt
-	$5,600 annual Property Taxes	= $ 5,600 annual property taxes
-	$1,500 annual Insurance	= $ 1,500 annual insurances
-	$3,000 hvac repair + $800 water heater	= $ 3,800 repair/maintenance cost
-	$1,200 lawncare + $400 pest control	= $ 1,600 landlord expenses
	Profit on BRR(R) Rental Property	= **$ 6,220 annual rental profit**

If you are unsure about the amount to charge for rent, start from the bottom of the formula and work your way up to the top. Insert your best estimates for the property expenses using historical bills or tax reports and insert your expected profit. This can help you figure the minimum amount of rent you must charge to meet your profit goals. If you do not plan to finance your investment, remove the mortgage payment from the formula.

Investors who purchase property using cash will have greater out-of-pocket costs to acquire the property but avoid a mortgage payment and owing interest to a lender. Although upfront costs are higher, cash paying investors net a higher monthly cash flow than investors who use bank financing. Alternatively, investors who finance investments have a greater ROI when using the Cash-on-Cash formula because their initial cash investment is lower than the investor who pays cash. They also benefit if they hold the property for the life of the loan (5-30 years) and use the tenant's rent to eventually pay off the note. At whatever point the property is free and clear of debt, the investor will eliminate the mortgage expense and their cash flow increases.

Measure Return on Investment

To measure your annual **Return on Investment** you may use a formula called the *Cap Rate*. The Cap Rate is a common metric to measure the relationship between the net operating income of a property and its cost or value. The Cap rate assumes a cash purchase and does not factor in debt such as mortgages.

Cap Rate = Net Operating Income / Initial Investment

In this scenario let's assume your initial investment was paid in cash and you spent $250,000 on this investment. $200,000 was used to purchase the property and $45,000 was paid for improvements and $5,000 were paid in closing costs. We will use the same operating expenses shown in the previous formula, but we will exclude the mortgage payment and repair costs. Remember that NOI is calculated as your Rental Income – Property Expenses and should not consider mortgage principal, interest expense, amortization, depreciation, or capital expenditures.

$36,000 annual rental income
- $ 2,880 annual property mgmt.
- $ 5,600 annual property taxes
- $ 1,500 annual insurance
- $ 1,600 landlord expenses

= $ 24,340 Net Operating Income

Cap Rate = $24,340/ $250,000 = 9.7% Return

Now let's assume a different scenario. What if you financed the same property instead of paying cash? The cap rate does not factor in debt or any financing, so this will not be the appropriate formula to use. Instead, measure your return using the cash-on-cash formula which factors in your annual cash generated against your initial cash invested:

Cash on Cash = Annual cash flow / Initial Cash Invested

To determine your Cash-on-Cash return, take annual cash flow after the mortgage and all property expenses have been deducted from the rental income and divide it by your initial cash investment. Remember the annual cash flow was $6,220. Assume the bank was willing to finance 80% of the purchase price and 80% of the improvements and required you to invest a 20% down payment.

$200,000 + $45,000	= $245,000 Purchase Price + Improvements
$245,000 x 20%	= $ 49,000 Down payment paid in Cash
$49,000 + $5,000	= $ 54,000 Down payment
+ Closing Costs	= Initial Cash Invested

Cash on Cash = $6,220 / $54,000 = 11.5% Return

This means the property's annual return will be 11.5% of the initial cash investment. This cash-on-cash formula factors in debt and allows investors to make quick computations of anticipated profit of an investment based on available data. As you can see, in this same scenario, the cash investor received a lower return than the investor who financed.

There are also opportunity costs to consider because the cash used to purchase this property could have been invested elsewhere earning a higher rate of return than the cost of capital. If the average out of pocket cost to purchase a property is $54,000, then the cash investor could have financed four to five rental properties with the $250,000 cash they used to purchase one property without financing.

Gains from Property Value Appreciation

Investors who hold the property long term anticipate an appreciating asset with an amortizing debt that is being paid off by the rental income. Investors benefit by owning the asset while the rental income generated is used to pay the debt. The difference between the market value of the asset and the debt owed on that asset is the equity which you can add directly to your net worth.

Your accountant will record the property value differently when reporting your balance sheet and will use a term called ***book value***, which is the original acquisition cost plus capital improvements made to prepare the asset for use minus accumulated depreciation. The market value may fluctuate over time, but these gains and/or losses will only be recognized at the time of sale.

In order to know the true market value of your property, you may need to order periodic appraisals and watch the market data of properties that sell near yours. A wise investor will hold their property until the market value has increased significantly and the property can be sold profitably. Investors that hold their properties for more than twelve months will avoid short-term capital gains tax as well. For properties owned longer than twelve months, the owners will be subject to long-term capital gains taxes which charge 0-20% tax rate against the profits. Taxes should be considered prior to selling your property. *I advise you to consult a tax accountant prior to listing your property for sale.* We will consider taxes in a later chapter.

At the opportune time, you may decide to sell your property for various reasons. Here is a method that you can use to compute your gain at sale:

Formula to determine Your BRR(R) Return on Investment when selling your property:

Sale Price of Property
- Outstanding Mortgage Payoff Amount
- Selling Costs (Transaction Fees, Attorney Fees)
- Closing Costs
- Real Estate Broker Commissions
- Title Fees
- Negotiated Buyer Credits or Concessions in the Contract
- Unpaid Property Taxes Prorated

Net Proceeds at the time of Sale

- Initial Investment (cash down payment or capital invested)
- Capital Improvements (don't double count if repairs were financed)
- Capital Gains Tax

Net Profit Earned on BRR(R)

Remember that the Buy, Rehab, Rent strategy also has the option to refinance the property to liquidate the equity that has been generated from the property's appreciation or improvements. Some investors refinance the property immediately after completing improvements and renting the property to recoup some or all their upfront invested capital.

As the property continues to rise in value, you may be able to continue to refinance the property to liquidate increases in equity via a cash out refinance loan. Banks generally allow you to cash out 75%-80% of the equity. Any cash that you liquidate will need to be repaid as part of your increased mortgage balance; however, the debt should be covered by rental income that is generated from the rental property, allowing you to profit from your property while your tenant is indirectly responsible for repayment of the debt. Furthermore, the equity that is liquidated can then be used to purchase more properties, expanding your portfolio and multiplying your profits.

Formula to determine liquidated equity when refinancing your property:

Market Value of the Property x 75% - 80%
- Outstanding Mortgage Payoff Amount
- Closing Costs
- Title Fees
- Unpaid Escrow Balances

Proceeds from cash out refinance at the time of Sale

Fix and Flip Properties

The Fix and Flip strategy allows the investor to benefit through short term appreciation, any increases in value because of improvements to the condition of the property, and local demand for a property of its quality, design features and price. Flipping properties differs from the BRR(R) method because the investor purchases the property with the intent to sell it rather than hold and rent it after the rehab.

The idea of flipping a property is derived from the concept of flipping a pancake. The strategy assumes that the market is hot enough for you to flip it quickly to a new buyer at a higher price. Because of the short-term ownership model, investors implementing the fix and flip investment strategy should prepare to pay short-term capital gains tax, which will be calculated as ordinary income and charged at the tax rate determined by their income tax bracket. Flipping properties can generate high investment income, and subsequently higher taxes as well. So, factor in the cost of taxes ahead of time and be prepared to pay a substantial amount of your profits in taxes to the IRS.

Formula to Determine Your Fix and Flip Profit

Sale Price of Remodeled Home

- Outstanding Mortgage or Construction Loan Payoff Amount
- Selling Costs (Loan Fees, Attorney Fees)
- Closing Costs
- Real Estate Broker Commissions
- Title Fees
- Negotiated Buyer Credits or Concessions in the Contract
- Property Taxes Prorated

= Net Proceeds at Time of Property Sale

- Upfront costs out of pocket (down payment, etc.)
- Cost of Improvements (labor and/or materials) paid out of pocket
- Closing Costs Paid at time of Purchase
- Investor Paid commissions, or assignment fees paid at the time of Purchase
- Other audit accounts or notes payable associated with property
- Holding Costs (Interest, Electricity, Gas, Water, Utilities Connection Fees)
- Insurance Premiums
- Marketing Fees

= Profit Earned on Fix and Flip

New Construction

Some developers focus on acquiring land and building new structures such as houses, hotels, and commercial strip centers, that they sell after completing construction. Reasons why developers might focus on building new construction versus rehabbing an existing structure include realizing a higher resale value, lower acquisition cost, duplicability, ease to scale, location, and availability of land. Some developers may also strategically hold their property for rental income and sell after the property values in the surrounding area have risen. Here is a formula to determine the new construction profits, assuming the land is already developed and suitable for building and that the investor sells the property after the property is built.

Formula to Determine Your New Construction Profit

Completed Construction Sales Price
- Lot Acquisition Cost
- Total Hard Costs (Site Work, Foundation, Framing, Systems, Finishes, Final)
- Total Soft Costs (Survey, Design Fees & Blueprints, Permits, Legal Fees, Warranty)
- Holding Costs (Insurance, Utilities, Interest Expense)
- Real Estate Broker Commissions
- Title Fees / Closing Fees
- Negotiated Buyer Credits or Concessions in the Contract
- Property Taxes Prorated

Profit Earned on New Construction

Land Development

Land development involves buying raw land and developing it for commercial or residential use. Land development can be a profitable investment strategy because land may increase in value over time as result of the developer's improvements to its infrastructure and/or platting the land and subdividing it into smaller lots that can be sold individually at a higher price than the land originally cost. Some developers can group land from various owners and sell larger plats of it at a higher price than the individual parcels.

Formula to Determine Your Land Development Profit

Cash flow from Sale of Developed Lots
- Cost to Acquire Undeveloped Land, Escrows and Fees
- Cost of Environmental Studies
- Cost of Land Survey
- Cost for Architectural Planning
- Third Party Appraisals Fee
- Attorney Fees
- Engineering and Design Costs
- Professional Service Agreement with Municipality
- Permits & Fees
- Insurance and Bonding Costs
- Cost of Infrastructure Materials and Labor
- Landscaping and Maintenance of Property
- Selling Costs and Commissions
- Holding Costs

Profit on Land Development

Short-term Rentals

When you own a property and use it as a short-term rental, you not only benefit from monthly rental cash flows but also from the increase in equity over time. Remember, equity is the difference between your asset value and the debts you owe. Over time, equity in the property grows because you are using the monthly rental income to pay off your debt obligations each month while the property simultaneously rises in value due to market appreciation. Even if the market experiences decline in the short-term, empirical data proves that over long periods of time, the market rises consistently, and properties become more valuable.

The goal of investing in a short-term rental investment strategy is to generate a higher nightly income than you would generate by renting the property with a yearly term. Even if the rental is not booked every single night of the year, the average nightly rate multiplied by the average number of nights booked should equate to a higher cash flow than a fixed rental payment with a long-term tenant. When it comes to profitability, short term rental profit is correlated to the property's occupancy. Therefore, it is extremely important to maintain consistent reservations, a positive customer experience, and obtain 5-star guest reviews.

Some cities are starting to approve more restrictive housing policies, permitting requirements, and added taxes imposed upon property owners of short-term rentals. Be sure to include all these costs for the city ordinances/permits when computing your potential profit.

If you occupy your home and rent the bedrooms or guest home while living in the property, you may generate even greater profitability by performing the cleaning services and utilizing the same utilities, subscription services, and maintenance work that you would already be expending for your own use. Homeowners that live in coastal areas, destination locations, or areas with expensive housing costs can cash in on their spare bedrooms in exchange for the discomfort of house guests. I have a friend who helped pay for her wedding by temporarily renting out her 3-bedroom home in the months prior to her wedding day. These newlyweds settled into their residence happily because they used this smart investment strategy to avoid the debt other couples commonly incur.

Formula To Determine Your Short-Term Rental Profit

Cash flow from Nightly Rentals
- Web Hosting & Booking Fees
- Monthly Rent or Mortgage Expenses
- Utilities (Lights, Water, Gas, Cable, Internet)
- Furniture & Equipment Rentals (If Applicable)
- Property Management Fees (paid per booking or % of revenue)
- Cleaning Fees (Fee Per Booking X Number of Bookings)
- Landlord or Renters Insurance
- General Liability Insurance
- Subscription Services (Netflix, Hulu)
- Landscaping, Pool Cleaning and Maintenance of Property
- Refunds and Guest concessions
- Repairs
- Parking fees (If applicable)

= Monthly Profit
x 12 months

= Annual Profit on Short Term Rentals

When you own a property and use it as a short-term rental, you not only profit from monthly rental cash flows, but you also benefit from the increase in equity over time. Remember equity is the difference between your asset value and the debt you owe to operate your business. As stated previously, your equity in the property grows because you use the monthly rental income to pay off your debt obligations each month while simultaneously the home rises in value due to market appreciation. Even if the market experiences declines, over long periods of time the market rises consistently, and properties become more valuable.

Equity Growth Formula:

       Market Value of Property
+   Value of Furnishings, Appliances, and Equipment
-   Outstanding Mortgage Payoff Amount
-   Outstanding Debts or Taxes Due on Property

       Equity Remaining in Property

Similar to the Buy, Rehab, Rent strategy, investors who own their property may choose to refinance it in order to cash out the equity generated from the property's appreciation or improvements.

Formula to Determine Liquidated Equity When Refinancing Your Property:

Market Value of the Property x 75% - 80%
-   Outstanding Mortgage Payoff Amount
-   Closing Costs
-   Title Fees
-   Unpaid Escrow Balances

       Proceeds from Cash Out Refinance at the Time of Sale

MODERATE INVESTING

Turnkey Rental Properties

Refer to the BRR(R) to determine how to profit from a turnkey rental property. The difference with this strategy and what you learned in the BRR(R) strategy is that a turnkey property does not require improvements or repairs. It is rent ready at the time of purchase, saving the investor the cost of improvements. This does not necessarily mean that improvements will not be required over time. Only the initial cost of preparing the property for rent is avoided.

Formula to Determine Your Turnkey Rental Income Profit:

    Monthly Rent Amount   x 12 months

- Mortgage Payment (Principal and Interest Only) x 12 months
- Annual Property Management fees
- Annual Property Taxes
- Annual Insurance
- Annual Maintenance and Repair Costs
- Annual Utilities or other Landlord Paid expenses

Annual Profit/ cash flow from turnkey Rental Property

Equity Growth Formula:

    Market Value of Property
- Outstanding Mortgage Payoff Amount
- Outstanding Debts or Taxes Due on Property

Equity Remaining in Property

Wholesaling

A wholesaler profits by playing the middleman between a property owner and an end buyer. The wholesaler charges an assignment fee by assigning a right to purchase a property to another investor who is willing to pay a premium. A wholesaler can also earn money by purchasing a property and then reselling it immediately to another investor at a higher price without performing any repairs. The wholesaler marks up the price of the property by the amount of their fee in exchange for their services finding the deal. Wholesale profit is subjective and varies per deal. The amount a wholesaler can charge boils down to the amount of money that can be added to the property and still leave meat on the bone for the end buyer to profit from resale or rent after the repairs are complete.

Formula to Determine Wholesale Deal Profit

Choose the *lesser of these two formulas* as your maximum purchase price:

Quick version:

    After Repair Value x 80%
- Estimated Cost of Improvements
- Estimated Closing Costs
- Your Wholesale Fee

    Maximum Price Offered for Wholesale Property

**Or Use this More Detail Version:*

    After Repair Value
- Estimated Cost of Improvements
- Estimated Closing Costs and Commissions at time of Purchase
- Estimated Closing Costs and Commissions at time of Sale
- 6 months Bank Interest (purchase price * current int rate (6/12)
- 6 months Holding Costs (insurance, all utilities)
- Profit Investor Expects to Earn (you can use an estimate like $40,000)
- Your Wholesale Fee

    Maximum Price Offered for Wholesale Property

The wholesale fee or assignment fee that you can charge is your profit.

RRR Reside, Rent, Refinance

Investors who execute the Reside, Rent, Refinance investment strategy apply the same formula to determine profitability as turnkey, short-term rental, or BRR(R) investors. The RRR strategy allows a property owner to occupy the home as their primary residence first and later convert their home into an investment property. The homeowner's profit is determined by the method they implement at the time they convert their home to a rental. If the home needs repairs, the BRR(R) formula may be the best way to factor in the cost of improvements. If the property is rent ready, then the turnkey formula is more suitable. If the homeowner chooses to rent their property as a vacation or short-term rental, the short-term rental formula is most suitable.

Formula to Determine RRR Rental Income Profit:

        Monthly Rent Amount
- Mortgage on Rental Property
- Property Management fees (If applicable)
- Property Taxes
- Less Insurance
- Reserves for Maintenance/ Repairs
- Utilities, Lawncare or Other Landlord Paid Expenses

        Monthly Profit that Property Owner Keeps

Again, the same formula applies for computing the equity that you can cash out when you refinance the property. The amount you can cash out will be a percent of the market value as determined by an appraisal that your lender will order. The LTV will typically be 75%-80% of the appraised value.

Formula to Determine Liquidated Equity When Refinancing Property:

Market Value of the Property x 75% - 80%
- Outstanding Mortgage Payoff Amount
- Closing Costs
- Title Fees
- Unpaid Escrow Balances

    Proceeds from Cash Out Refinance at the Time of Sale

PASSIVE INVESTING

Buy and Hold Land & Distressed Property

With the buy and hold investment strategy, an investor will hold their property for an indefinite period and sell when it is appropriate according to their investment goals. If this is your strategy of choice, you need to periodically evaluate the market conditions to determine if the timing is suitable to sell, develop, or lease the property. As you hold the property year to year, continue to estimate the unrealized gain or loss, and consider selling in a year when most advantageous for your bottom line. Consider tax savings and liabilities separately. Consult a tax accountant or real estate tax specialist prior to selling to determine the benefits or consequences of your financial wealth plan.

Buy and Hold Land /Distressed Property Profit Formula:

      Market Value of Property
+   Value of Improvements
-   Initial Investment
-   Holding Costs
-   Interest + Financing Costs (If applicable)

Unrealized Gain/Loss in Property

Formula to determine your Buy and Hold Rental Profit (if occupied)

        Monthly Rent Amount
- Mortgage on Rental Property
- Property Management fees (If applicable)
- Property Taxes
- Less Insurance
- Reserves for Maintenance/ Repairs
- Utilities or Other Landlord Paid Expenses

_____

_____Monthly Profit that Property Owner Keeps

Equity Growth Formula:

        Market Value of Property
- Outstanding Mortgage Payoff Amount
- Outstanding Debts or Taxes Due on Property

_____

Equity Remaining in Property

Private Lending

In a private lending investment strategy, the investor takes the position of the bank in a conventional mortgage loan. The investor charges a fixed interest rate with a term. The debt may include an interest-only period, may be amortized over a period of time or may also include a balloon payment at the end of the term.

The investor collects interest payments based on the frequency set in the note and charges penalties if the payment agreements are not met. The amount of interest collected will be determined based on the note. In the example below, I assume a 12% annual interest rate. If the borrower repays the debt in six months, then the investor only receives 6% interest, or 12% annual interest divided by 12 months times the 6-month term.

Formula to Determine Private Lending Investment Profit:

      Loan Amount
x   12% Interest for the Term of 6 Months.
_____

      Interest on Amount Loaned

Assume you loaned $500,000 with interest only for a term of 6 months:

      $500,000
x   12% Interest
_____

      $60,000
/   12 months in a year
_____

      $5,000
X   6 months term
_____

= $30,000 Interest Income

At the end of the term the $500,000 should be repaid as agreed.

REIT Investments

To invest in a REIT, purchase shares using a publicly traded investment platform. Hold the shares until they increase in value to the amount that meets your investment goals, and then sell them. Some REITS have a minimum holding period, so understand the investment time horizon before you invest since the shares may not be easily divested.

The greatest advantage of a REIT is the regular dividends paid to shareholders. Real Estate Investment Trusts are one of the most popular options for investors seeking regular income. To be a REIT, the trust must distribute 90% of the income generated at least once annually with some paying dividends monthly or quarterly. The income paid will consist of rental income and capital gains from the assets sold. The U.S. Internal Revenue Service will require the REIT to pay at least 20% of their distributions in cash, so in tightening economies where commercial vacancies are high, expect to receive some payouts in the REIT'S own stock.

——Stock Exchange-Traded Equity REITs ——Broad Stock Market (Russell 3000 Index)

There is no formula to determine your return for a REIT, but average returns over a twenty-year period were between 11.1% and 12.4% annually, according to a REIT.com study from 2016. See chart above.

Joint Venture or Partnership Investments

In a joint venture between two companies or a partnership between two or more members, all parties own an agreed upon percentage of the business income. Some partners may be responsible for losses while others may not. The partnership agreement signed by all parties spells out these terms. The contract terms specify the frequency of income distributions to the partners. The profit of the business is passed through to the members of the partnership based on the share of cash flows, losses or capital gains each partner is entitled to receive.

Formula to Determine Joint Venture/Partnership Profit:

```
        Profits of Business
    x   % of Net cash flows or Equity
    ─────────────────────────────────
        Your Share of Cash flows or Equity
    -       Initial Investment
    ─────────────────────────────────
            Earnings
```

Example:
```
            $100,000
    x       20% of Net cash flows
    ─────────────────────────────────
            $20,000 cash flow
    -       $15,000 Initial Capital Invested
    ─────────────────────────────────
            $5,000 Earning
```

You may be entitled to a share in equity.

Crowd Funded Investments

As a passive investor investing into a crowdfunding portal, your earnings will be based on actual performance of the offering rather than the targeted return in the offering documents. If you invest in the debt on the development, your rate of return will be a fixed interest rate agreed upon within the note. Common equity owners are entitled to a percentage of the overall investment's profits. Earnings are derived from the rental income and the income from a profitable sale of the property, sometimes years in the future.

Formula to Determine Crowdfunded Investment Profit:

For Equity Investments:

		$1,000,000	Total investment profits over 5 years
x		.05%	Your % of Equity of the Total Deal
		$50,000	Your Share of the Profit
−		$10,000	Initial Investment
		$40,000	Total Investment Yield

For Debt Investments:

		$10,000	Amount of Debt Contributed to Fund Deal
X		7.5%	Interest Rate in Note
		$750	Fixed Interest Annually
X		5	Number of Years Held
		$3,750	Total Interest Income over the 5 years

LEASING YOUR PROPERTY FOR INCOME

Many of the investment strategies taught in this book involve the leasing of property to businesses or individuals who pay a rental fee in exchange for use of space and certain rights of occupancy and possession. A *lease agreement* is a verbal or written agreement, often guided by state law, which conveys property or land for a period of time called a *lease term*, in exchange for payment or services. Some property owners lease space to multiple tenants who occupy the same building, like a retail strip, while others such as single-family investors typically issue one lease agreement per property.

There are new shared housing models that allow rentals per room, versus per unit, like hoteling long-term, to accommodate the growing demand for housing in a market with limited inventory. I foresee this model of leasing to become more prevalent, especially with workforce housing demand on the rise, the rising cost of housing, and an influx of corporations moving thousands of employees to major cities, but still with the average wage earners hardly able to afford inner city living. The option of sharing space will become a preferred housing model to avoid the travel time commuting to work.

I am currently working on a project with a shared-housing tech firm called Roommate Me and partnering with a local chamber of commerce and corporate CEO to develop spaces for employees to live close to work, even if they must share an apartment. As a young corporate professional, I lived in a townhome with two co-workers. We each paid rent to allow our housing costs to be affordable.

A traditional lease of this sort requires all occupants to guarantee the full amount of the lease. Real estate developers, tech firms, and thought leaders are taking this model and pushing the industry into housing concepts that will better accommodate families, seniors, medical professionals, and homeless populations in the same way with formal lease agreements that limit the payment of rent to each individual's portion of space within the unit or home. I am excited to be a part of a group pushing these new housing concepts forward because the earth is not getting any bigger, but the population is.

Real estate rentals can be a reliable source of residual income if you have great tenants; however, many investors have left this business because of nightmare situations with difficult tenants who damage property, skip out on the rent, or worse. Let me save you some time: expect the best, budget for the worst, and always maintain your insurance policies.

Be sure to look back at the section where we reviewed insurance policies, particularly the loss of rents or rent protection, and always enforce the requirement for your tenants to have rental insurance. Even the best tenants can fall on hard times and be at the mercy of economic downturns, job loss, or other crises. Properties in the safest neighborhoods can be victims of theft or vandalism, and unexpected damage from storms or system malfunctions can render your property uninhabitable. When properly insured, you can be financially protected in these circumstances and maintain your property in the interim. Screening your tenants upfront is also extremely important to avoid problematic situations. Placing a property manager as an agent between you and your tenant is also wise if you have a difficult time collecting money from others.

As a landlord, you become obligated to maintain your property in a safe, habitable condition and to follow state law and property codes in the way you communicate with a tenant and access your property. Every state has different landlord/tenant laws, so a great starting place to better protect yourself from liability and ensure you are operating legally is to review the local property code for your market. The landlord/tenant laws will have specific requirements for property entry, communication and notices, rent collection, repairs, termination, eviction, and more. Understanding the rules upfront is the best way to prepare for a positive rental experience.

Let's discuss the steps to find great tenants and close your lease:

1- Determine Your Lease Conditions
2- Determine Your Tenant Criteria
3- Review Your Insurance Policies
4- Market Your Property
5- Screen Applicants and Make Selection
6- Complete a Written Lease Agreement
7- Establish a Payment Method
8- Inspection the Property

Determine Your Lease Conditions

Your lease agreement will include important terms such as the allowable uses of the property, rent amount, late fees and penalties, rental term, names or type of occupants, number of parking spaces, rules and restrictions, pet policies, and insurance requirements. There are numerous other terms spelled out in a lease agreement. Review the standard lease agreement for your state to decide your lease conditions prior to leasing your property. As the property owner and landlord, you dictate the lease conditions to your tenants, and you establish a minimum criterion that your real estate professionals must honor during their marketing and solicitation of a tenant for your space.

The rent amount should be no less than the amount of your mortgage, property taxes, insurance, and landlord expenses combined. Also add a profit to the sum of the combined expenses so that you earn residual income, one of the benefits of owning rental property. Although your investment ambitions may lead you to set your asking rent at an obnoxiously high rate, the market will establish a ceiling set by what a willing tenant on the open market would be willing to pay for a property of your size, condition, zoning usage, bedroom count, and the amenities offered such as a swimming pool, garage parking, or nearby recreational facilities, golf courses, etc. Some cities may have rental rate caps that restrict rental increases, such as in Los Angeles. Evaluate the going market rates in your target location prior to purchasing property. It is also imperative to complete a financial pro forma *before* closing to ensure the property is profitable under normal market rental conditions.

A smart next step: Research the standard rental lease agreement for your target market. Read it and think through the lease conditions that are ideal for your property.

Determine Your Tenant Criteria

Your next step to successfully lease property is to outline the tenant criteria desirable and acceptable to you to ensure a positive and mutually beneficial landlord/tenant relationship. This criterion usually sets minimum standards and becomes the basis for how you evaluate and select applicants who express interest in renting your property. Tenant criteria for a residential property may be based on the applicant's credit score, credit history, ability to pay the rental amount as measured by household income, rental history, landlord references, criminal history, or any number of other general measures that landlords use to screen tenants. Tenant criteria for a business tenant might include business revenue, years in business, business type, intended use of property, parking requirements, business and credit references, credit profile and overall financial capacity to uphold the lease agreement.

It is up to you to define the minimum standards to qualify to rent your property. Beware that it is unethical to discriminate against people because of their race, skin color, religion, national origin, sex, disability and/or family status. The Civil Rights Act of 1968, which included the Fair Housing Act, went further to protect people from discrimination during the sale, rental, and/or financing of housing based on these criteria.

According to HUD.gov, "It is illegal discrimination to take any of the following actions because of race, color, religion, sex (including gender identity and sexual orientation), disability, familial status, or national origin."

- Refuse to rent or sell housing
- Refuse to negotiate for housing
- Otherwise make housing unavailable
- Set different terms, conditions or privileges for sale or rental of a dwelling
- Provide a person different housing services or facilities
- Falsely deny that housing is available for inspection, sale or rental
- Make, print or publish any notice, statement or advertisement with respect to the sale or rental of a dwelling that indicates any preference, limitation or discrimination
- Impose different sales prices or rental charges for the sale or rental of a dwelling
- Use different qualification criteria or applications, or sale or rental standards or procedures, such as income standards, application requirements, application fees, credit analyses, sale or rental approval procedures or other requirements
- Evict a tenant or a tenant's guest
- Harass a person
- Fail or delay performance of maintenance or repairs
- Limit privileges, services, or facilities of a dwelling
- Discourage the purchase or rental of a dwelling
- Assign a person to a particular building or neighborhood or section of a building or neighborhood
- For profit, persuade, or try to persuade, homeowners to sell their homes by suggesting that people of a particular

protected characteristic are about to move into the neighborhood (blockbusting)

- Refuse to provide or discriminate in the terms or conditions of homeowners insurance because of the race, color, religion, sex (including gender identity and sexual orientation), disability, familial status, or national origin of the owner and/or occupants of a dwelling
- Deny access to or membership in any multiple listing service or real estate brokers' organization

The Act exempts owner-occupied buildings with no more than four units, single-family houses sold or rented by the owner without the use of an agent, and housing operated by religious organizations and private clubs that limit occupancy to members.

It is fair and reasonable to deny tenancy to a person or business because they do not qualify for the minimum standards that you set. It is both illegal and grossly unethical to change the leasing criteria for different individuals because you want to prevent them from renting your space.

Does rental discrimination still exist? The simple answer is yes. These laws were created because so much blatant discrimination existed. However, the unfortunate reality is that discrimination and bias still occur without detection. 55% of housing discrimination complaints are based on disability. I have been told directly to my face by a leasing agent, "We don't want your kind in our property." I have been told by another leasing agent that my business use was not acceptable to the property owner because it would make it difficult to obtain an anchor tenant if we were in the building; however, after the property remained vacant for over a year the leasing agent could not provide me an explanation for why we were not selected because we were the only business to apply.

I have seen minorities, particularly young males, have a more difficult time being approved for rentals because they are considered a threat simply because of their skin color and physical appearance. I have seen single mothers discriminated against because landlords automatically assume they will experience hard times and be unable to pay, even if the household income meets the rental criteria at the time of the application. Larger families are also discriminated against because of the fear that many children will more easily damage a property. Housing discrimination goes on and on. Commercial property discrimination is even more overt because it is not protected by the Fair Housing Act.

I say all this to emphasize that rental criteria should be based on general factors unrelated to the listed items that are federally protected. If you are unsure if your tenant criteria are discriminatory, reach out to the Department of Housing and Urban Development or ask your local real estate agent or your licensed property manager to review the criteria before posting it. Conversely, make wise decisions when it comes to criminal and eviction history. Past mistakes are not always an indication of the future, but consistent or recent bad behavior can be a red flag. Some landlords charge a fee for higher risk tenants such as a double deposit for evictions or broken leases.

A smart next step: Write a list of your minimum rental criteria and think through the ideal tenant relationship you want to develop.

Review Your Insurance Coverage

Certain property uses are considered riskier than others and require additional insurance. Certain breeds of pets are also considered riskier and may require an additional rider to your standard landlord policy. As a general rule, prior to renting your property, review your insurance policies that are in effect to be sure you have the proper coverage. Discovering you are improperly insured after you rent your property, makes it too late to change the rental rate because the contract has been signed… unless you have the type of agreement that passes on insurance cost to the tenant.

In most cases you should understand your property expenses fully before accepting a tenant to be sure that your tenant is insurable. This is particularly true when you are dealing with commercial leases. For example, if your tenant wants to lease your land to breed pit bulls, and you think that is a phenomenal idea, then you could be held liable if your tenant's pit-bull were to break out of the fencing and harm someone. The cost of additional insurance for that use might not be feasible for the rental rate you agreed to charge. Yes, this is an extreme example. You get my point.

A smart next step: Review your current insurance coverage and speak with an insurance broker about their recommended policies for your property. If you do not own a property yet, get a head start and have a conversation about your intended investment.

Market Your Property

In certain high demand markets, you do not really need to market your property because of the backlog of renters looking for places to lease. In these unique situations marketing can be as simple as posting an address online or sticking a for-rent sign out front and waiting for the phone to ring. However, traditional property marketing will include cleaning and staging the home or commercial space, obtaining high quality professional photos of the interior and exterior and sometimes aerial views, publishing the property listing online, marketing to off-market private parties or inside networks, conducting private property showings, and holding both public and broker open houses.

These are just a few of the ways properties are marketed. Whether for rent or for sale, the process is the same. A licensed real estate agent can assist you with marketing your property for rent and will be skilled at getting your property leased to a qualified tenant that meets your rental criteria. Real estate agents charge a broker fee for listing property. This fee can range from a small percentage of one month's rent to a percent of the gross rental income for a multi-year lease. These rates are negotiable, but every market usually has a standard listing fee.

A smart next step: Research the going listing fee to market a property rental in your target area.

Screen Applicants and Make Selection

Once you market your property, at least one or more interested applicants should come forward to lease. Screen the applicant even if you only have one to lessen the likelihood of negative outcomes in the future. Websites, such as Transunion's SmartMove tool, allow landlords to quickly complete a rental screening for residential tenants based on the tenant's background, income, public rental history, public criminal history, and the overall rental rating TransUnion uses to determine if this tenant is a good choice. I cannot recommend this tool and the reliability of their assessment, but I can say that I have used this tool in the past to screen tenants. The tenant must approve of the background check, and the tool offers a service to send a link for the tenant to pay for the screening fee.

Since I am "old school," I also interview every tenant in person and give them a face-to-face explanation of my company's rules, regulations, expectations, penalties for violating the policy, and grounds for eviction. I do this to create a relationship upfront. I want my tenants to know that I care about them and their families, and I also want them to care about me and mine. When property rental seems transactional and robotic, tenants may be less inclined to treat the property with respect or to break a lease agreement.

No one that I rent to can ever say they did not understand the requirements of living or doing business in one of my properties. I make it clear. For example, smoking of any kind inside my rental property is automatic grounds for eviction. The tenant signs that agreement during our face-to-face meeting. When I complete a rental inspection and smell smoke in the property, I can take the signed paper to the eviction department. The tenant will have no defense. This has happened before, and as much as it hurt to evict a tenant, I found peace when the tenant admitted they knowingly breached the rental agreement. This is my rental criterion; yours may be different.

Again, a licensed real estate agent or property manager can assist you in screening applicants. They can take the tenant's written application, collect the tenant's photo identification, and check stubs or income documentation, rental history references, business tax returns, and business plans. Even if you hire a professional to assist you with screening, understand that the final decision is yours. Always speak up and make your selection. Some people rely on their gut decision versus what the application shows on paper. That is okay, too. Ultimately, you have to live with the decisions you make, so be sure you are in charge of those decisions.

A smart next step: Research available tenant screening tools, for a comprehensive credit-based renter recommendation.

Complete a Written Lease Agreement

Once you find a tenant and are ready to move forward with a written lease agreement, you can use a promulgated lease form prepared by attorneys from your local real estate commission or real estate association. Or you can hire a licensed real estate agent, property manager or attorney to draft the agreement on your behalf. These forms are available to download online and completed using the terms and conditions you negotiated and agreed to with the tenant. Since the lease terms are legally binding and sometimes complicated to understand, it is best to utilize the professional services mentioned previously to assist you in completing the lease agreement. However, you are more than welcome to draft a lease if you choose to do so on your own.

Complete every section of the lease agreement and leave nothing blank. Most importantly, be sure that all tenants and you sign a lease and initial in all places required. Verbal agreements do not hold up in court, so always have a written lease agreement on file.

As the landlord you have the authority to add provisions to the lease if there are conditions or restrictions you require of all tenants and occupants. These additional provisions to the lease may be added as a separate written addendum that is attached to the lease agreement and signed by all parties. In my standard lease agreement, I have one to two pages added to specify the rules of occupancy and the lease violations that will result in eviction. I discuss these conditions in person and have the tenants read over them. Then all parties sign, acknowledging their acceptance of these rules.

After a lease expires, be sure to renew or terminate it. Otherwise, your lease may automatically revert to a month-to-month agreement. Month-to-month lease agreements may have less protection for you as a landlord and may leave you in a situation where your tenant is only required to give you a 30 days' notice or less before they move out. If you plan to sell your property, end your existing lease agreement, or raise your rents, then you must send notification of your plans in writing within a given timeframe as specified by state law. Some states require a 30-60 days' notice of non-renewal of lease, notice to vacate, or termination of lease due to violations or eviction.

A smart next step: Print a sample lease agreement and fill it in from start to finish. Familiarize yourself with the agreement. If you have not already done so, read the state property code regarding lease notices, renewals, terminations, and eviction procedures. Finally, write a lease addendum of rules, regulations and lease violations that summarize your expectations of all tenants, occupants, or visitors.

Establish a Payment Method

One of the greatest aspects of owning a rental property is collecting rent. Within your lease agreement you specify your acceptable methods of payment. Those might include cash, check, money order, bitcoin, online payment method, or a payment portal via your property management company. It is best to select a payment method that is simple for your tenant and can be done online or through a smartphone. If you manage many properties, you may want to invest in an online payment portal such as PayRent.com, or request that your tenants make payments via autopay to ensure you limit the headache of managing and collecting multiple rent payments. Digital payment systems such as Zelle can be used; however, keep in mind most of these systems have a maximum daily limit that may be less than your rent amount and may cause your tenants to split payments into multiple payments, which could be a nightmare for accounting purposes.

It is wise to separate your rent payments from other business or personal transactions, and to maintain a separate account for security deposits. If you are a property manager, you may also be required by state law to keep a separate escrow account for security deposits. Commingling is illegal and occurs when a tenant's security deposit is deposited with the landlord or managing partner's business or personal funds.

A smart next step: Research payment systems and select the best method to collect rent that works for you. Open up a bank account to collect rents and a separate account to collect and hold security deposits.

Inspect the Property

Before your tenant moves in, complete a visual inspection of the property to ensure that it is move-in ready. Your space should be clean, safe, and empty unless being rented with furnishings, and all systems should function and perform as built. Provide your tenant with a move-in inspection checklist to acknowledge any existing damage to the property prior to their lease start. The tenant should return a signed inspection checklist within the first week of occupying the property. If there are existing paint nicks, broken windows, scuffed floors, or visible damage, this will be acknowledged upfront so the tenant will not be held responsible for these items when they move out.

You should also continuously inspect the property during the lease term. I typically inspect once quarterly using an inspection checklist to document new damage, or changes to the property condition. It may be simpler to coordinate your inspections during your pest control sprays or during scheduled maintenance to limit your visits to the property and inconvenience to the tenant. You will also need to inspect the property at move out and create a repair checklist for your handyman to make ready the property for the next tenant.

It is always best to find out about issues with the property in advance so that you are not surprised at the end of the lease. Also, regular inspections allow you to address concerns early on so that minor issues do not become costly major repairs. Things to pay particular attention include air filters, septic tanks, moisture or water damage, signs of leaks, infestation or rodent droppings, unapproved occupants or pets, hazards such as loose floor planks or cracked tiles, or other safety issues such as a tenant having a cooking plate in a bedroom or unsecured weapons.

A smart next step: Research a local handyman company and save the contact so that you can be prepared to make quick repairs if you discover issues during your inspection.

MANAGING YOUR INVESTMENT

Managing your investment and managing your property are two separate things. It is not only important to maintain your property in good working condition, free of hazards, and leased at market rates, but also for you to ensure that your investment performs to expectation and that you adjust as the industry, economy, and your local market changes. Situations will always come up, and the level of your management will dictate the level of your profitability. Managing your investment might include periodic communication with your investors to review financial performance, mortgage payments, bank correspondence, insurance coverage and tax assessments. Reviews can also cover market and valuation changes, periodic increases to rent, property maintenance, accounting and tax filing, and mitigation of property related issues. Management also includes adjusting your investment strategy, changing vendors and contractors, and revising budgets to real time information.

Whether you manage your investment personally or hire a financial manager and/or property manager to manage your investment, you still need to manage the people that you hire. Imagine you hire an 18-year-old to babysit your children for the weekend while you go away on a work trip only to return to discover that your children have eaten nothing but pizza, ice cream, and soda for three days. While you may be grateful that your sitter was able to keep your kids alive in your absence, the condition of your kids' teeth may be more of a concern to you. This is the same way you should think about your investment. I do not want to create a false expectation that you need to be 100% involved in the management of your investment, because I understand that you have careers, family, travel, hobbies, and many other things to do with your life besides watching over your property investments. People highly trained and passionate about doing this sort of work can help if you do not have the time or passion to do it yourself. However, certain details only you might notice because it is personal to you. That is why your presence is important and your oversight necessary.

A word of warning: read the reports that your professional accountant, real estate agent, property manager, attorney, inspector, contractor, and handyman send you. Be as present as possible and be in-tune with the details and intricacies of what is happening with your investment. Avoid assuming this is a "set and forget" business, or you may come back to a complete mess.

I have an exceptional financial manager, but every now and then I find errors in the accounting reports, miscategorized accounts, or missed payments. I cannot entrust the responsibility of my investments 100% to someone else because I am responsible for the outcome. I even scrutinize my contractors' work. Although they provide top notch quality, my scrutiny sets an expectation of excellence. I have even asked my general contractor to redo work that was below the quality I expect so that they understand I value my properties and will not settle for mediocrity.

Managing your investment also includes watching your market for changes that may impact your investment. Whether you rent property or are involved in another investment strategy, you need to value continual mastery of that investment strategy so that you can know when laws change, the market hits highs or lows, or rents and property values have increased or decreased. You must be aware of what is going on in the region that might impact your property, your tenant and their industry, business performance, and ability to continue the lease commitment. Imagine the shopping mall industry during COVID lockdowns. Every investor was watching the news to see how the government restrictions and health crisis might impact the large retailers' ability to stay in business.

The larger you grow, the more your teams may expand to help you manage your investments. As a single property owner, it may be simpler to manage the demand of property ownership on your own. Later will come a time in your investment journey to outsource certain services.

METHODS TO MAXIMIZE YOUR INVESTMENT PERFORMANCE

You should periodically evaluate your investment performance and seek new methods to maximize the value and cash flow of your property. Through property improvements, creative financing, new rental approaches, and concentrated investments, you may be able to earn higher yields than a "set and forget" approach.

Upgrade Your Property

Making improvements to the property is one of the fastest ways to increase property value. During your ownership journey, you will evaluate the cost/benefit differential of potential improvements and their subsequent impact on rent amounts and overall property value. Some improvements will be necessary because of wear and tear, damage, and required maintenance, such as roof replacements, plumbing repairs, and HVAC upgrades. Other improvements may seem unnecessary expenditures but could have a very real impact on the appraised value of the property and could influence the amount of cash you are able to obtain during a refinance or sale of the property. Here are some improvements that could yield a higher ROI or inversely impact value if neglected:

- Modern Appliances, including water heater
- New Windows, including Weather Impact and Commercial Grade Windows
- New Roof Systems, including Impact Resistant Roof Materials
- Upgraded Counters such as Granite or Marble Stone
- Upgraded Flooring Materials
- Modern Lighting
- Well maintained and secure Fencing
- Paved Driveways and Sidewalks
- Lawn Sprinkler Systems
- Landscaping, including manicured lawns, shrubs, trees, and flowers

- Pool Upgrades, including well maintained equipment, pergolas, decks and patios
- Technology such as video, security, or sound systems
- Front Doors, painted or refurbished
- Exterior Façade Updates
- Garages and/or covered parking, quantity of parking spaces for commercial property
- Freshly Painted Interior

Quite often property owners overlook these improvements, but they are the top items dinged on appraisal reports that lead to appraisal adjustments and reductions in value. Properties that include these updates may also be rented at above market rates because of the elevated perception of value.

It is important to evaluate the cost of improvements and select durable, quality but moderately priced materials unless you are investing in a luxury market. For example, a hand-scraped hardwood floor that will last for many years and will increase marketability would be a much smarter investment than glass-front kitchen cabinets, which might yield a lesser return. Shopping discontinued items, holiday sales, and bulk pricing can allow you to snag a great deal on high end materials.

If you seek to refinance or sell your property, review the condition of the items mentioned in the list and determine if investments into these improvements could yield a higher sales price and net greater returns. It is also obvious that maintenance to property helps it to maintain its value, so tighten your doorknobs, faucets, and door hinges, install lightbulbs, change filters, upgrade fixtures and finishes, repaint and repair damaged walls, trim, and baseboards, and clean your property before any photos, property tours, inspections, or appraisals.

Consider Alternative Rental Approaches

Numerous non-traditional approaches exist to generate rental income that may yield higher than market rental rates. Which ones you use may be limited by zoning regulations, so always check the zoning laws in your area before renting your property.

Though not an exhaustive list, Out-of-the-box residential uses that yield premium rental income include:

- Boarding Homes
- Assisted Living Housing
- Drug and Alcohol Recovery Housing
- Transitional Living or Halfway Housing
- Co-Living, Hostel, or Dormitory Style Living
- Retirement Communities
- Trailer Communities
- Off-Grid Communities

These sorts of unconventional approaches allow you to rent land or property at a premium due to the unconventional services, aid, or number of residents allowed in a single space. If you have an interest in these sorts of property uses, I encourage further research as we will not cover these topics in this book.

Collaborative Area Development

I advocate strongly for joining investment groups and clubs that target investments in developing markets. These collective groups can capitalize on the overall area development resulting from mass investment. While traditional logic might believe that limited competition in your target area maximizes your investment returns, I have seen how a group of like-minded investors investing in the same targeted market can drive value and mutually benefit everyone playing in that area.

One benefit of collaboration is sharing market data such as private appraisals, off-market lease rates, building plans, funding opportunities, construction pricing, and other relevant information. Collaborative investment also allows investors to synergize cohesive exterior facades, advocate for policy changes and municipal infrastructure investments, and to function as a collective voice to influence area planning objectives.

I honestly believe that unity is the answer for most of our community issues. When someone wins, too often they hold their cards close to the chest in fear that someone might steal their strategy or take over their market. In reality, there is enough property on earth's monopoly board for all of us to win. Working together with others has yielded my greatest results.

Development Incentives

City governments and financial institutions may offer grants and low-rate loan financing to incentivize development in underserved communities. Projects that provide affordable housing, economic development, or homeless housing may qualify for subsidies, tax credits, or property tax abatements, all of which can hugely impact investment returns for those willing to invest in these areas.

A good place to start is to research *Qualified Opportunity Zones (QOZs),* which are federally designated areas marked for economic distress that may be eligible for preferential tax treatment. Municipalities also have designated high opportunity areas such as Dallas' *Neighborhood Empowerment Zones (NEZ)* or Chicago's *Neighborhood Opportunity Fund,* both of which provide development incentives to investors to drive investment in these areas.

Research development incentives in your area to see if you qualify for grants or low-interest rate loans that decrease project cost and increase returns. I recently qualified for a $450,000 incentive in my city. The subsidy made a commercial development project feasible. I was shocked to learn my company presented the first project in ten years to receive this funding. I believe it was partially due to owners simply being unaware that they could ask the local city government to help fund their projects and a lack of understanding about how to go through the process. Soon after this award, my company received a 10-year tax abatement for a residential project as part of the Neighborhood Empowerment Zone (NEZ). This allowed me to partner with the Salvation Army and other local homeless housing agencies to re-house several homeless individuals in my newly renovated 4-bedroom house. This is an active project that I hope will come to fruition and was made possible by the local incentives.

LISTING YOUR PROPERTY FOR SALE

Selling a property can be a complex and time-consuming process that takes weeks to several months to complete. When it is time to divest your asset, you need to prepare the property so that you can maximize your return on investment and net the most cash possible. Before selling, consider the obligations of selling, such as partner approval, capital gains tax, the cost of moving and terminating leases and service contracts, community property, and distribution of proceeds. A methodical approach to selling is always preferred to a fire sale. So, start early and plan your sale to avoid discounting your property due to marketing blunders or haste.

Hiring a licensed real estate agent in your local market area is a great first step to selling your property. Even before you are ready to list, I encourage you to schedule a consultation with a local market expert to gather market data, including sales comps, and to get a third-party opinion of value and condition. Have a REALTOR lay eyes on the property and give ideas to help you prepare the property for sale.

Once you are ready to list, be prepared to sign a listing agreement that outlines the agent's roles and responsibilities. This agreement also describes pertinent property data and makes the public aware of deficiencies that must officially be disclosed. The listing agreement also specifies commissions or fees that are due at closing for the marketing services the broker provides.

Real estate agents can also assist you with hiring staging companies to decorate and furnish the property to stand out amongst other listings. Agents also have resources to connect you to vendors for repairs and can tell you top-selling property features so that you can know the best improvements or decor to yield top dollar for your property.

One of the best parts about hiring a real estate agent is that you gain extra helping hands to assist in the process, which can be quite hectic. I found myself at one point washing dishes, vacuuming, and cleaning a client's entire property myself to get the sale. Do not expect a real estate agent to do your dirty work, but in extreme situations real estate agents have been known to go out of the way to assist clients in selling their properties. Since an agent's commission is tied to the sale, their goal is to ensure the property sells for top dollar so that both owner and agent benefit. If you need a referral to a licensed real estate agent in your local market, request one at referrals@CommaClubCommunity.com.

If you have partners in your company, it is important to obtain any required approvals to sell as detailed in your partnership agreement. If a vote is required, call a meeting and obtain the necessary votes to approve the sale. The company agreement also specifies the signing authorities, that is, which parties need to sign closing documents.

Based on the company agreement and the shares of ownership specified, the escrow agent distributes sale proceeds accordingly. Be sure your company agreement is updated to reflect the most current ownership structure prior to signing a listing agreement to sell your property.

In **Community Property** states, spouses are entitled to an undivided half interest in property and consequently may also need to be notified of property sales and sign at closing, even if they are not listed on the deed or in the company agreement as a member or owner. The title search of public records will identify spouses of property owners. Therefore, if required, inform your spouse of property sales and proceeds collected from the sale.

Prior to selling, give proper legal notice to tenants, particularly if you expect them to vacate the property before you market it. Laws that protect tenants do not allow you to terminate a lease simply because you want to sell. Some landlords sell property with current leases in place, so they need to inform tenants of property showings to gain access, gain lockbox permissions, enter the property to make repairs or prepare the property to sell.

Listing a property for sale while tenant-occupied can be an advantage for investors looking to buy a cash flowing rental property. However, it can also be disadvantageous to the seller if tenants are uncooperative, messy, or vocalize property dissatisfaction to prospective buyers. I have toured several dreadful property listings with annoyed tenants who did their best to ruin the property showing and scare away buyers because of fear of losing their housing. As a commercial office tenant, myself, continuous unannounced showings into my workspace often left me feeling threatened and annoyed. If you plan to sell tenant-occupied property, communicate with your tenants. Inform them whether you plan to continue their lease or if they need to plan their relocation at the end of their lease term.

Remember to cancel service agreements with property managers, maintenance crews, utilities providers, security, grounds keepers, pest control, and cleaning companies and other contracted services upon closing the sale. You do not want to be left with additional bills after you no longer own the property. Some service contracts, such as security, may have a fixed term but may be transferred to the new owner if you inform them as part of the selling process.

Knowing when to sell is an individual decision. Some investors prefer to amass a portfolio that they transfer to heirs upon marriage, college graduation, or in their wills. Others decide to hold the investment for a term and sell when the market hits an ideal height. For others, their immediate strategy is to buy and sell property or shares to benefit from the short-term gains of property divestment. Regardless of your strategy, the goal is to sell higher than the purchase price, to recoup your investment, and profit from the increases in value generated during your ownership.

TAX CONSIDERATIONS FOR REAL ESTATE INVESTING

Real estate investments may trigger certain tax benefits and liabilities, including tax credits, allowable expense write-offs, or capital gains tax obligations when you purchase, lease, improve, and/or sell property. In order to avoid unexpected outcomes during tax season, plan for these changes before registering companies and investing in real estate.

Capital Gains Tax

Capital gains tax is a tax on the profit realized on the sale of stocks, bonds, real estate and property. The capital gains tax rate depends on how much profit you generate and your annual earnings, which dictates your tax bracket. Capital gains are taxed at 0%, 15%, or 20% as of 2022 at the time of this publication. Tax rates and income thresholds are subject to change.

The purchase and sale of property is public record. It is required by law for the settlement agent to report the gross proceeds received by the seller to the IRS using Form 1099-S. The IRS provides an exemption from the Form 1099-S reporting requirement for the sale of your principal residence if you are married and your *gain from the sale* is $500,000 or less. If you are unmarried, gains of $250,000 or less are exempt. Investors owning properties that are not their principal residence should be prepared to pay capital gains tax in the year of a property sale.

Because capital gains tax is considered a cost of sale, it is important to compute the estimated capital gains tax on the sale of property prior to initiating the sale to understand how it will impact the net proceeds the investor will receive. Consult your tax advisor to compute your capital gains tax, if any, to make an informed decision before selling your investment.

Depreciation Recapture

Depreciation is an annual income tax deduction that allows you to recover the cost or other basis of certain property over the time you use the property. It is an allowance for the wear and tear, deterioration, or obsolescence of the property. One of the benefits of owning rental property is that individuals and companies can write-off depreciation expense when filing taxes to reduce the taxable income for 27.5 years or other lengths of time depending on the asset class.

In the year that you sell the asset, the depreciation previously reported will be recaptured and will be taxed as ordinary income with a maximum tax rate of 25% as of 2022. To calculate the amount of depreciation recapture, the adjusted cost basis must be calculated and then compared to the sale price of the asset. The original cost basis is the price paid to acquire the asset. The adjusted cost basis is the original cost basis less any allowable depreciation expense incurred for as many years as the asset incurred depreciation.

If a house was purchased for $100,000, and the owner used the straight-line depreciation method dividing the total price by 27.5 years, then it was depreciated by $3,637 annually. This amount will be deducted from the taxable income, thus creating a savings for the property owner at tax time. However, at the time of the sale, this accumulated depreciation that was untaxed throughout the years of ownership must be recaptured and taxed because the IRS never forgets a favor. Follow the steps to understand how this works.

Step 1: Compute Depreciation Expense

Annual Depreciation Expense = Original Cost Basis $100,000 / 27.5 years

Annual Depreciation Expense = $3,637

Step 2: Compute the Adjusted Cost Basis

If the asset was owned for 3 years and then sold, the adjusted cost basis would be computed as:

Adjusted Cost Basis = Original Price $100,000 − Accumulated Depreciation ($3,637 x 3)

Adjusted Cost Basis = Original Sales Price $100,000 − Accumulated Depreciation $10,909

Adjusted Cost Basis = $89,091

Step 3: Compute the Realized Gain on Sale

If the property is sold at the end of the third year for $150,000, then the realized gain is the New Sales Price − the Adjusted Cost Basis.

Realized Gain = New Sales Price $150,000 − Adjusted Cost Basis $89,091
Realized Gain = $60,909

Step 4: Determine the Depreciation Recapture Amount

The *Realized Gain* from the asset sale must first be compared with the *Accumulated Depreciation* and the smaller of the two figures is considered the *Depreciation Recapture.*

Realized Gain $60,909 versus Accumulated Depreciation $10,909. The smaller amount is $10,909 so this amount will be considered the Depreciation Recapture Amount.

Step 5: Compute the Capital Gain

This realized gain will be divided into the portion of depreciation recapture (taxed at the maximum of 25%) and the remaining portion of capital gains (taxed at a certain tax rate depending on amount of the gain and the investors annual income level).

Let's assume in this scenario the capital gains tax is 15%. The IRS determines the tax rate, so be sure to consult your tax advisor.

Realized Gain $60,909 – Depreciation Recapture Amount $10,909 = Capital Gain $50,000

The Capital Gain is computed as the net of the Realized Gain less the Depreciation Recapture Amount.

Step 6: Compute the Tax

Remember, capital gain tax will be either 0%, 15% or 20% depending on the individual's income as of 2022. These amounts are subject to change with time so check the latest IRS information for capital gains tax rates. For this scenario, let's assume the capital gain is taxed at 15% and Recaptured Depreciation is taxed at 25%.

Capital Gains Tax = Capital Gain $50,000 x Capital Gains Tax 15%
Capital Gains Tax = $7,500

Recaptured Depreciation Tax = Recaptured Depreciation $10,909 x Tax Rate 25%

Recaptured Depreciation Tax = $2,727

As you can see, this is an extraordinarily complex process of computing tax due on property related gains. This explanation by no means provides an exhaustive explanation of tax benefits and liabilities relating to property ownership, so I encourage you to discuss your individual tax situation with a licensed tax professional. For referrals to a tax advisor, contact Referrals@CommaClubCommunity.com or identify a professional licensed in your area.

1031 EXCHANGE

A 1031 Exchange is a tool that real estate investors use to swap out investments and to defer capital gains or losses and the subsequent capital gains tax and depreciation recapture tax due in the year a property sells. The exchange is based on Internal Revenue Code 1031. It benefits the investor by allowing them to roll their proceeds into more properties to expand their portfolio versus using a portion of sale proceeds to pay taxes.

Because capital gains tax can stagnate trade, the government has provided this tax relief to encourage trade and stabilize property value. When ready to sell a property, you can exchange the property for a new investment of like-kind that is of higher value than the property being sold to completely defer taxes. For example, you have the flexibility to change investment strategies and exchange a single-family house for a duplex or an apartment for raw land. Fix and Flip properties typically do not qualify for a 1031 Exchange tax benefit since they are held "primarily for sale."

According to the IRS Fact Sheet for Like-Kind Property Exchanges,

> *Whenever you sell business or investment property and you have a gain, you have to pay tax on the gain at the time of sale. IRC Section 1031 provides an exception and allows you to postpone paying tax on the gain if you reinvest the proceeds in similar property as part of a qualifying like-kind exchange. Gain deferred in a like-kind exchange*

under IRC Section 1031 is tax-deferred, but it is not tax-free. The exchange can include like-kind property exclusively or it can include like-kind property along with cash, liabilities and property that are not like-kind. If you receive cash, relief from debt, or property that is not like-kind, however, you may trigger some taxable gain in the year of the exchange. There can be both deferred and recognized gain in the same transaction when a taxpayer exchanges for like-kind property of lesser value.

A 1031 Exchange may not be the best option for every investor and will depend upon your unique financial situation. If you are in a lower tax bracket, deferring taxes to a future year might raise your tax liability if you pay the deferred taxes in a year that causes your overall liability to enter a higher tax bracket. For example, suppose you are in the 0% capital gains tax bracket as a result of your income in the year you sell a property. However, if in future years your income increases, the deferred capital gains may throw you into a 15% or 20% tax rate.

You may wonder how long you can defer your tax liability? You can defer the capital gains tax due until the exchanged property is sold and the gain is realized unless you initiate another 1031 exchange and continue to defer the taxes into perpetuity.

Here are some quick facts about 1031 Exchange:

- If interested in using the 1031 tax code, you must initiate the 1031 Exchange BEFORE you sell the property.
- You must also collaborate with a qualified intermediary to facilitate the 1031 Exchange.
- You must identify a replacement property within 45 days of selling your property.
- You must close on the replacement property within 180 days after you sell your property.
- You can sell your property and buy multiple properties with the proceeds. If you are exchanging for more than

three properties, contact your Exchange Facilitator to discuss additional rules that may apply.
- There are fees to facilitate a 1031 Exchange. They can be as little as $500. Customary real estate closing fees can be paid with the exchange funds.
- You can acquire new property in other states than the location of the relinquished property.

The Comma Club Community will share more expansive tax education taught by tax strategists who specialize in maximizing investor returns. Visit the Comma Club Community to learn more about resources in development.

COMMENCEMENT

We have come to the end of this book. It is time for you to apply in the real world what you learned conceptually. We discussed the strategies to acquire, finance, lease, manage, and sell property, and we explored many possibilities to generate income through real estate ownership. You have been informed, inspired, motivated, encouraged, and equipped. Now, the next steps are yours to continue the journey toward success.

Remember, success is a journey and not an event. There are no guarantees, and there is always risk. However, when driven by a great sense of purpose, you can face the uncertainty with hope instead of fear. You discovered your *why*. Let your *why* continually prompt you to act. By now you should have selected the beneficiaries of your impending wealth and thought further beyond your lifetime to begin a legacy that will outlive you.

Now, get out there and possess the land. Take dominion of territories and govern them with wisdom and accountability, stewarding earth's most precious resources and wielding them for good. A proverb says, "Commit to the LORD whatever you do, and your plans will succeed." My best advice is to dedicate your plans to the LORD so that you can experience the same successes that I have been blessed to experience .

I will not leave you alone for the next steps of your ownership journey. For more information on available support, visit

CommaClubCommunity.com to join the Comma Club Community, a network of new investors. Comma Club offers an online education platform with resources to support you throughout your process including courses, coaching, and an interactive community. My goal of establishing this platform is to create a support community for new investors to engage with experienced investors, industry professionals and other newbies to launch their journey into the world of real estate investment and produce real results. This platform provides a forum where members share their experiences, seek guidance and access expert training to excel in their investment journey with the purpose of building long-term multi-generational wealth. Comma Club offers courses that will cover a breadth of real estate related topics where novice investors learn the fundamentals needed to build residual income and increase their net worth through ownership.

The Comma Club Community is ready to applaud you as you build wealth and grow the commas in your net worth over the many decades that I hope you will own property. We will collectively root for your success as you arise from your current economic state to become a thousandaire, a millionaire, a billionaire, and even levels of wealth that are beyond computation. I pray you inherit the incomparable eternal rewards for faith in Jesus Christ and for advancing his Kingdom on the earth which reflects love for God and for humanity, peace, hope, goodness, generosity, kindness, and humility. The Comma Club Community is at inception, but I will not stop until I see my vision magnified to the fullness of what I know is necessary to make property ownership more accessible and wealth more equitably distributed in America and beyond.

Now let's get to wealth building! How many Commas? You decide.

GLOSSARY

A:

Acquisition Cost – The cost of purchasing real property including discounts, incentives, closing costs, softs costs and improvements made before its first use.

After Repair Value (ARV) – the estimated value of a property after completed renovations, not in its current condition.

Attorney Closing – officer who hosts the Closing, prepares the deed, pays outstanding bills, and transfers title to the Buyer

Appreciation – how much value your house gains over time, or the opposite of depreciation

Address of record – The validated and verified location (physical or digital) where an individual can receive communications using approved mechanisms.

Appraiser – a person authorized to appraise all types of real property without regard to complexity or transaction value for federally related transactions and non-federally related transactions.

Appraised value – an evaluation of a property's value based on a given point in time an authorized appraiser

Appraisal – a fair market valuation of property, such as real estate, a business, collectible, or an antique, by the estimate of an authorized person.

Appraisal Report – a detailed document that outlines a property's value based on its quality, condition, location, and surrounding market conditions.

Assessed Value – a property's determined valuation to calculate the appropriate tax rates.

Accumulated depreciation – the total amount an asset has been depreciated up until a single point.

Actual Cash value – the amount equal to the replacement cost minus depreciation of a damaged or stolen property at the time of the loss.

Asking price – the amount a home seller wants a buyer to pay to purchase his home.

As-Is Value – The estimate of the market value of real property in its current physical condition, use, and zoning as of the appraisal's effective date.

B:

Beneficial Ownership - In domestic and international commercial law, a beneficial owner is a natural person or persons who ultimately owns or controls an interest in a legal entity or arrangement, such as a company, a trust, or a foundation.

Book value – a property's net worth as shown on the balance sheet or statement of net worth until the final sale takes place.

C:

Cash flow – refers to the movement of money in and out of a business.

Capital Contribution – an amount of money or assets given to a business or partnership by one of the owners or partners.

Capital Expenditures – spendings used by real estate companies to invest, purchase, renovate, and maintain physical assets such as properties, technology, or equipment.

Cap rate – as known as capitalization rate is the rate of return on a real estate investment property based on the income that the property is expected to generate.

Closing – the final phase of mortgage loan processing in which the property title passes from the seller to the buyer.

Community property – any property acquired by a couple during their marriage (with a few exceptions) is equally owned by both spouses.

Control – to have power over something

D:

Deed of trust – a form of evidence that a debt exists. In most situations, it is the documentation of a transfer of property to another person or party for them to hold as security.

Demographics – the data that describes the composition of a population, such as age, race, gender, income, migration patterns, and population growth.

Depreciation recapture – the gain realized by the sale of depreciable capital property that must be reported as ordinary income for tax purposes.

Dissolution – the act or process of ending a business or partnership.

Debt service – the total amount of debt you pay each year

Distressed Property – property listings that have one or many of the following characteristics: they are in foreclosure, have been foreclosed upon and are being sold by the original lender, homes being sold by homeowners who owe more money than the home is worth, or the condition is in severe disrepair.

E:

Expenses – the cost of operations that a company incurs to generate revenue.

Effective Gross Income (EGI) – the net rent generated by a property after adjusting for tenant improvement and other capital costs as well as lease commissions and other sales expenses.

Equity – the difference between the worth and the amount owed on a piece of property.

F:

Farmland - a real estate niche that deals with the purchase and sale of Arable land

Feasible- the analysis you conduct before undertaking development to find out if it is viable.

Financial Industry Regulatory Authority FINRA – a private American corporation that acts as a self-regulatory organization that regulates member brokerage firms and exchange markets.

Formation – a structure or arrangement of something.

G:

Going hard- a contract that is no longer in an option or contingency period.

H:

Historic property- landmarks, landmark sites, or districts which are significant in the history, architecture, archaeology, or culture of the state, its communities, or the nation.

I:

Industrial building- a building, which is wholly or predominantly used as a warehouse or for Manufacturing/assembling, processing activity or distillery.

Inspector - a licensed individual authorized to perform a real estate inspection for a buyer or seller of real property but is required to do so under the indirect supervision of a Professional Real Estate Inspector.

Internal rate of return (IRR) – a metric that tells investors the average annual return they have either realized or can expect to realize from a real estate investment over time, expressed as a percentage.

Investment Risk – probability of an expected return or loss on invested capital measured by the level of assurance or uncertainty of those results.

L:

Lease agreement – an arrangement, made between two parties, that allows one of those parties to use an asset belonging to the owner.

Lease term – a duration of time set out in the lease that designates the minimum amount of time a person is expected to remain in the same rental unit.

Loan Guarantee - A loan guarantee, in finance, is a promise by one party to assume the debt obligation of a borrower if that borrower defaults. A guarantee can be limited or unlimited, making the guarantor liable for only a portion or all of the debt.

Liquidity – The ease in which an investment can be bought or sold and if the price will be sold above or below market value.

M:

Market Value – the amount for which something can be sold on a given market

Management – the conducting or supervising of something such as a business, team, or process.

N:

Neighborhood Empowerment Zones (NEZ) – an area so designated for the purpose of providing economic incentives, including a tax abatement.

Neighborhood opportunity fund – funds to support commercial corridors in underserved neighborhoods.

Net operating income – measures an income-producing property's profitability before adding in any costs from financing or taxes.

New construction – a newly constructed habitable structure improvement requiring a permanent foundation. This excludes accessory structures such as sheds and incidental outbuildings.

O:

Option - the exclusive right to purchase a property for a period of time. An option is usually formally executed by an option contract and requires reasonable consideration such as a fee.

Option Period - a period of time to consider, inspect, and evaluate a property before deciding to execute an option to purchase.

Ownership – the state of owning or possessing something, as well as the right or act of being the owner.

P:

Parties – the individuals involved in the transaction

Promissory note – a signed document containing a written promise to pay a stated sum to a specified person or the bearer at a specified date or on demand.

Purpose – the reason for which something is done or created or for which something exists.

Pocket Listing – an off-market listing, or a property marketed to potential buyers through private channels rather than on the multiple listing service (MLS).

Pro-forma – a report that details a property's projected net operating income (NOI) and cash flow projections using its current and potential rental income and operating expenses.

Q:

Qualified opportunity zones (QOZs) – a QOF's qualifying ownership interest in a corporation or partnership that operates a QOZ business in a QOZ or certain tangible property of the QOF that is used in a business in the QOZ.

R:

Ranch - a specific type of farm which usually carries cattle or sheep, and their primary focus is optimal care of the animals.

Raw Land- Undeveloped land, often called raw land, is a vacant area without any public utilities, buildings or even driveways.

Real Estate Settlement Procedures Act (RESPA) – seeks to reduce unnecessarily high settlement costs by requiring disclosures to homebuyers and sellers, and by prohibiting abusive practices in the real estate settlement process.

Reconstruction – re-creates vanished or non-surviving portions of a property for interpretive purposes.

Redevelopment – occurs when new construction is added to previously occupied land, or the land structures need to undergo renovations.

Refinance – the process of paying off an existing mortgage loan using a new loan.

Regulation Crowdfunding (CF) – a Securities and Exchange Commission regulation that enables eligible companies to offer and sell securities through crowdfunding including real estate sponsors.

Rehabilitation – Restoring real property to an improved state

Realized gain – when an investment is sold for a higher price than it was purchased.

Replacement cost – the cost to construct or replace at a given time, an entire building of equal quality and utility, using prices for labor, materials, overhead, profit and fees in effect at the time of the appraisal.

Replacement Reserves – funds set aside that provide for the periodic replacement of building components that wear out more rapidly than the building itself and therefore must be replaced during the building's economic life (short lived items).

Remodel – the process of changing the functionality and the design of an area.

Renovation – updating an existing structure with cosmetic changes.

Restoration – the process in which you return the building to its original condition.

Return on their investment (ROI) – a metric that real estate investors use to determine their return on an investment property.

Right of First Refusal – a fairly common clause in some business contracts that essentially gives a party the first opportunity at making an offer in a particular transaction.

S:

Scope of work – detailed outline of all planned construction and renovations of a project.

Security – Anything that is put up to secure a loan, it may also be known as collateral in many loan documents.

Setbacks – usually refers to the distance a house or structure must be from a property line.

Subject property – the property for which a borrower intends to get a loan.

T:

Taxation – municipal revenue obtained from taxes.

Tax matters partner – a member of a partnership who is responsible for representing the business to the IRS in a specific tax year.

Tear down- demolish something, especially a building.

Term – a fixed or limited period for which a partnership, contract, or investment is intended to last.

Time Horizon - This means how much time you plan to hold the investment and how easy it will be to return the cash that you have invested.

Turnkey- a move-in ready home that doesn't require any major repairs or improvements before it is livable.

U:

Utility Reimbursement – the amount, if any, by which the utility allowance for the unit exceeds the total tenant payment of the family occupying the unit.

W:

Waterfront- any land on the edge of a body of water while beachfront is located on or adjacent to a beach.

Y:

Yield – Rate of Return expressed in the formula annual income / initial investment. Yield can also be measured as Cash on Cash which is Annual Cash flows/ Cash Invested. A very common measure of investment performance in commercial real estate is the Capitalization (Cap) rate which is expressed in the formula Net Operating Income/ Current Market Value.

REFERENCES

Bureau, U. S. C. (spell out USC) (2021, October 26). "Wealth and asset ownership," *Census.gov*. Retrieved February 7, 2022, from *https://www.census.gov/topics/income-poverty/wealth.html*.

Chen, J. (2022, February 2). "Real Estate Investment Trust (REIT)," *Investopedia*. Retrieved February 7, 2022, from *https://www.investopedia.com/terms/r/reit.asp*.

Esajian, P. A. U. L. (n.d.). "How To Navigate the Real Estate Assignment Contract," *Fortune Builders*. Retrieved February 7, 2022, from *https://www.fortunebuilders.com/real-estate-assignment-contracts'*.

Exchange Commissions. (2017, May 4). "Regulation Crowdfunding," *SEC Emblem*. Retrieved February 7, 2022, from *https://www.sec.gov/smallbusiness/exemptofferings/regcrowdfunding*.

HomeFirst Communities. (2020, March 13). "What is a manufactured home, exactly" *HomeFirst*. Retrieved February 7, 2022, from *https://homefirstcertified.com/what-are-manufactured-homes/*

https://www.noradarealestate.com/blog/dallas-real-estate-market/

https://www.visualcapitalist.com/20-years-of-home-price-changes-in-every-u-s-city/

https://www.sba.gov

https://www.jpmorganchase.com/impact/racialequity.

"Racial Disparities in Lending," Retrieved from. *https://themarkup.org/show-your-work/2021/08/25/how-we-investigated-racial-disparities-in-federal-mortgage-data*

"REIT Performance," Retrieved from: *https://www.reit.com/news/blog/market-commentary/comparing-average-reit-returns-and-stocks-over-long-periods.*

"IRS Fact Sheet on Like-Kind Exchanges, Retrieved from ," *https://www.irs.gov/pub/irs-news/fs-08-18.pdf.*

–New Home Source.com. *https://www.thespruce.com/building-your-own-house-1821301)*

https://www.federalreserve.gov/econres/notes/feds-notes/disparities-in-wealth-by-race-and-ethnicity-in-the-2019-survey-of-consumer-finances-20200928.htm.

Bhutta, Neil, Andrew C. Chang, Lisa J. Dettling, and Joanne W. Hsu (2020). "Disparities in Wealth by Race and Ethnicity in the 2019 Survey of Consumer Finances," *FEDS Notes.* Washington: Board of Governors of the Federal Reserve System, September 28, 2020, https://doi.org/10.17016/2380-7172.2797.

https://crewnetwork.org/about/resources/industry-research/accelerating-the-advancement-of-women-in-commercia.

"The Devaluation of Assets in Black Neighborhoods," *The Brookings Report* . *https://www.brookings.edu/wp-content/uploads/2022/07/Devaluation-of-Assets-in-Black-Neighborhoods.pdf.*

https://kvia.com/news/texas/stacker-texas/2022/02/10/the-black-homeownership-gap-in-texas/

"Snapshot of Race and HomeBuying in America." Retrieved from: *https://www.nar.REALTOR/research-and-statistics/research-reports/a-snapshot-of-race-and-home-buying-in-america*

https://www.whitehouse.gov/briefing-room/statements-releases/2021/06/01/fact-sheet-biden-harris-administration-announces-new-actions-to-build-black-wealth-and-narrow-the-racial-wealth-gap/

www.ingramcontent.com/pod-product-compliance
Lightning Source LLC
Chambersburg PA
CBHW020633230426
43665CB00008B/158